D1036992

THE

BERIA
PAPERS

Alan Williams

SIMON AND SCHUSTER
NEW YORK

SBN 671-21589-2
Library of Congress Catalog Card Number: 73-8996
Designed by Irving Perkins
Manufactured in the United States of America
Printed by The Murray Printing Company, Forge Village, Mass.
Bound by The Plimpton Press, Norwood, Mass.

1   2   3   4   5   6   7   8   9   10

FOR DAVID BURG,

ANN, RICHARD

AND VIVIAN

I saw the vulture face of Beria,
Half hidden by a muffler,
Glued to the window of his limousine
As he drove slowly by the curb hunting down a woman for the night.
—Yevgeny Yevtushenko, Soviet poet

Paper One

Gagra, June 1949

Woke with the sun, my body filled with vigor and burning for a woman. This Black Sea air works its usual wonders on my constitution. (Even last night's liter of fermented mare's milk has left me with a perfectly clear head.) Only the Professor seems miserable.[1] He appeared at breakfast looking puffed and green, like an old corpse. He said it was his spleen playing him up, but I told him I knew better. "Beso, my friend," I said, "it is your bourgeois conscience that makes you so sick! Some of the things you told me last night could get you twenty years!" For a moment I thought he was going to drop dead of a heart attack there and then, for he cannot remember half the things he did say last night. He has a weakness for slushy nineteenth-century romantic literature, but at least I can credit him with being honest. I quite like him. In fact, I'd have been sorry if I'd killed him today—an unfortunate incident that almost ended in tragedy for Beso, but one which, on reflection, makes me half split my gut laughing. (At least they won't be able to say I lacked a gallows' humor!)

[1] Professor Beso Emerto of Tbilisi (formerly Tiflis) University, a leading Soviet literary critic.

9

It happened in the morning after I had finished with the usual batch of telegrams—including a bombardment of messages from Zarknovitch, that officious worm who goes on pestering me with details about Project Borodino.[2] One cannot even enjoy a holiday in peace. I shall be glad to be rid of him—he is worse than a nagging wife!

Then Nadoraya[3] came up and told me that the speedboat was ready. It had arrived overnight by train, straight from the shipyards in Rostock where it had been custom-built by our German comrades, who had been informed that it was the latest prototype of our high-speed naval patrols for keeping an eye on the Turks. I winked at the Professor, who was on the terrace with me when Nadoraya arrived, and told him that it would never do letting our poor starving comrades in our Germany know that such a superb piece of craftsmanship was merely a plaything for me! I thought it might cheer him up to know he had a little secret dirt on me—but the old fellow only seemed to grow more miserable. I really think he may feel uncomfortable in my presence! Anyway, I felt like being generous, and invited him along for the maiden voyage, telling him that at ninety knots his hangover would be blown away like a cobweb!

The boat was down on the jetty, guarded by four of my Georgians. A man I didn't recognize was translating from a manual and giving instructions to the captain in charge. He was introduced as the German mechanic. As soon as I appeared he jumped to attention and saluted, then stood as though he were made of wood. I laughed and asked him what he thought of my little toy. Did he not think it was just the thing some Western playboy would have to amuse his girl friend? (I could see at once that this German dolt took the hint, for he blushed and began trembling.)

Then I turned and winked at Nadoraya. "That's what we need, Colonel—two or three beautiful girls! Redheaded virgins from Svanetia!" And Nadoraya and his Georgians all laughed with me,

[2] Code name for first Soviet A-bomb project.
[3] Colonel in charge of Beria's 200-strong personal bodyguard of Georgians.

but the German was struck so dumb that he could only stand and gape at me.

Then Rafik,[4] who is something of a mechanic himself, showed me over the boat. I must say those Germans are still masters of technology. The machine is a real work of art! Slender and beautiful as a bird, white all over except for a pointed black prow like a vicious beak, as though the whole boat were crouching in the water ready to spring up and attack. The body is made of some new alloy that the Americans have invented for their aircraft—very light and strong—the engine is a 125 h.p. inboard; the controls are of stainless steel set in black rubber; the interior is done in varnished walnut; and the boat is equipped with the latest radiotelephone, a radio compass, depth-finder, and even radar.

I must have shown my delight, for at once the atmosphere became more relaxed and soon I even got the mechanic to smile when I joked that it was just as well we had spared at least a few Germans after '45!

Nadoraya then came aboard with me, and together with the mechanic I took her on a couple of runs at quarter-throttle just out from the shore. She handled magnificently, like a well-trained animal, but I was irritated to see this German watching all the time as though waiting for me to do something wrong.

When we got back I ordered Rafik to fetch some cushions to put along the two banquettes in the stern, and to bring down the icebox with four bottles of well-chilled wine. Then I called the Professor aboard and we set off.

The water was very flat, absolutely calm right out to the horizon, and we had a wonderful run for three or four miles. The shore sped past as though we were traveling in a fast car. As usual, of course, I knew that guards would be watching us through telescopes and that several other high-powered boats would be ready at intervals every few miles in case we got into any difficulties.

We were almost out of sight of Gagra—about four miles from

---

[4] Colonel Rafik Sarkisov, Beria's aide-de-camp.

the shore—when we came on this boat trailing a dinghy. I thought at first it was a coast-guard patrol, until I saw a girl swim alongside the dinghy and two men pull her aboard. I cut the throttle in time to reach for my binoculars and get a good view of her. My God, what a creature! A true statue of a girl, all golden brown in a dazzling white bathing costume; and when the men pulled her over the side her buttocks jutted into the air like two ripe plums. It was the Professor who told me who she was—one of our top long-distance swimming champions of the U.S.S.R.

I was already planning my line of attack, when she balanced herself on the end of the dinghy and dived gracefully back into the sea. I watched her strike out with a strong steady crawl away from us, while the boat with the dinghy remained stationary. I eased the throttle out, steering in a long curve away from the girl, but not too fast so as to attract attention. The only obstacle to my plan was damned Beso. I was already cursing myself for having brought him, and wondering who would ever miss the old hack.

I slowed the boat right down till she was just ticking over, then I told him to open a bottle of wine. The girl was now perhaps six hundred yards from the dinghy. I let Beso take a healthy slug, then told him to go back and see if the screw was not fouled up. I was wearing only my trunks now, but he was still in his suit and sandals, and when he was leaning right over the side, with his head almost touching the water, I jumped forward and gave his arse a great shove. He went in so fast that he didn't even have time to shout, and when he came up he was spitting out water and flapping like a great fish. "Help me, Lavrenti, I can't swim too well!" he shouted.

I laughed and threw him one of the lifebelts. "You'll float, my friend!" I shouted back, then went forward to the controls. The boat with the dinghy was some way off now, but even if they didn't see him, I knew that sooner or later one of the guards on the coast would spot him and send out a patrol to fetch him. It wouldn't do the old fool too much harm to get a soaking in good Black Sea water!

12

Then I pulled the throttle full out and made straight for the girl.

I must say I was really proud of my skill as I cut around in front of her, just missing her head with a great white wave, then pulling up within arm's reach of her. She looked up at me with a startled expression, almost of terror, and for a moment I wondered if she recognized me. But I called down to her not to be afraid, and grabbed her under the armpit, where I felt a nice clump of wet hair.

Her body was even more splendid than I had first thought: a true athlete's body, with long muscular legs, a small waist and flat belly without a stretch mark or ounce of fat, and big breasts pressing against the inside of her costume like a pair of half-melons. But I remembered that as a privileged citizen she would be accustomed to a certain decorum, and I decided that the best tactic would be to play the perfect gentleman. I knew that she would have guessed I was someone important on account of the boat, but since I wore only my bathing costume—without my glasses, uniform and medals—I don't think she had recognized me. I told her only my first name, and that I was a naval officer on holiday from Odessa, which seemed to impress her, as well as put her at ease. I offered her some wine, which she accepted with a lovely smile. Then I got out a toweling robe from one of the lockers and wrapped it around her, refilled her glass and invited her to sit beside me on one of the cushions. She pulled off her bathing cap, and I saw that she was a real beauty. Her hair was the color of ripe barley—a girl in a dream! Then I remembered the guards along the shore with their damned telescopes watching every move, so I went back to the controls and headed straight out to sea.

Every girl, no matter where she comes from, loves speed. This boat, I told her, was the fastest in the world. I saw her eyes shining with excitement, and reckoned it would be plain sailing from now on. At full throttle it took us less than three minutes to be out of sight of land.

13

I had quite forgotten about the wretched Professor, and was only concerned that the guards on the shore might try to follow. I thought of using the radiotelephone, but did not want to arouse the girl's suspicions—even talking Georgian. Finally I decided to trust my boys to keep their distance and not make fools of themselves. After all, they know me well enough!

I cut the engine only when the horizon was completely empty. The sea was still very calm, and the sudden silence added a certain excitement. I joked about it, asking her how it felt to be alone with a man so far from the shore, and she smiled—rather secretively, I thought—and accepted another glass of wine. I then pulled her down next to me. Her skin was still rough from the sea, where it had dried in the wind, and I could taste the salt on the back of her neck. I could also sense that she was a strong girl, and hoped for her sake that she would not try to struggle.

We talked a little, and I found she was a good Komsomolka,[5] but with my experience I also detected a certain worldliness about her which was encouraging. And her smile excited me to a near-frenzy. I judged my moment well, and suddenly unzipped the back of her white costume and peeled it off to her waist, taking one of her gorgeous breasts and squeezing it in my palm, and talking all the while. I talked kindly but sternly, and she listened to me most seriously, her eyes gray and very wide, with the innocence of an intelligent child. Soon I could feel myself growing stiff inside my trunks until my prick was straining like a trapped beast and I could bear it no longer. I shouted, "Enough of this!" and, seizing the back of her neck with one hand and the top of my trunks with the other, I bared myself in front of her, my prick rearing up like a great pepper pot. I pulled her head down toward me, and to my delight she offered no resistance, but instead went to work on me with an expertise which, had it not been for my raging lust, I would have found almost degrading. As it was, her tongue was like a quick flame, her lips suddenly closing with a delicious pressure, while her hot saliva ran down into my loins. I

[5] Member of the Young Communist League.

14

let it until I felt the climax growing dangerously close, then I dragged her head up by her hair, making her yell, and flung her face downward on the cushions. I ripped her costume from around her legs, then spread her out on her belly, and with my knees pressed between her thighs, entered her roughly from behind. She was tight at first, still damp from the sea, and I worked on her gently so as not to make her raw; but she was a ripe girl and soon she was moving with me, the inside of her thighs becoming warm and sticky as though smeared with fig-juice. And all the time I was able to study her body under the dazzling light—the golden fur at the base of her spine, the curve of her, and the pale freckles on her shoulders; and as I studied her I pinched her, first her nipples, then her belly and hips, and the tight muscular flesh of her buttocks, until she grew slippery, and I could hold out no longer, just exploded inside her—an orgasm that left me quite dizzy, as though it were the liter of last night's mare's milk that had been boiling up inside me and which I now shot deep into her!

She didn't want it to finish, but lay there groaning, so I gallantly terminated her pleasure with my hand. When it was all over she annoyed me by beginning to cry. I gave her more wine, but this only made her cry more, so again I had to talk sternly to her, telling her that I was an important man and that if she behaved herself and was sensible I would see that she was included in the Athletes' Parade in Moscow on July 18. This seemed to calm her down, and after some more wine I started the engine. She began saying that she must go back to her boat, but I told her not to worry and took her directly back to Gagra.

My Georgians were waiting on the jetty. They treated the girl like a visiting dignitary, and I soothed her further by assuring her that I would arrange everything with her bosses, while she remained my guest until tomorrow.

Up at the villa I was informed that the Professor had been dragged from the sea by one of the patrol boats and was suffering from exhaustion. I gave instructions to have him allocated a first-class sleeper on the night train back to Tbilisi. I think I know my Beso well enough to be sure he will not commit any indiscretion.

My little Ludmilla—as she is called—stayed for a fine feast that night, and I really savaged her afterward; but she seemed to be learning quickly and there were no more tears.

I had Rafik see her off in the morning, to complete her training on the boat with the dinghy. She told me that it is her birthday in eight days' time, and I have made a note to have roses and chocolates sent to her hotel here in Gagra, where she is staying with her team manager.

PART
ONE

If I had known how it would turn out, I never would have done it.

—CLIFFORD IRVING

Charles E. Whitmore, vice-president of Atlantic, National & General Consolidated, looked up at the green eye winking at him across the desk as a voice chirped, "Your one-fifteen luncheon appointment with Mr. Miskin, Mr. Whitmore."

Slowly, with the care of a scientist handling a piece of delicate equipment, Whitmore laid a gold pencil along the margin of foolscap, closed the typescript, locked it in the drawer beside his knee, then spoke back at the machine. "I'll be right down, Miss Keast."

He was a big man with a gray executive face and the movements of a semi-invalid. Today he took the exceptional precaution of locking the door, before passing beside the gallery of glass-fronted offices full of muted typewriters and printed jokes on the walls, emerging into a vestibule of color of crème de menthe where a battery of beautiful receptionists was drawn up behind gilt-legged desks like a guard of honor.

Whitmore moved silently past them. At the elevators he was obliged to join the lunch-hour crush, where several faces nodded to him; but Whitmore's pale eyes returned no glimmer of greeting. He was like a man used to traveling first-class, to whom all fellow passengers were a necessary imposition.

Outside the marble-walled entrance hall a limousine waited with its engine running, chauffeur on the curb. Whitmore sank into the upholstered gloom, protected from the glare of Madison Avenue by the smoked glass as the car crept a couple of blocks away to the quiet chilled restaurant where the vegetables are delivered fresh each morning off an Air France flight.

His guest had already arrived, bobbing out of the dark with a white smile. Whitmore grunted and sank down opposite. A waiter appeared like a shadow and placed a glass of cold milk in front of him. Sy Miskin sat with his hands cupped around the stem of his untouched martini.

"Well, sir, what's the verdict?" Miskin was a short spry man with a head too big for his body; when he spoke it wagged about like the head of a toy dog you see dangling in the rear window of cars. His features were soft and plump, but with wide greedy nostrils and gray eyes staring out of an artificial tan. He was Whitmore's editor in chief at Burn, Hirsch, one of the more respected publishing houses in the United States, established over a century ago, but now little more than an intellectual ornament to the conglomerate of Atlantic, National & General. Miskin himself, though not an intellectual, closely followed contemporary literature, which meant the current best sellers, and could pass all the tests on the round of literary parties, while remaining an old-fashioned wheeler-dealer, hard-nosed and crafty, especially in exploiting paperback deals, which he saw as the ultimate aim of publishing.

He had built his reputation on less than half a dozen books, none of which had had the least literary merit, but their world sales had totaled more than ten million. Their authors he had nursed with skill, becoming not only their editor, but agent, manager and all-purpose fixer: cajoling, bribing, trapping them with complicated cross-deals, movie options, fast lawyers, foreign tax dodges that were just legal, until they could not move until he moved. And move he did, from house to house, taking all his authors with him and upping the ante each time.

He was an optimist. He had the unquestioning self-confidence of a successful gambler. And now the big hand had arrived: the pot that was going to make him famous overnight. Only first he had to convince Whitmore to put up the stake money—three million dollars for a single project. And time was running short.

Whitmore took a sip of milk. When he spoke he chose his words gravely, like a doctor delivering a prognosis.

"I'm not quite through yet, Sy—about two thirds of the way. But so far I'm not entirely happy. Half of it's porn—cheap, nasty, sensational filth, the kind of thing any dirt peddler on Forty-second Street might turn out."

Miskin licked at his martini. He knew his employer well enough not to try to rush him. Whitmore was a five percent man, used to a low yield on a high turnover; nor was he a man who would allow a small fluctuation in profits to upset his Baptist principles. As vice-president of A. N. & G. he must be seen to be not only doing good business, but doing it in a wholesome American manner.

Miskin paused for the waiter to take their orders, choosing plain steak, very rare, for himself, while Whitmore had his usual slice of boiled fish. When they were alone again he leaned forward, his voice soft and solicitous, sharing the older man's concern like a sympathetic lover. "I entirely agree with you, C.W. It is filth. And that's just the reason why we've got to publish it."

Whitmore stared across the table, waiting.

"Publish it," Miskin went on, "precisely because it *is* the kind of stuff the back-alley boys turn out—only in this case haven't. Because this dirt peddler of ours happens to have been, up to less than twenty years ago, the second most powerful man in the world—and probably one of the most evil men in history."

Whitmore sat in the dim light like a shapeless stone lying in deep water.

"Always assuming the thing isn't a hoax," he said at last. "Because I don't want to find ourselves with another Clifford Irving on our hands."

"We've had it thoroughly checked. You've seen the report by Professor Krull of the Harvard Center for International Affairs? He reckons it's genuine."

"Would he be prepared to stake three million dollars on it?" said Whitmore, with a sour smile.

"He's the top man in the field, C.W. And we've also had a linguistic expert check the original and he can't find any mistakes. Nor can the forensic boys. The paper is at least fifteen to twenty years old—they can't be more precise than that—and they've even checked on the make of typewriter used. It's prewar. As for the typing, all they can say for sure is it's very faded. I tell you, it's the genuine thing!"

"These experts are like economists," Whitmore growled. "You call them in, and by the end of the day you've got more opinions than you've got heads giving them. Look at the Khrushchev book. How many of your experts are still going around saying it wasn't written by the old guy at all, but was just a big plant—either by the Russians or by our own people? I never did get to the bottom of that one; I don't think anybody did."

"The Khrushchev book made money," said Miskin, "even on two million bucks—and the stuff wasn't all that hot, either."

"This is different, Sy. The Khrushchev property, as I understand it, was a straightforward political memoir. And even if it had been proved a phony, all you'd have had would have been a few red faces around the *Time-Life* offices and a deficit on their balance sheets. But if we go ahead and publish this stuff of yours, and it does turn out to have been written by some dirty-minded hoaxer—with some expert help, I grant you—then we're going to be in bad trouble. And I don't mean moneywise, or even from a moral angle." Whitmore took another sip of milk.

"I'm talking about a bigger issue. Apart from the dirt, there's a lot of political explosive in this book, and highly unstable explosive at that. If it is a fake, Burn, Hirsch are going to be in bad trouble. And I'm not referring to accountants, or even stockholders. I mean the State Department. Putting out slanderous lies about the Soviet leaders—" He broke off as the waiter brought their food; then took a deep breath and shook his head. "Nope. Before we get into that kind of game, I'm going to need more than just the okay from some egghead from Harvard and a few linguistic experts. I want some positive, independent evidence before I ante up on this one."

"Such as?"

"A witness. Someone on the inside. This Rafik fellow, for instance. Colonel Sack-something . . ."

"Colonel Sarkisov. He's dead."

"Someone else, then—one of the other Georgian guards, for example?"

"They were all killed in July '53."

"*All* of them?"

"To a man. Real Roman style—in a pitched battle with Red Army units while holding out on the Count Orlov estate near Moscow. Krull has put it all in his memorandum."

Whitmore sat picking at his boneless fish.

"There must be other people—servants, chauffeurs, one of the doctors maybe? Even one of the girls? They'd be grown up by now, but one of them might be induced to talk—for money. I imagine the dollar goes a long way in Russia."

Miskin gave his practiced smile. "You ever been to Russia, C.W.?"

"Not in so many words," said Whitmore.

Miskin nodded. "It would take weeks, months, before we got even the smell of a lead. But more likely the KGB would get onto us first and sling us out on our ear—or worse. The press might be able to dig up something after we publish, but for the moment we just don't have the time." Miskin glanced at his watch. "My contact's calling me at four—ten o'clock tonight, Swiss time—when I'm supposed to be ready with a straight yes or no."

"You'll have to stall him."

"He's a very determined customer, I warn you. And he's got one of the top lawyers in Zurich acting for him."

"Swiss lawyers aren't American lawyers," Whitmore said. "Besides, we've got the typescript."

Miskin cut himself a slice of red meat and said quietly, "Only half of the typescript."

Whitmore stared at him. "Half? Did I hear *half*, Sy?"

Miskin's expression was bland. "I thought I told you, C.W. My contact made it one of his pre-conditions—that only half the work left Switzerland. He reckoned it would be enough for us to make a judgment."

"But what about the stuff I've been reading this morning? It's a diary, right through from the end of the war to the time of his death—sometime in '53, didn't you say? I'm up to the fall of '51 already."

"That's right, but you'll have noticed that there are gaps—several days, sometimes weeks—between the entries. Before my contact handed over the original, he took the precaution of dividing it into two sections, each dated consecutively, leaving our half—the pilot section, so to speak—sufficiently complete to keep the general thread of the narrative, but still leaving out a good deal of the meat."

"Son of a bitch," Whitmore muttered, then added, "and we don't get the second half until we sign up, is that it?"

"Correct."

Whitmore's liver-spotted hands tapped a slow tattoo on the tablecloth.

"Supposing," he said, "we offer him less. Say one million straight cash—then go ahead and publish what we've got."

At least Whitmore's suggestion showed that he was beginning to bite.

24

Miskin said judiciously, "It's not a course I'd advise, C.W. For a start, I don't think he'll take anything less than the asking price—and Krull's verdict will only have strengthened his hand. At the same time, if he gets to think we're holding out on him, he just could take the property elsewhere. He might even make separate deals in different countries. And if any of them were to beat us into print by just one day, we'd be screwed. Besides," he added, in slightly pained tone, "I don't think it would look at all good for us to come out with only part of the book, in what would amount to a pirate edition. After all, I have my own reputation to think of."

"Okay, okay," said Whitmore quickly. "So how do we stand on copyright?"

"We bring out an immediate edition in the original Georgian —say five hundred copies. In fact, I've already made the necessary arrangements. It's going to be expensive, but it's the only way to establish exclusive world rights within the Copyright Convention, which covers most respectable countries outside the Iron Curtain."

"Who owns the rights now? Your contact in Switzerland?"

Miskin took a moment to reply.

"For all intents and purposes, yes. Of course, it's not as though we were dealing with the author. Here the author doesn't come into it, and I don't think we need bother too much about any relatives. There's a wife and son who've changed their names. No doubt they'll be made to issue the routine denunciations—imperialist slanders on the Soviet Union, and so on—but I don't see them trying to kick up a fuss over royalties, since the author is a mass murderer who's dead anyway."

"Does the contact expect royalties?"

"No. He's selling outright and he owns the property."

"Who says he does? Who's to say he didn't steal it? Or that what he gave you isn't just a copy—one of several copies? What's that thing they call their underground press in Russia—the stuff that's typed out and passed from hand to hand?"

25

"*Samizdat*. But there's no question of that here. If it had gone into *samizdat* we'd have all heard about it by now. But that's hardly the point, C.W. In a deal like this, one must rely on a certain degree of mutual trust." He broke off to order coffee and the check.

Whitmore stared glumly at his plate, wiped clean like a cat's. "You're talking about trusting a total stranger in a deal involving three million dollars, remember."

"Exactly!" Miskin cried. "And that's why I think he's on the level. With money like that he's not going to horse around. Why should he? He doesn't want a messy legal situation any more than we do. No—he wants a straight quick deal, no tricks, no conditions. And that's what I advise we give him."

"I still need more time, Sy. Forty-eight hours, at least. And don't tell me he won't wait that long, however determined he is. If he's in that much of a hurry, there must be a catch somewhere—and you can tell him so. Now, he calls you at four. Then what's the program?"

"I take tonight's plane to Geneva, arriving in the morning, and drive out to the Hotel du Lac in Vevey, where I meet him and his lawyer. I bring the contract with me, signed by you, along with the banker's draft—or a covering letter confirming that the draft is on its way. He signs, hands over the second half of the material, and the deal's clinched."

"Is the contract ready?"

Miskin tapped his inside pocket. "All set, except for the title. I'll fill that in when we sign. I don't want even our own legal people to see that. Just the name would be enough—and it only needs a whisper to the press . . ."

"All right. Now listen. You tell him you'll be on tomorrow's plane instead. Tell him I haven't quite finished reading it, that I need to consult further with Krull—the usual stall. Play it cool —nothing to make him suspicious, just let him know we're being cautious. After all, he chose us, and if he's at all shrewd he's not going to expect us to be that darned trusting.

"Just one thing," Whitmore added when the waiter had left them with their coffees. "You *are* sure we're first on his list? I'd hate to think he's been hawking the stuff around."

Miskin spread his hands out palms upward, with a smile of mock resignation. "As I told you, C.W., we only have his word for it. But I think we can safely assume he's started at the top."

Whitmore accepted the implied compliment with a brief nod, then stood up, his coffee undrunk. "Okay, Sy. You be on that plane tomorrow. Meanwhile, when you talk to this contact of yours, check where the call's coming from and try and find out where he's staying."

He turned and was gone, guided across the room by a posse of waiters. Miskin realized, when it was too late, that he had left without signing the contract. Whitmore was a cautious old bastard who would want it read by his own lawyers first, small print and all.

When Miskin got back to his office, in the brownstone house on East Forty-fourth Street which had been the firm's premises since it was started in 1892, he fixed himself a stiff Scotch and soda and sat down to wait for the call from Europe.

It came through punctually to the minute, on his unlisted private number so that it did not have to pass through the office switchboard. Miskin was mildly irritated when the operator informed him it was a collect call from a number in Annecy, France. He accepted it, and the voice came on, high-pitched and heavily accented: "Mr. Miskin?"

"Speaking."

"This is Gregory. Is everything okay, Mr. Miskin?"

"Everything's fine, Mr. Gregory."

"You have talked with your boss?"

"I've talked to him."

"So. You arrive tomorrow morning in Geneva?"

"Now, just hold it a moment, Mr. Gregory. There are just a few things—"

"What things? Everything is settled?"

"A few minor details still have to be checked."

"Details! What details?"

"Things my boss has to talk over with Professor Krull—"

"Krull!" It was a metallic shriek. "He is not satisfied?"

"Professor Krull is perfectly satisfied," said Miskin patiently. "It's just that these things can't be rushed—"

"Your boss is showing the material to other people!" the voice shouted. "Okay, so if Krull is not enough—"

"Will you please let me finish?" said Miskin. There was a crackling pause. "Everything will be settled in the normal way. On Saturday morning."

"The banks are closed Saturday!"

"Don't worry about the banks," Miskin said soothingly. "We'll take care of that. Just have the material ready—with your lawyer —and we all sign up like good boys."

"Mr. Miskin." The voice was quieter now. "If there is any trouble, any hanky-panky . . ."

"Now, listen, Mr. Gregory, I represent—"

"You are an American businessman, and I am selling you something that is worth more than gold. If you try to cross me . . ."

"Are you drunk, Mr. Gregory?"

Another metallic pause. "That is not your business! No, I am not drunk, but I am drinking. So. You arrive Saturday morning. Same time, same place? And no tricks!"

Miskin grinned wearily to himself. "No tricks," he repeated. "And by the way, I'd like to know where I can get hold of you if anything important crops up."

For a moment the line went dead, as though a hand had been placed over the mouthpiece. Then the voice said, "I'll give a check call to your office, Mr. Miskin. Tomorrow morning—mid-day New York time."

"Where are you staying, Mr. Gregory?"

"I'm moving around," the voice said hurriedly. "Now, this de-lay—these points with Krull—"

"I'm sorry, I'll explain everything when I see you, Mr. Gregory. Goodbye." He heard another crackling exclamation, and hung up. There was nothing to do now but wait.

At the same time that Miskin was fending off Gregory on the line from Annecy, Charles Whitmore was keeping the appointment he had made that morning with a senior Treasury Department official in the Galleon Room of the St. Regis Hotel. The last of the late-lunch stragglers were leaving, men with loud laughs and anxious eyes. The two of them had the place to themselves.

Whitmore's companion, Mike Sanger, was a tall man with a good profile, in a dove-gray suit and neutral tie. He was head of the department that dealt with counterfeit, tax evasion and large-scale international fraud—work that brought him into close contact with the police forces of most West European countries. It was in this capacity, as well as that of a close family friend, that Whitmore had sought him out at a few hours' notice.

He came straight to the point. "As I said on the phone, Mike, this is a highly delicate and confidential matter. Three weeks ago our editor in chief at Burn, Hirsch—fellow called Miskin— was over in Europe at the Montreux Bookbang. Sounds very un-Swiss, but that's the way it seems they do business in the book world these days. On the last day Miskin was in his room when he got a call from the lobby. Some foreign guy who said he had a hot property. He turned out to be some kind of East European—a Pole or a Russian. Miskin, whose family originally came from over there, has a nose for these people. The guy was very excited and nervous—gave his name simply as Gregory, and said he'd been in Vienna, where he'd come into possession of a document which had been smuggled out of Hungary. Wouldn't say how—just that he wanted to sell it. The price was, and still is, three million dollars."

He began to stir his sugarless tea. The Treasury man waited, sensing that for once in his career the old man found himself on unfamiliar, even dangerous ground.

"To cut it short," Whitmore went on, "the document purports to be the private diaries of Beria, Stalin's police chief."

Sanger whistled. "Should be mighty interesting! If they're genuine."

"That's where I need your help, Mike."

"Advice or action?"

"Both. I'm in a spot. Before flying back, Miskin met next day with Gregory and his lawyer—some big wheel from Zurich called Dettweiler. Seems even he doesn't know the exact nature of the material, and was just there to witness Miskin's signature on the receipt of the typescript—or rather, half the typescript. It was written in Georgian, some kind of language I've never heard of, nothing like European or Russian. Miskin had some trouble getting it translated—particularly as it had to be done in the greatest possible secrecy.

"Anyway, Miskin has shown it to Professor Krull at Harvard, who said, while reserving final judgment, that he thinks the stuff's genuine. Meanwhile, Gregory's putting on the pressure. He wants the deal clinched by Saturday morning, when Miskin's flying over—ostensibly to sign. Otherwise Gregory threatens to find another buyer. The competition could be pretty fierce."

Sanger gave a wry smile. "I'd say it sure would! You've read it, of course?"

"Most of it. Reads like a pornographic horror story. Rape, murder, violation of little girls—you name it, this guy did it. Or said he did it. I should add, Mike, that there's a lot of political stuff—including some very compromising details about the present Kremlin leaders."

"Sounds like a thoroughly commercial property," Sanger said dryly, taking out a leatherbound pipe and a pigskin pouch. "Or perhaps too commercial to be plausible?"

"That's the trouble. Fact is, Mike, I'm in a squeeze. If the stuff really is genuine—however filthy—I just can't afford to pass it up. On the other hand, if it turns out *not* to be genuine, the very nature of the material would be enough to blow Burn, Hirsch into orbit, and it'd take a long time for the pieces to come down."

Sanger began to pat tobacco into the bowl of his pipe. "And you want my advice?"

"I may need more than advice," said Whitmore.

"Right. You say you've got to decide by Saturday, which, for purposes of clearing the check, means Monday. First I'd try for a second opinion, but not another Soviet expert. I'd be inclined to try the material on a psychologist—someone with a full knowledge of the political background who could give you a balanced judgment on whether a guy like Beria would write diaries like these in the first place. I haven't read them, but it does seem out of character for a secret-police chief to compile what sounds like highly incriminating evidence against himself. Perhaps, in the case of a man with the blood of millions on his hands, he was driven by an irresistible impulse to confess, get the stuff off his chest, even if he did risk passing it down to posterity."

Whitmore was beginning to look impatient. He said, "Okay, the psycho-couch angle can wait till later. What I want now are facts. Can you get a lead on this guy Gregory—who he is, where he lives, what he does—before Saturday morning, if possible?"

Sanger pulled at his pipe. "By Saturday morning, Chuck? You're asking for the sky. Unless Gregory is his real name, in which case, if he's an alien or a refugee, the Swiss'll have a record of him. Or the Austrians will. You said he got the material in Vienna?"

"That's right. And Miskin said he spoke fluent German with the lawyer."

"Okay, I'll get our people to run a check all around—with the Swiss, Austrians, West Germans, French, British. Nothing dramatic, just a simple request on a personal basis. We do it all the time." He had a notebook out. "First, where is the meeting taking place on Saturday?"

"Hotel du Lac, Vevey, at noon. He's supposed to have called Miskin at four this afternoon. I'll check before we leave where the call came from. He might even be staying at the hotel now, quite openly."

"He might," said Sanger. "If he was an amateur and on the level. But—supposing he's a professional—bona fide or a forger, it doesn't matter for the moment. There could be all kinds of murky angles to a deal like this. More than just the plain old profit motive—even far-reaching political issues. Either an attempt to discredit the neo-Stalinist elements in Russia today or, as you say, a plot to upset the whole power structure of the Soviet bloc. Past association with Beria could still mean political suicide for a lot of important people out there. That's why anyone concerned in this thing is going to have to tread damned carefully."

He paused, eyeing the old man dubiously over the bowl of his pipe. He knew that Whitmore's political views were indifferently conservative; the niceties of distinction between the various warring factions within world Communism would be hopelessly lost on him.

Whitmore seemed aware of this, for when he spoke it was with a certain humility. "I'm a businessman, not a politician. And I'm not in a position at this time to make a full evaluation of the political score. But if it does worry anyone, then there'll be plenty of time to sort that angle out before publication. I deal in facts and figures. And the figures are simple enough—three million by Monday morning. What I need now are more facts. What about the banking side? Even if we can't track this Gregory down before the deadline, can we keep some kind of tabs on him afterward?"

"Through a numbered Swiss bank account?" Sanger was busy again with his pipe. "You'd be dealing with the holy of

32

holies there. You know how it is with the Swiss—the customer's always right, providing he pays the bill."

"I thought we'd got the Swiss to ease up a bit there—open some of those numbered accounts to our Internal Revenue boys?"

"True. But only in a few extreme cases, and usually only after an indictment by a grand jury. But in this case, even if we could prove fraud, I doubt if we could make it an extraditable offense —unless, of course, Gregory or any of his associates, if he has any, turn out to be American citizens."

"Okay. But this guy Gregory first has to open the account?"

Sanger nodded.

"So how does he do it?"

"With money. Just like with any other bank—only if anything the Swiss make it even easier."

Whitmore made an impatient gesture with his hand. "Look, Mike, don't play me for a simpleton. I'm talking about the formalities—identification and so forth. He's not going to walk in with a suitcase of C's, for God's sake!"

Sanger pulled steadily at his pipe. "Has he specified any particular bank?"

"The Volkskantonale Bank, Zurich. They have a branch in New York."

"I know them. One of the smaller Swiss outfits, not one of the banks that have so far played with the Internal Revenue Service here."

"So what does Gregory need to identify himself—without giving us his real name?"

"Just a letter of introduction, addressed to him personally, which he takes along in the presence of his Swiss attorney."

"Just the one name—Gregory?"

"He can call himself Joseph Stalin for all they care. It's the number that counts, not the name. Just plain Gregory will be all they need for the draft."

"I suppose," said Whitmore slowly, "your contacts with the CIA wouldn't help here?"

Sanger laughed. "For God's sake, keep *them* out of it! If they get even a smell of this, they'll want to take over the deal and as likely as not screw the whole thing up. So if you want my help, Chuck, it has to be on the understanding I'm not doubling up with the 'Company,' as they call themselves."

Whitmore looked depressed. "So it seems I don't have many options?"

Sanger knocked out his pipe. "We have a very good man in Geneva, also in Vienna. I don't suppose much can be done tonight, but we'll get a line on Gregory—if that is his name—sometime tomorrow. And I'll have a tail put on your man Miskin the moment he touches down. You got his flight number?" Whitmore gave it to him.

Sanger closed his notebook and they both stood up.

"I'll just make that call to Miskin," Whitmore said, "to see if he knows where Gregory's staying."

He was back in a couple of minutes, looking even more gloomy. "Negative. He called from Annecy, France. And he's moving around. That is, if Miskin's telling the truth."

Sanger nodded and shook hands. "So long, Chuck. And don't worry too much. Leave it to me. I'll call you the moment I hear anything."

Sanger called Whitmore the next day just before five. "Gregory looks like a bum steer, I'm afraid. No one under that name has registered into any Swiss hotel or *pension* in the last few days, and there are no reservations in any of the big hotels for a Gregory over the coming weekend. All the other countries have drawn a blank."

Whitmore grunted, said nothing.

"Anything new your end, Chuck?"

"Nope."

34

"Well, I'll keep in touch."

Whitmore sat for a long time staring at the leather desk-top. Half an hour ago he had given Miskin his final instructions: that only ten percent of the asking price—$300,000—be paid to Gregory on the first signature, which would be for a month's option on the property. Whitmore reasoned that this would give Burn, Hirsch time to check out the book further, as well as await some further evidence that might clinch the matter one way or the other. The contract stipulated that at the end of thirty days Burn, Hirsch would be free to drop the option if evidence had been produced to cast serious doubts on the work's authenticity. At the same time, however, Gregory would be bound not to dispose of it elsewhere.

Deep in his mind Whitmore was not happy. In the past, as long as Burn, Hirsch produced perhaps one really profitable book a year, everyone was content. Political books weren't their line anyway, unless the politics were wholly decent, or ancient history. And the diaries of Comrade Lavrenti Pavlovich Beria looked as if they were far from either.

Sy Miskin's TWA flight touched down at Cointrin Airport, Geneva, at 10:20 on Saturday morning. Pierre Jadot, of the Police Financière Fédérale, watched it land from the spectator's terrace and made his way down toward Arrivals, where the chief immigration officer gave him a nod when his subject came through.

Miskin left the plane with a jaunty step. He had ambushed a hangover with a half bottle of Veuve Clicquot Brut and was now freshly shaved and ready for any tantrums that Gregory might offer. He passed through Customs and Immigration without incident, his luggage consisting of one Louis Vuitton overnight bag and a black attaché case. Outside the airport, the taxi turned onto the *autoroute* along the lakeside toward Lausanne.

Miskin was tense but happy. Even the weather seemed to

herald success: the air clear and sharp after the stagnant heat of Manhattan. Vevey smelled of freshly cut flowers, the streets like well-swept floors. It was still only 11:30. At the Hotel du Lac he left his overnight bag at the desk and had coffee and a martini in the bar. He had reservations for that night in the Hotel des Bergues in Geneva, as well as on the evening plane back to New York.

Upstairs the door of Suite 96 was opened by a short, powerfully built man in a black beard. "Mr. Miskin! You are on excellent time. Come in, please!"

For a moment Miskin did not recognize him. The man he knew as Gregory was wearing the same shiny blue suit that he had had on at their last meeting, but the beard was new. It was also false. The man was sweating, and the gauze foundation was beginning to peel loose from under his ears. Miskin wondered if he ought to mention it. Negotiating with a man like Gregory was not easy in normal circumstances; negotiating with him in a transparent disguise threatened to be tragicomic. Miskin was afraid he would start laughing—and negotiating over three million dollars was no laughing matter.

But before he could say anything, Gregory seized his arm and waved to a man sitting by the window. "You know Herr Dettweiler, of course? We have some nice champagne for you. Or would you prefer whisky? I am drinking Zubrowka myself—Polish liqueur-vodka, very strengthening at this time of the day!" His huge bulk bustled around Miskin, almost tripping him up as he closed the door.

Dettweiler came slowly out of an armchair and shook hands. "I am pleased to meet you again, Mr. Miskin. Your journey was agreeable, I hope?"

"Fine." Miskin flashed his teeth. "Everything all right this end, Mr. Gregory?"

Gregory had lumbered over to a coffee table where there was an open champagne bottle in an ice bucket. "All absolutely tickatee-boo!" he cried, with a ghastly American twang. "You would like some champagne?" he said again, and without waiting for the answer poured out a glass, losing half of it in a pool of foam. He filled it up and lost as much again handing it to Miskin, then refilled his own glass from a yellowish-green bottle which, Miskin noted with misgiving, was more than half empty. The Swiss lawyer showed Miskin into a chair, while Gregory remained standing, constantly moving about.

"I see no reason why we should not approach the business immediately," Dettweiler said. "You have all the necessary papers?"

Miskin patted the attaché case in his lap. "But first, I wonder if Mr. Gregory here would mind introducing himself a bit more." He gave a light laugh. "I mean, I can't very well go on calling you Mr. Gregory, can I? It sounds sort of silly."

"Why silly?" Gregory stopped his pacing and was staring down at him, his big rheumy eyes flecked with red.

Miskin shrugged. "Well, what's your other name, for instance?"

"John. John Gregory." There was defiance in the man's bulky stance.

"That's not your real name, is it?" Miskin said, with only the shade of a smile this time.

"If I tell you it is my real name, do you not believe me?" said Gregory, his accent growing thicker with excitement.

Miskin glanced at Dettweiler. "Do I understand this is the signature I get on the contract?"

The Swiss nodded. "It is."

Miskin squeezed his lips together. "I don't want to create problems," he said, still looking at the lawyer, "but, as I made clear at our last meeting, my employers are very insistent that they know whom they're dealing with. Three million dollars is a very great deal of money to hand over to a total stranger."

"Mr. Miskin," said Dettweiler, in a voice so low that Miskin had to lean forward to catch his words, "as I think *I* made clear at our last meeting, my client is acting only as an agent—sole

37

agent for the property in question. If you are satisfied as to the genuine nature of that property, it is unnecessary to pursue inquiries of a personal nature. I am Mr. Gregory's attorney and will speak for him."

Miskin drank some champagne. "Okay. But I don't think I have to impress upon you, Herr Dettweiler, that if anything should go wrong with this deal, you've got Atlantic, General & National to answer to—and they've got one helluva lot of pull, even over here!"

Nothing changed in the lawyer's face. "You are not, I hope, intending to threaten me?" he said in the same soft voice, and Miskin's head bobbed forward. He was beginning to enjoy himself.

"Oh, I'm not threatening anybody, Herr Dettweiler. I leave that to my employers. And as you say, you're Mr. Gregory's attorney, which is fine by me. But I'd remind you that your client hasn't told you everything, either."

"What does that mean?"

"He hasn't told you the nature of the property, has he?"

The Swiss looked quickly at Gregory, who had swallowed his drink and stood watching Miskin with a suspicious glare.

"It was not part of the deal!" Gregory shouted. "We discussed it all last time. You say you do not want to make problems, and now you are making them!"

"All right, all right." Miskin had had his fun; he had sown just the right doubt in Dettweiler's mind to have weakened the alliance, so that from now on the Swiss would be acting more as a referee than as an opponent. Gregory on his own was no doubt going to prove trouble enough when it came to the business of the ten percent option.

Miskin unlocked his attaché case and took out a folder tied with red ribbon, and a typed letter with the heading of A. N. & G. Consolidated, signed by Whitmore.

Gregory stood over him, breathing hard. "Shall I call the bank?"

38

Miskin glanced at his watch. "I'm afraid the banks are closed."

"Ours is staying open."

Miskin looked up at him with his bland smile. "There's really no need for that, Mr. Gregory. The draft won't be through till at least Monday morning."

"Monday! You said today—Saturday—the very latest!" Gregory swung his huge hands and gaped helplessly at Dettweiler, who looked in turn at Miskin.

"It's all right, gentlemen, don't panic. Just a small hitch with exchange control." Miskin gave them his whitest smile. "Even in the United States, you know, we have a few regulations about moving big sums of money from one country to another."

"It would have helped," said Dettweiler, "if we had been informed of this problem earlier."

Miskin shrugged and picked up the letter again. "I should also explain," he began, "that my employers have made certain changes to our original—" As he spoke, Gregory lunged forward and seized the letter out of his hand.

"Now, just a moment, Mr. Gregory!" Miskin stood up quickly. "Give that back—it'll get damaged." It was his turn to look to the Swiss for help.

Dettweiler nodded. "Give it back, please, Mr. Gregory."

Miskin took it and sat down again, smoothing it out on his knee; then he passed it to Dettweiler. The Swiss read the letter through without expression; he was about to hand it back when Gregory snatched it out of his hands and stood reading it himself, his face turning red.

"*Yob tuoyu mat!*" Gregory let the Russian obscenity escape without apparently realizing it; the next four words came out in a roar of rage and saliva: "*Three hundred thousand dollars!*" He gaped breathlessly at Dettweiler. "It is a goddam double-cross! Three million—that's what we agreed!" He swung around on Miskin and waved the letter under his face. "Swinish, filthy trick—you American businessmen, all the goddam same! Thiev-

39

ing dogs at a bone! But you won't get it." He gave a ferocious cackle. "You won't get it, because we take it elsewhere. Dettweiler, call Berlin, Paris, London, Milan and the big Japanese boys. Separate deals with all of them. And we tell these American dogs to fuck their mothers!"

"Don't be silly," said Miskin. He turned to the Swiss. "I think you'd better tell your client, Herr Dettweiler, that even big American corporations are not in the habit of handing over three million dollars without certain guarantees—"

"Guarantees!" the Russian roared. "You have the goddam typescript—you have Krull's expert opinion! What else do you want? Beria's ghost to sign the contract?"

"Shut up," said Miskin, with a quick glance at Dettweiler; but the lawyer's face betrayed nothing. "And take off that damned beard!" Miskin added. "Whom are you trying to fool?"

Gregory rolled his eyes and blinked. "It was in case of photographers," he muttered, then turned and stumped into the next room. They waited in silence until Gregory reappeared, wiping his face where a few shreds of cowgum still clung to his sweaty stubble like dried jelly.

"What Burn, Hirsch is offering," Miskin said, half turning to the lawyer, "is a thirty-day option for ten percent. Even if we don't publish, your client keeps the money. I don't think even he can argue that this is unreasonable."

To his surprise Gregory was silent.

"I appreciate Herr Gregory's annoyance," said the Swiss. "This is not what I understand you agreed on the telephone from New York?"

"I'm afraid your client has misinformed you, Herr Dettweiler. I never discuss any deal on the phone. That's not the way we work. As it is"—and Miskin tapped the letter in his hand—"the decisions are no longer mine. They're now coming right from the top."

Gregory had poured himself another glass of Zubrowka and came stumbling back, a trickle dribbling down his chin. "You said three million. In Montreux you said it! You have a book worth perhaps ten million—unique, without price. And now you turn on me—betray me!" He stopped and muttered something in Russian, then strode over to a table and grabbed the telephone. "The deal is off," he shouted over his shoulder at Miskin.

"Put that thing down, you damned fool," Miskin said wearily.

Gregory stopped. Through the silence came a sound like a trapped wasp from the receiver still in his hand.

"Put it down," said Dettweiler.

Gregory hesitated, as though contemplating whether to smash the instrument against the edge of the table. Then slowly he replaced it in its cradle.

"We'd better get one thing straight right away, Gregory," Miskin said. "I'm not fooling around. We've got half the material back in New York, which gives us a certain claim to it. So before you start calling Paris and Milan and Tokyo, just remember that what you'll be offering will be secondhand now. Nobody likes a Dutch auction, and even if they still want the material they're going to have a fight on their hands—our lawyers in New York will see to that." He paused and sipped some champagne. "You've got a good deal, Gregory. Don't go and louse it up now. You might not get another chance."

The Russian's manner changed: he became almost meek, moving his hands awkwardly about, while Miskin handed the contract to Dettweiler.

"Perhaps you'd better be looking through these. But first, for your client's sake, I think I'd better spell out certain conditions we have deliberately omitted from the contract."

"Conditions? More conditions?" said Gregory.

"So far we've made no conditions," said Miskin, "except to give you an option for thirty days—and I might tell you that I had to fight to get that much."

Gregory stood twirling his tiny glass in one hand and rumpling his hair with the other, but he said nothing.

41

Miskin went on. "Since Mr. Gregory refuses to tell us any-thing about himself, we obviously must insist on some positive evidence as to the authenticity of the material."

"You have Krull's evidence," Gregory said.

"We have Krull's opinion," said Miskin suavely. "And no doubt we could get other, equally reputable experts who might contradict him. In fact, it's a sign of our faith in the material that we haven't so far done so." He paused. Dettweiler sat very still, his hands folded in his lap like napkins.

Miskin turned toward Gregory. "You said at our last meeting that you got the material in Vienna, from a source in Hungary. We've got to know about this source. And how it got to Hungary in the first place. Out of Russia, presumably?"

While he was speaking, Gregory had come closer until Miskin could now smell him—sweat leavened by eau de cologne. He sighed and sat down on a sofa between them. Miskin detected a certain relief in his manner.

Dettweiler said, "You did not mention these conditions at our first meeting."

"I was not in a position at our first meeting to know what conditions my employers would make." Miskin looked back at Gregory. "I should add that no reputable publisher—certainly none of the ones you've thought of calling—would touch the material without some hard guarantee as to where the stuff came from, and how."

Gregory stared at the floor, his big alligator shoes crossing and uncrossing themselves under the coffee table. "The way it got out of Hungary is not important," he said at last. "A tourist from the West—he brought it out in his luggage. There was very little risk. There are so many tourists in Hungary during the summer, the frontier police hardly ever search anyone."

"How did he get hold of it?"

"From someone in Budapest."

"Who?" There was silence. "I must know, Mr. Gregory, otherwise I am not authorized to sign this contract."

The Russian shifted his great bulk and one hand made a vain effort to smooth down his hair; then pulled from his pocket a thick envelope which he thrust at Miskin like a weapon. Across the front was typed in red: "S. Miskin, Esq. Personal and confidential." "Inside is an affidavit—a document signed by a great friend of mine, a Hungarian. It is very valuable." He paused. "We are not talking now as businessmen, Mr. Miskin, but as human beings. If that man's name is ever discovered, the consequences would be terrible. I don't have to tell you." And Miskin nodded sympathetically.

"He is a very fine man," Gregory went on, "an old Communist who fought in Spain with Pal Maleter, the general the Russians shot after the 1956 uprising. In the war he fought with the Red Army and won the Order of Lenin. Then later he held a high post in the Hungarian Communist regime until the purges in the early fifties, when he resigned and was sent to prison. He came out in 1955. He now lives in retirement and writes poetry."

"Did he bring the material out of Russia?"

"Yes." Gregory's stubby fingers picked at the cowgum behind his ears. "It is all in the affidavit."

Miskin sat holding the envelope, but made no move to open it. Finally he said. "He's an old renegade Communist with a jail sentence behind him. Yet he was allowed into Moscow. How come?"

"It's all in the affidavit," said Gregory again.

"And his name?"

"His name too."

"And you got all this from the tourist, the guy who brought it out to Vienna?"

Gregory nodded.

"How did you get onto this tourist?"

"He is an old friend."

"And the Hungarian?"

Gregory poured himself some champagne. "I know him—

that's all that matters. The details are not important."

"Everything's important," said Miskin.

Gregory shrugged. "I met him behind in Moscow—a long time ago. We correspond regularly."

"Okay. So what was in it for him—a fat commission, I suppose?"

Gregory's mouth dropped open. "Holy Christ, no! He is not a goddam merchant—he did it from idealism! You've read the material, you know what's in it—that it is the last nail in the coffin of Stalinism. When it is published, those old neo-Stalinist pigs will never dare lift their heads again. That is why my friend did it—not for your goddam dollars!"

"But not the same with you, eh? You're really hungry for those dollars?"

"It is not the same, I am a businessman!" Gregory sprang up and began pacing again, slopping champagne on the carpet.

"Okay," said Miskin. "Now this Western tourist. We're going to need his name."

"It is not necessary. He is a professional man—he has a reputation to keep."

"The hell he has! Since when was it a crime over here to smuggle manuscripts from behind the Iron Curtain?"

"Bah, you understand nothing!" Gregory came stamping back to the sofa. "When this sort of thing gets out there are always filthy stories. These Kremlinologists, they are a kind of academic Mafia—they hate anyone from outside, anyone who threatens their position. They invent conspiracies, as with Solzhenitsyn. They were furious because they hadn't got him for themselves, so they spread the most foul rumors—that his books had been planted in the West by the KGB to compromise him."

"The information you give us will be treated with absolute confidence. You have my word for that," said Miskin, and to his relief the Russian sat down.

"It is quite simple," Gregory went on. "You just say that it came out of one of the satellite countries through a highly confidential source. The public is not so stupid about these matters. In fact, what would make them suspicious would be if you told them too much."

Miskin sat fingering the sealed envelope, balancing it delicately by the corners. "All right, we'll forget about the contract for the moment. Only this"—he nodded at the envelope—"we'll have to check. It'll be done with the greatest discretion, don't worry. Your man won't have anything to fear. But I must warn you, Mr. Gregory"—and he glanced meaningfully at Dettweiler —"that if anything *doesn't* check, there'll be trouble. In fact, we'd regard it as a clear breach of contract."

"No, no, you have nothing to fear! It will check okay!" Gregory cried. "Only I warn you too: if this man's name ever gets out—one word in the press, and I will get you, Mr. Miskin! I will damned well get you and break your goddam neck!"

Miskin decided to play it lightly. "I'll bear that in mind, John. But first I have to read this." He waved the envelope. "Do you mind if I use the bedroom?"

Gregory nodded at the door. "But no copies—no photostats."

Miskin smiled. "You think I carry a pocket Xerox around with me?"

Five minutes later he returned, sat down and carefully laid the envelope in his case, under the contract. "It's a good story. As I said, we'll have to check out a few things, but I think it'll be enough to satisfy my employers as far as the option goes."

"And the big contract—the whole three million?"

"For that we may need something more. Something really conclusive—and public."

"Such as?"

"We're going to want a witness. Somebody who can come forward and state categorically that these alleged diaries—" He checked himself in time, with a quick glance at Dettweiler, for he was still not certain just how much the lawyer knew about the precise nature of the material; Gregory had been very secretive with him at their last meeting. "Someone totally independent who can corroborate, on oath and in public—to the press and on TV, if necessary—that certain incidents in this book are true."

He was ready for Gregory's outburst, but none came. The Russian simply nodded; but there was the hint of satisfied cunning in his face, like a fat cat who has finished a saucer of milk. It worried Miskin; he had grown so used to Gregory's tantrums that this sudden tranquillity disconcerted him.

He now handed the contract to Dettweiler. "Perhaps you'd like to be looking through this." He turned to Gregory and smiled, and to his surprise the Russian smiled back.

"The title of the property has not been filled in," said Dettweiler.

Miskin continued looking at Gregory, his eyes friendly and inquiring. The Russian wiped a hand across his mouth. "The title of the property," he repeated. "Oh, yes. Something . . ." He hesitated, groping for the English word.

"Uncompromising," said Dettweiler, and Gregory gave a vigorous nod.

"It seems to me," Miskin went on, "that at this stage it would be only reasonable to let Herr Dettweiler into your complete confidence, John." The lawyer's work no doubt involved him in such tortuous deals with foreigners that perhaps he had become blasé. But Miskin had another motive: he wanted to nudge the Swiss further onto his side, for he still did not entirely trust Gregory. Miskin's sharp little homily about publishers not liking Dutch auctions had been largely bluff; he was aware that most of the big publishing houses in the West might be prepared to enter into some quite spectacular bidding for Beria's diaries. Dettweiler would no doubt know this, too, but it would still be in his interest to have the deal clinched as quickly as possible.

Gregory roamed around the room, both hands clasped across his head where his hair was now standing on end.

"We need a title that isn't in any way ambiguous," said Miskin. "For the contract, I mean. We can work on the published

46

title later." He glanced at Dettweiler. "The author's name will have to be mentioned. I suggest something simple. Why not *The Beria Papers?*" He was watching Dettweiler as he spoke, but the lawyer's face again betrayed neither surprise nor interest. Miskin turned back to Gregory. "If that's okay with you, John?"

"It is excellent—a really good selling title. It will make you real good money, Mr. Miskin."

"Well, if we're going to ante up three million bucks for it, I sure hope it does!" Miskin rejoined, with a knowing smirk at the Russian.

Dettweiler read the contract through with a rapid professional eye. He made several queries, but Whitmore's lawyers had left no loopholes, and the Swiss was finally satisfied. He handed the contract back, and Miskin arranged it beside the three copies along the coffee table. Then Miskin sat back, smiling at Gregory.

"Right! Now the rest of the property."

The Russian nodded. Dettweiler went into the bedroom and returned with a briefcase from which he took a parcel sealed in brown paper. "You wish to see inside?"

Miskin shrugged. "Just for the record."

Gregory snapped the cellulose-tape seals, broke open the brown wrapping and showed Miskin the coarse yellowed paper covered with the now familiar foreign script, faded and double-spaced, with occasional corrections in pencil.

"You will not require it to be translated first?" he said.

Miskin chuckled. "I think at this stage I'll just have to take your word for it." He picked up the bulk of paper, still in its wrapping, and laid it inside his case. Then he sat back and took out a gold pen.

"Right. Signatures, gentlemen."

They signed in order—Miskin, Gregory, then Dettweiler; first the top copy tied with red ribbon, then the three copies on thinner paper, which they signed in the same order. Miskin

47

noted that Gregory's was too legible for a normal signature.

When it was done the Russian suggested another bottle of champagne. Miskin glanced at his watch. It was nearly one o'clock. "I don't want to sound rude, John, but I have a lunch date with one of our authors who lives along the lake, and I'm late already!" His hands were swiftly gathering up the contracts as he spoke, leaving one of the copies for Dettweiler. "You'll excuse me, won't you? And don't feel too hard about our rough American business habits—we're all soft and mushy inside, really!" He held out his hand. "It's been a pleasure doing business with you, Mr. Gregory."

☙

Jadot saw Miskin leave, from his chair across the lobby facing the elevators, but made no attempt to follow him. His instructions had been to make sure the first subject, Miskin, kept his appointment with Herr Dettweiler at the Hotel du Lac, Vevey. He was then to keep a surveillance on a second subject, who had gone up to Dettweiler's suite half an hour before the first subject arrived. By arrangement with the manager, the desk clerk would inform him the moment this second subject appeared.

Jadot had been waiting for one hour and forty minutes when Gregory came down. During this time he had instructed the hotel receptionist to check all calls made to and from Suite 96. So far there had only been two, both outgoing to Zurich. Jadot had checked with his bureau in Geneva and had learned that they were Dettweiler's home and office numbers.

At 1:45 exactly the receptionist came over to tell him his taxi was waiting—the prearranged signal that his second subject had appeared. Jadot's instructions were to follow him to any hotel or frontier post and find out his identity and all personal particulars. These instructions did not indicate that the subject would be anticipating surveillance.

He went outside and got into his car, expecting the man to

take a taxi; but instead the subject walked down the lakeside and stopped at the landing stage for the pleasure steamers that plied between Geneva and Chillon. There was one already pulled up alongside, its deck packed with excursionists.

The subject looked at his watch, then seemed to hesitate. Jadot drove past him and parked farther along under the trees. In the rear-view mirror he saw the subject looking out at the lake, where a second steamer was now approaching from the direction of Chillon. He seemed suddenly to make up his mind, strode onto the landing stage and boarded the first boat. By the time Jadot reached it, the second steamer had drawn alongside and passengers were moving in all directions; and then Jadot lost sight of him. Jadot struggled forward against the crush and upset a woman's basket. She shouted at him in German, and Jadot, by nature a diffident man, wasted five vital seconds apologizing.

The movement of passengers was now subsiding. A whistle blew on the second boat; Jadot again saw the subject. He was on the second boat and was now wearing a beret too small for him. But the disguise was effective, and Jadot was wondering whether it had been intentional as he struggled forward again, ready with his police pass, and managed to jump across between the two boats. The engines had begun to throb, and they were beginning to draw away from the other steamer when Jadot saw the subject near the stern, where the gap between the two vessels was narrowest. Suddenly, with elephantine agility, the man vaulted across the rail and landed on the deck of the steamer which was still at the landing stage.

Jadot knew it would be useless to try to follow the same way. Instead he ran up to the little bridge. They were a good hundred yards from the shore before the captain agreed to turn around. Jadot was not hopeful. A full three minutes had passed before he was back on the landing stage, where the first steamer had also pulled away. There remained only a few people on the jetty, with no trace of the subject.

49

Jadot drove back to the Hotel du Lac and called his bureau, keeping explanations to a minimum. The subject's conduct on the boat amounted, in his opinion, to sufficient justification for a B-grade surveillance to be placed on all airports and frontier posts, road and rail, throughout the country. Later, if the surveillance continued to prove negative, a description of the subject should be circulated to all police posts, hotels and *pensions*.

Jadot's immediate superior was still at lunch, and it was nearly half an hour before he could be reached; but even then the man was reluctant to sanction such dramatic measures before referring the matter to higher authority. Since it was a weekend, the machinery of communication was more sluggish than usual, and it was ninety minutes after Jadot had lost his subject before a B surveillance was finally ordered.

The Bureau de la Police Financière Fédérale in Geneva teletyped its report to the Treasury Department in New York at 4:20 P.M., Eastern time. Mike Sanger was out on his thirty-foot yawl when the weekend duty officer called him at his beach house outside Westport, Connecticut, and he wasn't contacted until much later that evening. He plugged the phone into the tape recorder and had the duty officer read off the Teletype. Twenty minutes later he called Whitmore at his country home near Towners, New York, and played him the tape through without comment.

When it was over, Whitmore groaned. "So they loused it up! What sort of police force is that? The tail gets shaken and the guy slips straight through the net!"

"I know," said Sanger. He was tired, and the last thing he wanted was to have to start defending his colleagues in Europe, especially as he had only been doing the old man a favor in the first place. "I admit it doesn't look too good on the face of it, Chuck. But remember, you did insist that discretion was the top priority. Well, you got it. It's always possible that Gregory's

50

still in Switzerland—but if you want the Swiss to go on looking for him, the thing will have to be taken higher. That means the Police Criminelle, which in turn will mean making the thing official."

"But according to this report from Geneva, the thing now *is* official!" Whitmore cried. "So it looks like I lose both ways?"

"Only half official," Sanger replied carefully. "If they're to keep a continued watch on their frontiers, we'll have to give them some pretty good reasons. The Swiss have their tourist trade to think of. And they also don't like being hustled. And so far we haven't hustled them."

Whitmore scowled across the heavily draped room. "Why the hell did they take nearly two hours to alert the frontiers in the first place?"

"They had to go through the proper channels—and, in an unofficial capacity, that took time. The Swiss like to do things by the book."

"To hell with the book!" Whitmore muttered. "Just find this Gregory for me. I may have to be paying the guy three million dollars. As it is, it looks as though I'm already in for three hundred thousand—and that isn't government money, Mike, it's the corporation's!"

"Okay," Sanger said, "so what do you want me to do now?"

"Get the Swiss onto him—and everybody else. The British, Germans, French, Italians, Austrians—somebody must know who he is!"

There was a pause. "Listen, Chuck. I think you're going about this the wrong way. You're as good as asking for an international manhunt before Monday morning, with darned little to go on except a rough description and not even a photograph. And in the meantime you're going to have to come up with a story—not the whole story, perhaps, but enough to make the security angle mighty tricky. In any event, an awful lot of people are going to be involved, and not all of them will be as discreet as my contacts in Geneva. Sooner or later, even if you do find who Gregory is, the CIA boys are going to get onto it. They're pretty busy out there. Switzerland may be a holiday paradise to most people, but behind those beautiful ski slopes the place is swarming with just about every kind of spook in the business. And once the CIA boys are onto it, they're not going to let go. And you don't want that, do you?"

Whitmore shifted in his chair and swore inaudibly. "What about this lawyer guy, Dettweiler? He must be able to lead us to Gregory."

Sanger closed his eyes and said, "Chuck, lawyers are like doctors. Unless we could prove an extraditable offense, we couldn't even get the Swiss to pay him a courtesy visit."

There was a long silence; then Whitmore's voice came back, gruff and aggressive. "Mike, I've got a darned good mind to call the whole deal off—cancel the contract on the grounds of Gregory's suspicious behavior. The Swiss would back us up, wouldn't they?"

"You mean in a court of law?" There was another silence. "Chuck, you've asked for my advice. Well, I'm going to give it to you straight. The hand has been dealt, and the best thing you can do now is play it. Put your ante in for thirty days, in which time you may be able to dig something up. I'd say it was a sound business risk."

Whitmore released a loud sigh down the phone. "Well, Mike, it looks as though I've got to do as you say—ante up and play the hand. Thanks anyway."

"Sorry I couldn't do more. I'll keep in touch." The line went dead.

At 10:20 A.M. Monday, Swiss time, a draft from the Bank of America was received by the Volkskantonale Bank, Zurich, for the sum of U.S. $300,000 in the name of John Gregory, who would present himself with a letter of introduction from the vice-president of Atlantic, National & General Consolidated, in the presence of Ludwig Dettweiler, attorney at law in Zurich.

PART
TWO

And, after all, what is a lie? 'Tis but
The truth in masquerade.
                    —LORD BYRON

Paper Two

Moscow, December 1949

I am left exhausted, like a fish beached out of a sea of vodka and champagne. The festivities have been truly amazing, despite the weather and the economic situation.

The Boss[1] has ordained that his seventieth-birthday celebrations continue until the New Year, and a hysterical adulation is sweeping the city: crowds cheering every mention of him in cinemas and theaters, and there are reports of children singing carols with the names of Christ and God replaced by his! Indeed, one would not be surprised to see the Old Man appear on the rostrum in Red Square wearing the czarist crown!

His birthday party, however, was a tricky affair for me, on account of this wretched Kostov[2] business. For the Boss has been in a black mood ever since the trial, and at the very hint of the affair

---

[1] Stalin, whom Beria also referred to as the "Old Man" and in person as "Master," often using the Georgian word, *batano.*

[2] Traicho Kostov, a former Bulgarian vice-premier, who was one of the first victims of the postwar show trials in Eastern Europe, and the only one who retracted his confession in open court. He was hanged on December 21, 1949, Stalin's seventieth birthday.

his face turns puce, sweat breaks out all over his pitted forehead, and he even begins to shake as though he were about to have a seizure. I have not seen him so inflamed by anything since the Tito business—and that is saying a lot!

However, he was somewhat placated by the news that the traitor had been hanged that very morning, and I was able to cheer him further by informing him that my boys in Sofia had, on my personal instructions, arranged the noose so that the Bulgar took a good fifteen minutes to die. But the whole episode has left a sour taste in my mouth, since it reflects directly on the Service. (Of course I questioned the boys in detail, and it seems they gave K. the full works, but they must have seriously underestimated him—for this mulish Bulgar was no soft-stomached bourgeois intellectual; it appears he had been hardened by any amount of beatings at the hands of the fascists during the war, and that he had a constitution like pig iron. In any case, he cast a shadow over the Boss's birthday dinner as though the brute were mocking me from his freshly dug lime grave.)

The party at Kuntsevo[3] was a lavish affair: pork, lamb, duckling and pheasant, with the best wines from France, even fruit from the fascist nations—melons from Spain, and oranges and pineapples from South Africa—which the Boss made several jokes about during the evening.

As usual, the room was stiflingly hot, but none of us was allowed to even loosen his collar, let alone take off his jacket—for lately the Old Man has become a stickler for formal dress, however much buffoonery may ensue later.

He began the evening in a reflective mood, treating us to a long session of reminiscences, mostly about the Western leaders he had met. And although we had heard most of it before, we listened attentively, for while he appears on such occasions to be lost in his own thoughts, he misses nothing!

He told us that the one he liked most was the Canadian capital-

[3] A village outside Moscow where Stalin had his private dacha.

ist millionaire, Beaverbrook, whom the British made a lord. The fellow owns one of the biggest bourgeois newspapers in the West and is a great enthusiast for the old British Empire, which is fast dying. This seems to amuse the Boss. He told us he thought Beaverbrook a cunning rogue, but that he was not at heart an anti-Soviet, and the two of them had had some good jokes together, the Boss said. He even added that he could do with a man like Beaverbrook in the Politburo.

Churchill was too set in his ways—a born anti-Socialist whom he could only hope to outwit, but who would never have made a friend. Roosevelt had been no more than a weak-minded invalid —a true symptom of the American bourgeois classes. And de Gaulle he had detested—a giant pig-headed bore, full of pompous ideals for that nation of sybarites of his, who couldn't even drink a glass of wine without looking as though he had a bad smell under his nose.

Then, as the night mellowed, the Boss began directing those sly taunts of his around the table—mostly at the servile Voroshilov,[4] reminding him that he was lucky to be allowed to take the salute during the Victory Parade, after his performance in 1941, at which the wretched creature, all groomed and gleaming in his marshal's uniform and rows of medals, went the color of ash.

But, worse, the Old Man then began to treat us to another dose of his war talk—boasting, as he always does on such occasions, that it is by the sword that Socialism has made its greatest strides. The truth is, his self-confidence is still badly shaken, not only by the whole Tito business, but by the Berlin fiasco, and he is endlessly casting about for some sure way of securing his revenge. Unfortunately, as soon as he has a liter or two of wine inside him, he begins to see the solution in a glorious Armageddon. Once, after the statutory toast to the Victory of Stalingrad, he turned to

[4] Marshal Kliment Voroshilov, one of Stalin's oldest cronies, who was relieved of his command as People's Defense Commissar after the siege of Leningrad when Stalin accused him of being a "specialist in retreat." He died in 1970 and is buried alongside Stalin under the Kremlin wall.

me with his wolfish grin and said, "So, my good Prosecutor, when you have finished hanging the last of these Titoist scum, perhaps you can spare me a few of those nice new bombs of yours[5] so that between us we can liberate our comrades in the West!"

The trouble is, such words are not spoken in mere jest, for I know the Boss too well for that. And who can say that tonight's gossip will not be tomorrow's orders of the day? He even went on to propose toasts to "Our Russian forebears, Peter the Great and Ivan the Terrible, and to their historic exploits!"—as though the Old Man were a full-blooded Russian himself.

But honestly, such talk is enough to freeze even my blood! For these marshals and their aides are such groveling toadies that they would drag themselves on their bellies to the grave rather than question even the Boss's most outrageous designs. And the fearful truth is that despite Berlin and the Bomb, he still seriously underestimates the bourgeois forces. The Americans, he thinks, are too fond of their good living to raise their might again to help Europe; the British are finished; and so are the French and the Italians, where our comrades are already as strong as they were in Czechoslovakia. And Germany is too whipped to want to fight again.

I try to argue that while our land forces are superior to theirs, our nuclear capabilities are still inferior; but this the Boss brushes aside, claiming that the Americans are such moral cowards that they would never dare drop their bombs on Mother Russia. (Japan, he says, is different: a yellow race, inferiors, and the Americans are true racists at heart.)

Meanwhile, those greedy fox eyes of his are straining for a glimpse of the Mediterranean, the white coast of England, the palm trees of Africa, perhaps even the sands of Arabia and snows of the Himalayas! Yet all around him, while he eats and drinks and dreams his mad fantasies, our country lies frozen and half starved.

I was in a melancholic mood when the party finally broke up.

[5] Reference to Soviet A-bomb.

Poskrebyshev[6] and the Armenian[7] were as usual dead drunk and had to be hauled off to the toilets. I was pretty far gone myself, and glad to be in the car speeding back to the city. All things considered, the evening could have gone a lot worse. For, as the joke goes among us: at these sessions with the Boss, the difference between a rotten egg slipped under your seat and a bullet in the back of the neck is a slender one!

Moscow, January 1950

The New Year began with a beautiful trick on that viper Poskrebyshev. I laugh just to think of it!

He had it coming to him, of course: a really loathsome creature, creeping about with those high, hunched shoulders and gray pocked skin—he is like the carrier of some contagious disease. I cannot understand how the Boss tolerates him, except that he is an utterly dependable lackey.

Just after Christmas I was called in to discuss Poskrebyshev. The Boss was in a thoughtful mood, sucking at his unlit pipe, and hardly touching any wine. It is a mood I recognize well—very calm and determined, yet deadly, like an old fox before the kill—and at first I was sure that P. had had it. For it appears the Boss thinks his hireling has been getting too big for his boots: that while P. is always so courteous and cringing with all of us, he is a real foulmouthed tyrant among the ministries, where his very appearance strikes terror among the minions.

The Boss indicated that he wanted P. taught a lesson. Something private and subtle, leaving the matter to my best judgment and resources. I took my leave and supervised the arrangements myself, right down to the last detail, delegating only the technical formalities to Rafik.

[6] Alexander Poskrebyshev, Stalin's private secretary and one of the most powerful and sinister figures in the dictator's entourage. He disappeared after Stalin's death, but is believed to have died of natural causes.
[7] Anastas Mikoyan.

59

The plan I came up with had a really classical simplicity, worthy of the Old Man himself!

On New Year's Eve P. returned from the usual festivities in the Kremlin, where he had been hovering about like a shadow behind his master, accepting every glass of wine which the Boss mockingly foisted on him, and as usual getting sick as a dog by the end of the evening. But when he got back to his flat in the Arbat he found his wife was not there. (She is a modest little woman with a talent for the piano, especially the Chopin sonatas.) We let P. sweat it out till the small hours, then I had Rafik telephone to inform him that his wife had been picked up, on the Boss's orders, for anti-state activities. We had bugged the apartment and could hear the wretched creature sobbing for some time; then he began to pray—he actually *prayed* in the old style, like a good priest!

But next morning he was at work as usual—not even a minute late—padding about after his master, as sick as an old dog! The Boss was really cheerful that evening as he described his secretary's demeanor in eloquent detail, and I only cursed our engineers for being such incompetents that they were not able to install miniature cameras in the apartment so that we could watch the whole comedy as it unfolded!

We left P. in this torment for two days, and not once did he drop even a hint of her disappearance, although he must have been wondering how long it would be before the Old Man pounced again. Then on the night of the third day of the New Year came the master stroke.

P. returned to his apartment late, after we had pumped him full of champagne against his will, and we sent him out as usual quite drunk. When he got back I could just imagine him lurching up those four flights of stairs—then, on the last landing, hearing the piano music. He burst in, and there at the piano sat the girl— a big strapping blonde hammering away at Chopin's sonatas.

We could hear P.'s voice on the tapes, almost unintelligible as he cried out, *"Who are you?"*

And she replied, without stopping her playing, "Comrade Pos-krebyshev, I am your new wife—sent to you as a New Year present by Comrade Beria, with the seasonal greetings of the Security Service."

Oh, it was beautiful! We heard P. break down and weep like a child—and I have now been informed by the girl that he actually fell on his knees and tore at his remaining hair! He must have become quite demented, for even this scheming old *apparatchik* has a love for his wife.

Next day we put him out of his misery. I called him to the Lubyanka, and saw him personally in my office. His wife had had a pleasant stay, I told him, she had been in one of the best cells, in the old part—with even a big window overlooking the court-yard. Then I told him he could take her home now, and again he broke down and wept before I had time to throw him out.

MALLORY'S REPORT

It began like any other day. I was woken at eight o'clock by the BBC Russian news, the words almost inaudible through the roaring and whining of the Soviet jammers, which reached even as far as Munich.

Boris Drobnov, my Russian flat-mate, was already banging about in the tiny kitchen, preparing his breakfast of black tea, liver sausage, and two raw eggs beaten up in a tumbler with a dash of Worcester sauce and a slug of pepper vodka.

Lying in the back room, which was about the size of a large cupboard and about as dark, I felt as though I had a hangover, although it was more than twenty weeks since I'd last touched a drink. Today also marked the two remaining weeks left of my temporary six-month contract with Radio Free Europe.

My name is Thomas Mallory. At the time of these events I was thirty-seven, a graduate in modern languages of King's College, Cambridge, with five published novels, a brief turbulent marriage, and a modestly successful career as a free-lance journalist behind me. I now had $450 saved from my job with RFE, a long-standing overdraft at my bank in London, a five-year-old fish-eyed Citroën DS-21, and no fixed abode besides the hutch I now lay in—which Boris grandly called "the Joseph Stalin Guest Room."

He was late this morning with my coffee. As the newscast finished, I could hear him swearing to himself in Russian, then came the chatter of his Olivetti. When he finally appeared he was holding two sheets of paper and glaring with anger.

"Tom, read this. The bastard has done it again!" And he thrust one of the sheets at me. It was a typed letter in German, under the heading MANSHOLDT PROPERTIES, MÜNCHEN. I read:

DEAR HERR DROBNOV,
Yesterday, during your absence at work, I inspected Apt. C, 25, Elisabethstrasse, of which you are leaseholder. I found the condition of these premises disgusting. Furthermore, the quantities of paper stored in the apartment constitute a serious fire hazard.

If these conditions have not been rectified, you will be obliged to find alternative accommodation without further notice.

Yours faithfully,
ADOLF STOLTZ (Hausmeister)

When I'd read it, Boris handed me the second sheet, on which he'd written back in German:

HERR STOLTZ,
When you decide to address me in a civilized manner, I will agree to reply likewise.
BORIS DROBNOV

"I should do as he asks," I said sleepily. "It'll be one hell of a nuisance having to move your stuff somewhere else."

"My stuff!" he roared. "What this bastard German calls *Papieren*—they are my filing system, my library, my whole goddam livelihood!"

I knew from hard experience that arguing with Boris was not a profitable pursuit. Besides, I had some sympathy with Herr Stoltz. Boris' flat was perhaps unique—a reproduction in miniature of the cosmic chaos of Russia. There was little furniture, for he did not believe in permanent possessions; but every inch of wall space and a good deal of the floors—including the bathroom, kitchen and cupboards—were piled with books, magazines and rotting newspapers. My room was half filled with back numbers of *Pravda* for the last ten years, while thousands of press cuttings spilled from every shelf like curious yellowing vegetation. The only objects of value in the flat, apart from his radio and Olivetti, were an ikon, an antique Russian typewriter the size of a cash register with what looked like the skeleton of a bird inside it, and which had once belonged to the executed Soviet leader Lev Kamenev, who had given it to Boris' father; and a marble chess table stained with tea.

Boris was still standing by the bed glowering at me. He was a short man with broad fleshy features and hair that was both thick and balding, and totally resistant to comb or brush; his eyes were large and bulging under heavy lids like bruised fruit and had a disturbing tendency, when he became excited, to roll up inside his head until only the whites were visible, like a pair of plover's eggs.

Physically he was immensely strong and, although very fat, had the shoulders of a miner and the thighs of a wrestler. He wore mass-produced suits of artificial fiber that were always splitting under the arms and around the crotch, but flapped like loose canvas below the knees and across his massive buttocks. He sweated easily, and although he took some pains with his toilet, he never looked freshly shaved or entirely clean.

His three great passions, besides the study of Soviet affairs—in which he was an acknowledged expert—were food, drink and gambling. In the first he was both greedy and knowledgeable—a tolerable cook and an experienced international gourmet who kept the *Guide Michelin* by his bed, never traveling anywhere without it, and often spending long periods studying it and planning gastronomic adventures. He also attended regular wine auctions, where he bought vintage clarets which he "laid down" under his bed, hoarding them like gold bars.

His third passion, gambling, was less happy. After he'd first defected—escaping to West Berlin just before the Wall went up in 1961, while on a Soviet student delegation to East Germany —he had gone to the States, where he earned considerable sums lecturing, writing articles and being debriefed by the CIA; but over the last three years, while he'd been working for Radio Free Europe in Munich, all his savings had been swept away under the croupiers' rakes of every major casino in Western Europe. Fortunately, the nearest one to Munich was in Garmisch, from which he was banned for having been sick into the roulette wheel—an incident which he insisted had been provoked not by overindulgence in food or alcohol, but by "nausea at the obscene perfidity of fate."

It was this kind of conduct which had brought Boris into conflict with a senior American executive of RFE, whom he threatened with a writ for slander after hearing that the man had referred to him as having the social graces of a baboon.

The description was apt. I had lived and worked in close proximity to Boris for five months, and knew he was not a man to whom the social graces came easily. He was dogmatic, tactless and aggressively argumentative. "If there were palm trees in Warsaw and niggers in Prague, you Americans would have pushed the Red Army back to the Urals!" he had once bawled across a Washington dinner table at his host, a Senator with pronounced liberal views. Such outbursts were made all the more disconcerting by the fact that it was often difficult to tell whether he was drunk or sober; for, although a massive drinker, he had a head like stone, and I had never known him have a hangover.

Nor was this lack of finesse confined to strangers; for while I had probably come to know and understand him as well as anyone alive, there were moments when even I experienced despair. If Boris represented the one percent of the Russian population which was well educated, well informed and well

65

traveled, God only knew what the other ninety-nine percent must be like. During the five months I'd shared with him, I had put up with his tantrums and rages, his foul eating habits, the appalling smells he made in the lavatory, his drinking and weeping and roaring and endless arguing and complaining; yet beneath all this Slav boorishness lay an intelligent, kind, even gentle character, and a ferociously loyal friend whom I'd come to love like an older, eccentric brother; and although his zest for gambling made him financially precarious, I'd have trusted him with my last penny.

Over those five months we had worked together in the same office at Radio Free Europe—an ostensibly "independent" organization, with its headquarters here in Munich, which broadcast to the satellite nations of Eastern Europe. Boris and I were employed as "information evaluators." In my case this meant reading every serious newspaper and magazine published in the West, and drawing up a daily précis of their contents. Boris had the job of doing the same with the Soviet press—a more difficult job, since it entailed both reading between the lines and an astute deduction of random facts, until he was able to draw up a detailed analysis of some important development which had received only scant coverage in the official Soviet press.

Although we were both paid American newspaper rates, Boris was not happy. He felt his talents were being wasted. All around him men of less knowledge and experience were being promoted to executive positions, including our immediate overlord, the chief evaluator—a cheerful, stupid Estonian who had made the mistake in 1939 of fleeing east and had been rewarded by ten years in one of Stalin's camps.

Part of Boris' problem was of his own making: his special ability to rile people, particularly the Americans on the staff—solemn men with talc-dusted jaws and button-down shirts who failed to understand the Slav character. But he was also up against a more insidious obstacle. His father had been a leading scientist during the Stalinist regime, and from childhood

Boris had been groomed for high office—which in the eyes of the more bigoted members of RFE made him immediately suspect. For it was not easy for Boris to explain why he had renounced a life of assured wealth and power for the more precarious rewards of the West. While a student at Moscow University, he had become disgusted by the dishonesty, stupidity and intellectual claustrophobia of the Communist system; and his intimate and encyclopedic knowledge of Soviet affairs gave him a clear edge over the Kremlinologists—their jealousy and spite being exacerbated by the fact that most of them had never set foot in a Communist country.

On that March morning both Boris and I, without knowing it, had reached the crossroads—the male menopause which calls for a radical, even revolutionary move.

At 8:30 he brought my coffee—still fretting about Herr Stolts. I got up and shaved in a dim blistered mirror; sluiced myself down with a saucepan of tepid water, for there was no shower; dressed in what passed for my office clothes—an old suede jacket, turtleneck sweater and brown Levi's—swallowed a couple of antidepressant pills that I'd been taking since my crackup eight months ago; then went out with Boris to the garage at the back of the block, where I kept the Citroën, and drove us out through the Englischer Garten to the long gray building that looks like a cross between a private clinic and a top-secret military establishment, which is the headquarters of Radio Free Europe.

That evening we began to clear out the flat. First Boris decreed that no books or press cuttings were to be touched; but magazines of Western origin more than a year old could go. There was some argument about the back numbers of *Pravda*, which stood in my bedroom in three leaning columns that reached to the ceiling, with a fourth just having its foundations laid. At last it was agreed to throw them all out except one—the edition of November 23, 1963, with a hastily remade front page bearing a black-bordered photograph of the late President John

F. Kennedy and the uncensored AP story, datelined Dallas.

Boris made some coffee and opened a bottle of Mouton Roth-schild '67, which he drank out of a teacup—for he did not believe in bourgeois trinkets like glasses, and soon broke any he was given. He worked with a method all of his own, and the flat was soon in even greater disorder than before we'd started.

I was relegated to the less important "files" in my bedroom, the bathroom and cupboards; but everything I threw out had to be first stacked in the hallway and vetted by Boris before being carried down to the dustbins. And while I worked, I thought about my fragile prospects for the future. I'd planned using my savings from RFE to spend the spring and summer in a partly converted farmhouse on the wilder side of Tuscany—the property of my one really rich friend, who had made a fortune on the Australian nickel boom, part of which he'd lavished on a swimming pool and modern plumbing for the house; then he had lost interest, leaving it to molder on the vine-covered hillside, visited only occasionally by friends bound for the more opulent pleasure domes of the south.

Here, in monastic seclusion, I planned to write my sixth book. But with a difference. For I was now thoroughly disillusioned with the English literary trade: polite praise in the Sunday papers, followed by meager returns and stagnant sales. The market had been tapped and drained. Even pornography had grown too common to be profitable. So I had decided on a new tack. I would write the definitive, all-purpose Soviet propaganda novel, complete with every cliché in the Communist catechism—block sales and glowing reviews guaranteed. I would have bank accounts in rubles, zlotys, forints, Czech crowns, lei and dinas. I would spend winters on the Black Sea, summers in Warsaw and Leningrad, weekends in Budapest and Prague. I would live like a prince and, since the money would be blocked, pay no tax.

I had decided to ask Boris to join me in Italy for a month's holiday, during which I'd draw on his wisdom, as well as his cooking. About the book I'd been deliberately noncommittal.

It was now nearly nine o'clock and I was getting hungry. I'd cleared the Joseph Stalin Guest Room; tidied the kitchen; scoured the bathroom, in which I'd found, under a hoard of *Krokodils* behind the lavatory, a jar of contraceptive jelly with a label saying *"Not to be used later than June 1964"* (Boris' sex life was one of his few really closely guarded secrets). As an afterthought I went back into the guest room and pulled out the bed. Underneath lay a broken cup full of mold, a box of decomposed Russian sweets, some unpaid bills, and two thick packets wrapped in brown paper, the flaps stuck down with glue. I threw out the other rubbish and took the two packets into the living room, where Boris had finished his last mug of claret. I laid one of the packets on the desk and began tearing the other open. Inside was a ream of blank typing paper, thick and coarse like the wrapping and, despite the seals, yellowed at the edges. "We don't want to keep this, do we?" I asked.

Boris came over and stood peering closely at the paper. "Holy Christ," he muttered, "I must have brought it out with me. I threw in just about everything at the time." He ran his stumpy fingers almost lovingly over the top sheet. "Good old Soviet typing paper! We used to use it in the shit-house. Better than *Pravda—*" he chuckled gleefully—"not so smeary!"

"Well, kiss it goodbye," I said, picking up both packets and starting toward the door.

"We must keep just one of them," he called after me, "as a souvenir."

"Oh, for Christ's sake, everything in this flat's a bloody souvenir." I dumped both packets on the heap of rubbish in the hall. When I got back, Boris was standing in the middle of the room with both hands clasped above his head, looking at me with elephantine cunning.

"You know, *mon cher*, we really shouldn't throw away that paper. A person could have a lot of fun with something like that."

"I don't follow."

"No?" He lowered his arms and glanced at Kamenev's type-writer on the desk. "I wonder," he said slowly. "I wonder just how long the experts would take to find out." He shook himself like a great dog and said, "Come on, enough work! We go out for a good meal."

Even now I cannot decide whether it was then that the idea first took root, and whether we both thought of it simultaneously.

We did not mention the subject of the typing paper again until we were having dinner. Boris had taken me to one of his favorite restaurants, a Georgian establishment in Schwabing, decorated in the style of a nineteenth-century railway dining car, with banquettes upholstered in wine-red velvet, and a three-man band in Georgian national costume who played plaintive music on a lyre, flute and balalaika, while Boris ordered blinis with sour cream, shashlik and a bottle of expensive Georgian wine.

The choice of restaurant had been arbitrary; yet if we had gone anywhere else, things might have turned out very differently for both of us. As it was, the wine was the decisive element.

"A fine Mukuziani," Boris was saying, as he inspected the bottle which the waiter had just brought, its label bearing the strange Georgian script that looks like shorthand—something between Sanskrit and Arabic. "One of old Stalin's favorite wines," he added. "Sometimes he used to drink about three or four bottles in a night."

"How do you know?"

Boris shrugged grandly. "My father occasionally dined with him at his dacha." He rolled the wine around in his mouth and nodded vigorously. It was always a tense moment, for I had known him to send back wines in restaurants two, sometimes three times for no sensible reason.

"They were all goddam boozers," he went on, taking a hand-ful of sweet biscuits. "Beria, the police chief, was the worst—

70

he was just a damned drunkard, as well as a killer and a rapist. He particularly liked very young girls—between twelve and fourteen. His entourage used to call them 'green fruit.'" He gave a noisy giggle. "Very liberal he was, as far as the age of consent was concerned! The girls would be tracked down by his personal guards, stopped sometimes in the street and taken to Beria's mansion in Moscow, where he had them. If they resisted he gave them sleeping pills with wine, then afterward their parents would be interrogated by the security police. If they showed themselves reasonable they would be given money and a new flat, sometimes even a dacha or a house on the Black Sea, and if they kept quiet they were left alone. Otherwise the whole family was deported to a camp."

"Did your father tell you that too?"

"My father and others. Khrushchev mentions it in his memoirs. According to him that's what they originally charged Beria with when they arrested him—more than a hundred cases of rape." He looked up eagerly as the blinis arrived, and there followed several moments of reverent silence as the pancakes were ladled out of the flaming pan and heaped with sour cream. Boris began to eat like an animal, almost before the waiter had put down his plate.

"Beria was a Georgian—like Stalin," he continued, as I watched a gob of cream slide down his chin. "Extraordinary that such a charming race could produce two such monsters. And yet they loved them in Georgia. They actually loved the two butchers!" He thumped the table with his free hand and swallowed more wine. "You know, there were terrible riots in Tbilisi, the capital of Georgia, when Nikita denounced Stalin at the Twentieth Congress. And with Beria they were almost as upset, too. I happened to be on vacation in Georgia when it was announced that the old rapist had at last been purged. July 11, 1953, it was. And you know what the taxi driver did when it came through on the radio? He turned to us and cried, 'Beria! Beria! The last support of our people has fallen!'"

71

"Do you know much about Beria?" I asked. I had stopped eating and was watching him intently.

"As much as anyone, perhaps," he said, with fine immodesty. "My father worked under him for a time, on the A-bomb project. Every record of him has been scrubbed out since. You know the story of the *Soviet Encyclopedia*—the edition for 1953? A month after it was published, the editors wrote to all subscribers—home and abroad—instructing them to remove the four pages on Beria with the enclosed razor blade and to insert four new ones on the Bering Straits." He laughed and refilled his glass.

"Have you ever considered writing a book about Beria?" I asked.

"Oh, I've thought of it, but there's not enough material. There's never even been an official biography of him, you know —not even in Russia. He was a very secretive man—a real Byzantine schemer. Stalin's daughter says that at the end he had her father completely in his power. Holy Christ, if he'd ever written a book—a diary perhaps—what a goddam scoop that would be!"

"What a scoop indeed," I murmured, and took a sip of mineral water.

🚩

I said, "Did you ever hear about the three White Russians in Paris who forged Stalin's 'table talk' after he died? They just sat down one day and banged them off on a Russian typewriter and flogged them to a French publisher for fifty thousand dollars."

"Fifty thousand dollars for Stalin's table talk?" Boris shook his head. "It is ridiculous—a mere bagatelle!"

"That was only the advance. But, of course, being White Russians, they got drunk and told everybody."

"Were they arrested?"

"Not exactly. But they had to pay the money back—or what

was left of it. Being White Russians, they'd probably lit cigars with it."

Boris nodded. "But Beria—now, that's another story. The ultimate in evil. Something between the Borgias and the Spanish Inquisition, but ruling with tanks and telephones."

"Was he any worse than his predecessors?" I asked.

Boris chewed thoughtfully. "It is a matter of personality rather than degree. You have to understand the background, *mon cher*. The father of all modern secret police forces was Napoleon's Fouché, who was liberal. It was we Russians who perfected the profession—first under the czars, then with Lenin and the Cheka. Even the Gestapo was modeled on the Soviet pattern. Felix Dzerzhinsky was the first, a Polish nobleman turned Communist—a passionate, sadistic idealist. And whenever anyone tells you that Lenin was Socialism's saint, just remember that Dzerzhinsky was Lenin's creature, and spit in the idiot's eye.

"Then there was Yagoda, who took over in 1934—a rat-faced chemist and a killer in Stalin's image, who started the mass deportations and finished up getting shot himself in 1937. Next came Yezhov. Only four feet eleven inches tall, and known as the Bloodthirsty Dwarf. They say Stalin appointed him as a kind of joke, for this Yezhov was really insane. He actually slobbered at the mouth like a rabid dog! He was the one who led the Great Terror, known as the Yezhovchina, in which ten million people died. I tell you, Hitler and Himmler were amateurs next to Stalin and his mad dwarf."

"What happened to him?"

"Ah! There are many stories. Officially he is supposed to have died in a lunatic asylum. But I did hear, before I left Russia, that as late as 1952 he was seen working as a ferryman on the Don. Just imagine—this crazy little slobbering killer, rowing back and forth across the river like some demon boatman!" He finished his wine, while I lit a cigar.

"So you must understand," he went on, "that when Beria suc-

73

ceeded him at the end of 1938 he was actually welcomed as a *liberal*. And in a funny way this was true. For Beria was a man of strange paradoxes. As I said, he put an end to the worst excesses of the Terror, and when he took over the NKVD he even introduced reforms in the camps—he allowed prisoners to play cards and chess. He was also quite a cultured bastard, very fond of classical music. I heard once that he wept when he heard a great Moscow pianist play Rachmaninov's Second Prelude!"

"Hitler's supposed to have been dotty about *The Merry Widow*," I said. Boris ordered a vodka liqueur and some chocolates, while I sat back and enjoyed my cigar—one of my last indulgences since I'd been forced to give up alcohol after an attack of pancreatitis.

"Listen, Boris. How about you and me sitting down like those White Russians in Paris and knocking off a few pages of Beria's private 'diaries'? You translate them into Russian on Kamenev's typewriter and use that old Soviet paper, then we show them to some American publisher—just, of course, to see what they'd do."

"Holy Christ!" Boris' eyes rolled up in his head, and his mouth dropped open, full of half-chewed chocolate. "I'll tell you what they'd do—they'd go goddam crazy with excitement. Their shoes would burn through the floor!

"What a joke it would be," he added slowly. "A really terrible joke."

"But do you think we would have a chance of getting away with it? I mean, how difficult would it be to convince the experts—the Kremlinologists?"

"Those idiot bastards!" Boris spat out some chocolate and caught it with his lower lip. "Clowns and charlatans, they know nothing! They would fight over it like dogs at a bone, and if one of them said it was a fake, then half the rest would be sure to say it was genuine. That's how those people work. Besides, I know some nice personal details about Comrade Beria which the experts would find very difficult to challenge. For instance, my father was great friends with a famous Moscow actress, quite an elderly lady, but very beautiful and elegant, whom Beria used to fuck from time to time, and always sent flowers to on her birthday. But that would just be for openers, as the Americans say. I know lots of other stories—fantastic, horrible ones, but probably true. Really superb!" He slapped my arm across the table. "It is a beautiful idea, *mon cher*—a master stroke."

"And you think we could do it?" I said, not sure whether Boris was serious or not; but for some reason—and I am not by nature a cautious person—his next words made me uneasy.

"Of course we could do it, *mon cher*! It would need a lot of research, but we have that right here in Munich, in the Radio Liberty archives. Every public engagement of every Soviet leader and member of the Politburo is filed. All we would have to do is look up Beria's dossier and make sure that the entries in his diary coincided with these appointments. The rest would just need a lot of imagination.

"The funny thing is, the whole thing just *could* be true. For there have been rumors about a Beria diary. I heard them in Moscow at about the time he was purged. Of course, any papers he left were officially destroyed. But then you never know with Soviet bureaucracy. They are great ones for hoarding things, like squirrels; they might have just filed them away in some cellar and forgotten about them."

"But surely a man like Beria wouldn't have kept a diary?"

Boris paused. "I don't know. Normally, I agree, a man like that, a secret policeman, would be unlikely to commit anything to paper that was not absolutely necessary. But Beria was a funny fellow. He wasn't just secretive, he was also terrifically vain—particularly in his exploits with women. He used to boast of these to everyone, even foreigners. Visiting statesmen from the West were terribly shocked by him. Stalin encouraged him, just to enjoy their embarrassment. At the same time Beria was a great cynic, and like Stalin he had a good gallow's humor. My father once told me a story about him which he swears he heard from someone, another Georgian, who was there at the time. About one night at Kuntsevo when Stalin and Beria were very drunk, particularly Beria, who suddenly turned to Stalin and said in Georgian, 'You know, Master'—he never called him Comrade Stalin, always 'Master'—'you know, Master, there is only one thing wrong with the Soviet Union.' And when Stalin asked what that was, Beria replied, 'That a man like me can reach the position I have!' Stalin laughed all night—he thought it a tremendous joke."

"Whom did you hear these rumors from?" I asked.

Boris shrugged. "People in the university—high-up Party members. But they weren't really rumors, just gossip. They used to say that if Beria had kept a diary it would have been pure pornography. He was just the sort of man who would enjoy writing down everything he'd done, every filthy, vicious detail, like those perverts who like to watch films of themselves fucking. Beria was like that. I don't know if he did it on film, but he had that same streak of exhibitionism. Only he wasn't just a voyeur. He used to interrogate his victims personally, often torturing them and watching them die. He would have been the same with his women and his 'green fruit.' "

Boris leaned forward and rubbed his hands. "I have an idea for you, Tom. Why don't you scrap that idea for a novel, and write another one about two people like us who fake the Beria diaries? It would make terrific fiction!"

"Why fiction? Why not write the real thing?"

🖢

"We wouldn't need any accomplices, Boris. Just you and me."

"Just you and me," Boris repeated. "Yes, that's good. That's bloody good! But if we ever breathed a word!" He lowered his head still further and I missed what followed. We had moved on to a crowded *Nachtlokale* in Schwabing, full of students writing to German pop music, and we had to lean across the table and yell to make ourselves heard.

"We would go somewhere quiet—that hole you have in Tuscany—where no one would see us for six months, and we'd write the private diaries of Lavrenti Pavlovich Beria, Stalin's bloody right hand." He slapped me painfully on the shoulder. "My God, it would be a good joke!"

"How much would we get, do you think?"

"Millions of dollars, *mon cher*. Millions."

"No, seriously."

"Millions," Boris belched. "Nikita's memoirs brought two million. Beria's would get more, far more. Especially if it was good hot stuff—plenty of 'green fruit,' huh?"

I peered across the hazy floor where the dancers were spinning like tops. A very pretty girl in a flesh-clinging miniskirt and broad leather belt was gyrating with her back to us, the tips of her white panties wriggling a few inches from Boris' face. He glanced at them and planted a massive smack across one fully exposed buttock. The girl gave a shriek of pain. Her partner, a large young man with a black beard and a Castro cap, materialized out of the darkness and began shouting. Several other people stopped and also started shouting. Boris lolled back in his chair, his eyes rolling like a monstrous mechanical doll. I got to my feet as more men in beards and battle tunics with Ban-the-Bomb shoulder flashes arrived; then, all at once, they drifted away. There was no sign of the girl and the man in the Castro cap. I sat down again.

"They should call this place Chez Guevara," I muttered, as a blond man in a lounge suit stopped at our table.

"You must leave, please." He did not seem to raise his voice, even above the pounding music.

Boris took a moment to focus on him, then began to bellow, "Where is the manager?"

"I am the manager," the man said peaceably. "You will leave now."

"I am press!" Boris shouted, scrabbling for his wallet. "There, there! You see, press!" he cried, waving his *Presseausweis* like some dog-eared season ticket.

The man made a movement with his hand, and two waiters appeared as though conjured out of the smoke. I stood up quickly and thrust some money at one of them. "Let's go, Boris." The blond man looked very fit.

Boris was still bawling at them as I led him stumbling to the door and collected our coats. "It is outrageous! Bloody outrageous! A lot of petty-bourgeois swine playing at weekend guerrillas. It is not a real nightclub anyway—nobody wears ties." He was still shouting as we got outside and into the Citröen.

For the moment the diaries of Lavrenti Pavlovich Beria were forgotten.

I woke next morning with a strange sense of elation—something I hadn't experienced since my breakdown—and leaped out of bed without even waiting for Boris to bring my coffee. He'd already had breakfast, and I suspected that he'd been up for some time, because there were further signs of disorder in the sitting room: a fresh pile of books had appeared in the middle of the floor, surrounded by a mass of press clippings spread out like crazy paving. And as we were leaving I noticed that the two packets of Russian typing paper had disappeared from the rubbish still in the hallway.

It was only as we got into the car that he broke his silence. "You remember what we were discussing last night?" he said casually. "Well, I've been thinking some more about it. About the problem of language—the Mingrelian dialect that Beria spoke. Well, I think I have the solution. I know a group of old Georgians in Paris who run a very good restaurant. At least one of them must be a Mingrelian, and most of them have typewriters with the Georgian alphabet—all Georgians like to write in their spare time. Mostly poetry. You know that Beria wrote poetry as a young man, though no one has ever published it? Even Stalin, when he was studying in the seminar in Tiflis, is supposed to have scribbled a few verses."

"Wait a minute!" I cried. "What dialect did you say Beria spoke?"

"Mingrelian."

"Good God. There's a Russian girl—or rather, a Georgian girl —who's just got a bye-fellowship at King's Cambridge. I remember reading all about her in the papers. It made quite a stir at the time, my old college collapsing to Women's Lib, although she sounds rather a spirited girl. Apparently, according to a friend of mine there, she taunts all the old dons at the high table by quoting Stalin's dictum 'No fortress so firm that it cannot be stormed by Bolsheviks'!"

"A goddam Communist, then?"

"Quite the opposite. She got out of Russia a couple of years ago by marrying a Soviet Jewish doctor and emigrated to Israel. But the husband got killed in the Six-Day War, and now she's on her own, writing a thesis on dissident Russian literature."

"And you say she's Mingrelian?"

"Sure of it. I'd never heard the name before, and it stuck in my mind."

"Holy Christ, if you're right . . . ! What's her name?"

"Bernstein—Tatiana Bernstein."

"Tatana it would be—the Georgian version of the name. You have met her?"

"Never."

"You seem to know a lot about her," he said suspiciously.

"I was intrigued. She sounded as though she'd had quite a romantic past—studied as a young girl at one of the top Moscow ballet schools. And by her photographs she looks rather pretty."

Boris grinned. "So you suggest that instead of a ninety-year-old restaurateur we hire a pretty young Cambridge student?"

"She's a fellow. And she'll be working during the summer vacation. But we could try."

Boris sat forward with his hands pressed on his knees as we edged through the rush-hour traffic on Leopoldstrasse. "You could write to her and offer her some very lucrative but highly confidential translating work," he said slowly. "But she would be of no great advantage over one of my Paris friends, and less secure—unless—" He broke off with his mouth wide open. "Unless—" And he let out a shrill exclamation in Russian.

"Tom, I've got it! The perfect, absolute solution! The detail that will provide the ultimate proof that not even the most suspicious publisher or Kremlinologist will be able to challenge! Listen. We write, in Beria's diary, an episode in which he rapes a young girl from a junior ballet school—the one this girl went to. We will make all the details fit, and then, for a percentage, perhaps five, even ten percent, we get this girl to stand up in public and announce that she was the original victim of Beria's assault!"

He was so excited by his plan that he began to bounce up and down on the foam-rubber seat. "Holy Christ, it is superb! The absolute authenticity—unquestionable—quite brilliant, *mon cher!*" He was now bouncing with both hands clasped above his head, muttering to himself in Russian.

"You must write to her at once," he added. "Introduce yourself as an old student of King's and make her really hungry for this translation work. She's probably as poor as a wolf in winter!"

"We don't want to overdo it," I said. "In any case, it means running the risk of introducing a third and quite unknown person. Wouldn't it be much easier all around for you to write out the final draft in Russian? Beria wrote fluent Russian, I imagine?"

Boris lowered his hands and shook his head. "Much less convincing—and too risky. Beria would only have written such confidential diaries in his native tongue. In Russian it would mean a translation, and that would imply other people being involved, perhaps other copies going around, even in *samizdat*—which would immediately lower the market value. Besides, Mingrelian is such a rare dialect that whoever we showed it to would be instantly hooked! And with that old Soviet typing paper we at once have a tremendous advantage."

"What about the typing itself? They must have forensic tests to tell how old it is."

"We just use old ribbons—very faded. I have a whole stack of them in my desk."

"And where do I come in?"

"Ah, you are essential, *mon cher!* I will supply the facts and you will write the fiction. Have you ever written any pornography?"

"Not as such. Just the statutory screw so they can put a naked girl on the cover."

"Well, in these diaries you are going to give us some really hot stuff! Let your imagination run wild. Just put yourself in Beria's shoes: You are the second most powerful man in Russia, you just flick your fingers and you can have any girl you want! And when you've got them, including this little Mingrelian ballet student, Tatana, you can do anything you like with them. *Anything.*" He gave a grunt of pleasure. "Then we go to some big American publisher and ask for a couple of million dollars, paid into a Swiss bank account and no questions asked. Okay?"

"Fine," I said, "except that they're going to want to know how the hell we got hold of it."

"Simple. You have smuggled it out yourself from behind the Iron Curtain, from one of the East European countries. That is how all the illegal Russian manuscripts reach the West. But, of course, your contact is confidential. That is the very beauty of it! The greater the mystery, the more convincing the fraud. And believe me, if the stuff is real dynamite, those American publishers aren't going to be too keen themselves to prove it's

81

not genuine. But remember," he added, as I pulled up outside the offices of Radio Free Europe, "not a word to a single human soul!"

"Not a word," I said. "Secrets of the grave."

"Beria's grave!" Boris cried; and he was still chortling as we went inside and signed the register at the desk.

"First we must do some careful contingency planning," Boris was saying, noisily lapping up his *Bouillon mit Ei*.

In the last couple of days we had taken to lunching in a little restaurant in the middle of the Englischer Garten that was almost empty at this time of year.

"For instance," he went on, "there is the goddam CIA. We don't have to worry about the publishers—they'll be the first suckers. But the CIA boys are different. They may get onto us, of course, but with luck they'll think we're just agents for the original. In any case, it is important not only that the CIA people believe the book to be genuine. They must also be satisfied that they know—or think they know—where it comes from, and how. But if for one moment they suspect it is a fraud, then they can start making real bad trouble for us! Maybe they can't get us extradited and prosecuted, but those boys are very good at putting the squeeze on—can get us banned from a lot of countries, perhaps even do a deal with the Swiss and make it difficult for us to move our money around."

"Why should the CIA be so interested?"

"The CIA is interested in everything. And Beria's personal memoirs could tell those spooks at their headquarters in Langley, Virginia, a lot of useful things. Particularly," he added, with a sly grin, "if they contain spicy details about the current leaders in the Kremlin!"

"Oh no. We're not getting into that kind of racket, Boris. That one's strictly for the propaganda boys—the sort of thing the CIA might do themselves. Personal memoirs—seduction and rape—that's fine. But we're not going to start libeling the Soviet government. After all, you talk about the CIA. What about the KGB? What's their reaction going to be?"

"I don't think it matters what their reaction is," Boris said—just a little too promptly, I thought. "Whenever anything controversial like this gets published in the West, their reaction is always the same: it is a CIA counterrevolutionary plot. Remember *The Penkovsky Papers?*"

"I thought they *were* forged by the CIA."

Boris shrugged. "Who knows? That's the point—who knows anything about anything in these matters? It was the same with old Nikita—nobody will ever know for certain how much of that stuff was really his, or how much was added by the CIA, or the KGB, or perhaps both. But in Beria's case, most of the people who could prove that it was a fake are now dead. And those who aren't would probably prefer to lie goddam low! So whatever the KGB says, who the hell is going to listen?"

"I'm not so concerned with what they'll say, Boris. It's what they'll *do.*"

Boris gave his eloquent shrug. "So what can they do? Murder a few American editors on Fifth Avenue?"

"Not the editors, perhaps—but us."

"Bah! So what can they do to us? Hunt us down and kill us like they did Trotsky? In Beria's time, perhaps, but that's not their style anymore."

I waited for him to go on, but he seemed more interested in his *boeuf Stroganoff.* And I reflected that for someone who had fled the Soviet regime and had had the statutory ten-year prison sentence passed on him *in absentia,* he was being remarkably sanguine; for I did not somehow see the Soviet government and its intelligence service meekly accepting the publication of perhaps the hottest political "memoirs" of modern times—if my growing enthusiasm was justified—by issuing the routine cliché-ridden denunciations, and leaving it at that.

83

I tried another tack. "You say the CIA are sure to get onto us? How?"

Boris lifted his head and wiped a hand across his mouth. "Through the publishers. You see, I have been doing some thinking. About the provenance of the book. As I said, you will pay a little visit to one of the East European countries. I suggest Hungary." He raised his greasy hand. "No, don't worry! Hungary today is the most liberal of all those countries—despite your experiences in 1956. In fact, they give you a good excuse to go back, when the Americans start asking questions. And the Hungarians aren't going to worry. They get nearly one million tourists a year from the West, and they can't check on everyone. Besides, you didn't do anything very terrible there as a student—just took in a few bottles of penicillin.

"But there's another reason for choosing Hungary. You know when I said that the greater the secrecy about the source of the book, the better? Well, I think perhaps we ought to spice that secrecy with a few clues. Just to help string the spooks along. Give them a confidential affidavit from someone in Hungary to say exactly how the book came into his hands. And I think I know just the man. An old Hungarian Communist. A veteran of Spain, fought in the Hitler war with the Red Army—in which he's a colonel with the Order of Lenin—and used to be fairly high up in the Rakosi regime before he resigned in 1952, and spent a couple of years in jail. A very brave man—and a good joker too! He actually had your old Dean of Canterbury, Hewlett Johnson, arrested by mistake in 1950 while on a state visit to Hungary. You must get him to tell you the full story—it's a true classic!"

"You want me to meet him?"

He nodded. "You should get on well with him—he was one of the leaders of the Uprising, and was deported to Russia for six years. He now lives in Budapest on his Red Army pension and writes poetry in his spare time."

"How did you get to know him?"

84

Boris was silent for a moment, busy picking his teeth. "He was a great friend of my father's in the war. I was only a school-boy when I first met him. But after I defected, we kept in contact—through a third party. Then last year . . ." He paused again, and his heavy lids half closed over his eyes. "I must warn you, Tom, this is something I have never discussed with anyone before. It is the deadest secret. If you breathe a word—" He turned suddenly and called for a beer. I waited.

"Last year this Hungarian contacted me. He had managed to get into Russia, by a very clever, roundabout way, and had come into possession of a certain manuscript." He lowered his voice and now mentioned the name of a Russian writer, still at precarious liberty, whose works were banned in the Soviet Union but were published in the West and were now world-famous. "This Hungarian brought back his latest novel, which is due to be published in the autumn. What concerns us is how he got the manuscript out. He used a very ingenious method—which, if you are tactful with him, he may be prepared to describe in a signed affidavit for the Americans. And it will be that method which we say was used for smuggling out Beria's diaries."

"What's this Hungarian's name?"

"Laszlo Laszlo. It's not his official name, but it's what he's always been known as to his friends. We have a joke that he was born in Baden-Baden in 1919!" And he went into a small paroxysm of laughter.

I waited for him to finish, then said, "Boris, aren't you taking one hell of a lot for granted? For a start, unless the man's a maniac, he's not going to write out a signed confession of how he smuggled a world-famous manuscript out of Russia and hand it over to a total stranger."

"I will contact him with the necessary credentials. Don't worry. He will trust anyone I trust. He is a man of honor. We will, of course, offer him some money for his trouble, but he will probably refuse."

"All right. But supposing his name gets out? We could be dropping the poor bastard right in the shit if the Communists ever get to hear what he's been doing."

For a moment Boris looked almost worried, his eyes rolling shiftily around the restaurant. "No," he said, with more confidence than his expression betrayed. "The affidavit will be filed with an American attorney in the strictest secrecy. And if even a whisper gets out, we'll blacken both the attorney's name and the publishing firm right around the world!"

"And the CIA?"

Boris snorted. "You ever heard of the CIA giving anything to anyone? They wouldn't even hand over a tape recording to the Justice Department in the case of the Pentagon Papers. Those boys are as tight as a snake's arse-hole."

"I just hope so," I said. "So the publishers are satisfied, and so are the CIA. Where does that leave us?"

"Goddam rich," said Boris, with a happy smile.

"I mean, in the transaction? Do we negotiate through an agent?"

"No agent!" Boris cried. "We cannot afford to involve outsiders—besides the Georgian translator. Anyway, I'm not paying any goddam commission to some literary parasite. We deal direct—I with the publishers, you with Laszlo Laszlo."

"An agent would be useful," I said, "because we wouldn't have to be brought in at all. You said yourself they may find out who we are. Surely the fact that we've worked for RFE will make them doubly suspicious—especially you with your background and me being a novelist? They'd put two and two together pretty fast."

Boris sat back and patted his stomach. "Not really. You see, it will cut both ways. They will be suspicious whoever we are. But then they will reason this way: Who would be likely to get onto a thing like this in the first place, and how? Not just anybody. But RFE is exactly the sort of milieu where you would expect somebody to hear about such a deal. Equally, a

Russian or East European who did not know the West well would be just as likely to use someone at RFE as the contact. But in fact there is no reason for this problem to arise at all."

He drank some beer and leaned across the table, his breath smelling of the black sausage he'd had for breakfast. "When I said they might get onto us, I meant the CIA, not the publishers. There is no reason for the publishers to know anything until after the money has been paid. And if everything goes as I think it will, the deal should be clinched pretty quickly—in a few days, perhaps a week. They'll know the competition's going to be terrific and they won't want to mess around once they've come to a decision."

I nodded, but didn't say anything. It all sounded dangerously simple; but then hadn't all the great confidence tricks of history been simple—like the man who sold the Eiffel Tower for scrap metal, then returned two weeks later and sold it again? And I had to concede that on this first hearing I could find no obvious flaw in Boris' reasoning. But the fact that the whole idea was no longer some wild abstraction—a late-night fantasy over a bottle of good Georgian wine—but a serious conspiracy maturing in detail and logic with every hour, was something which I still couldn't entirely accept. No doubt Boris would blame it on my bourgeois upbringing; and no doubt he'd be right.

When we got back to the offices he insisted on entering after me, stopping off at the canteen first. "Better not to be seen always together," he muttered, like an overcautious lover.

Boris was already living the conspiracy to the full.

Five days later Boris took the first irrevocable step: he gave a month's notice to Radio Free Europe. For someone in his position, stateless and without private means, this must have been a drastic move; but Boris was already too carried away by his own self-confidence and conviction in our mad project to show the least anxiety.

His decision was prompted by the arrival that morning of a swift reply from Madame Tatana Bernstein, neatly typed in perfect English on King's College notepaper, thanking me for my letter and telling me, as I expected, that she planned to be working through the long vacation, but would nevertheless be interested in my proposal of some special translation work. She suggested that when the time came nearer, we might meet to discuss it in more detail.

The letter raised Boris' enthusiasm to a fever. In the flat he set to work, assembling what he called his "mobile data bank." Several hundred books, magazines, and stacks of press cuttings were arranged once again across the floor of the sitting room, making it almost impossible to enter; and here, for the next four weeks, he studied, copied, docketed, filed and cross-filed, and made thousands of words of notes, while I felt embarrassingly ineffectual. For not only was there little I could do to help, since most of the work was in Russian, but I had so far done nothing positive to commit myself, except to abandon in abstract the idea of my new novel.

Boris had lent me a number of books in English and German on the Stalinist era, and occasionally handed me a sheaf of clumsily typed notes in English. I also made my own notes, and by the end of two weeks considered myself reasonably well informed about basic events in the Soviet Union between the end of the war and June 1953, the date of Beria's downfall—the period which we had decided the "diaries" would cover. The entries would be consecutive but spasmodic, full of random reflections, abbreviated notes and self-revelations, punctuated by lurid personal anecdotes, many of them clearly written under the influence of drink. Boris' suggestion that we include incriminating details about the current Soviet leadership was not mentioned again.

Most evenings he now spent in the library of Radio Liberty, RFE's sister station on the outskirts of Munich which broadcasts only to the Soviet Union. The library is one of the most comprehensive of its kind in the world, containing up-to-date, day-by-day bulletins of every facet of Soviet life since the war. And the filing system was so efficient that Boris had little difficulty selecting only what he considered relevant. The Beria section was one of the least copious of all those on former Soviet leaders, including men of far less significance. But this not only made Boris' immediate task much easier, but would make it correspondingly difficult for the experts to dig up evidence later to disprove the authenticity of the "diaries." The one small hazard was that all persons entering the library had first to identify themselves, then fill out a form. It was a purely routine precaution against some fanatic trying to blow up the place, and was presided over by a young American Army sergeant, who, by the end of the first week, knew Boris well enough to treat him as an old regular, and waved him through without the usual formalities.

It was a detail to which neither of us gave much thought at the time.

♯

On our last night before leaving for Italy to use my wealthy friend's house in Tuscany, Boris treated me to dinner at one of Munich's most exclusive restaurants. During the meal he became patronizingly magnanimous.

"You are a poor writer, *mon cher!* The expenses for this little venture will be on me—repayable, of course, when our Swiss money comes through!"

I didn't argue. Boris' finances, like his sex life, had always been a mystery to me; I knew they were deviously cosmopolitan, with bank accounts in various countries, mostly with the proceeds from translation works, but the details he never disclosed to anyone, least of all to the Bavarian tax authorities. Tonight, however, I was to be privileged; and he now produced three thousand dollars in American Express traveler's checks, assuring me there were another three thousand in reserve if we needed them. He then passed me an unsealed envelope containing ten new hundred-dollar bills. "For Laszlo Laszlo. As I said, he may not accept them, but it is always as well to be prepared. As for the Mingrelian girl—or whoever we get to do the translation—we will pay another grand." My own savings of $450 seemed rather pathetic beside such opulence.

Back at the flat, we finished the last of our packing. For someone so disinterested in physical possessions, Boris had a great deal of luggage. The main item was a huge Revelation suitcase, extended to its full capacity and crammed with his "mobile data bank." It required the two of us to carry it out to the car in slow stages. There were also several battered briefcases, our three typewriters, and a canvas bag containing his summer wardrobe, which consisted of a number of outsize shirts and Bermuda shorts the color of Italian ice cream. At the last moment he squeezed in two bottles of pepper vodka and a jar of Polish pickled mushrooms.

Next morning, as soon as the BBC Russian news was over, we set off for Garmisch-Partenkirchen and the Austrian frontier. Boris, having obstinately refused to abandon his Russian citizenship, held only a German *Fremdenpass,* a stateless passport, which meant he had to get a visa for every country he visited, even in transit. On both the German and Austrian sides of the border the guards paid us more attention than is usual with tourists; but they did not inquire about what money we were carrying.

We had lunch in Innsbruck, and entered Italy through the Brenner Pass. It was late afternoon when we reached Verona, where Boris insisted on two exhausting hours looking at what he called "the flaming *barocco.*" We stayed the night in Bologna, and next morning were passing Florence on the Autostrada del Sole when he again insisted on stopping and doing the sights. He was not an easy traveling companion: restless and capricious, constantly urging me to go faster, but thinking nothing of dawdling several hours over a good meal with plenty of wine and liqueurs.

At last we headed south again, back on the *autostrada* toward Rome. The sun was already beginning to go down when we reached the Valdarno intersection leading up into the Chianti country where the farmhouse lay. We stopped first in the local town, Gaiole, where Boris produced a shopping list that was more like the inventory for a quartermaster's stores, and which took us an hour and fifty thousand lire to get through; then we started up a winding dirt track round the side of a steep hill covered in vines and *boschi* as dense as jungle. The bends in the track had been half washed away by winter rains, and the only habitation we saw was the tip of a pale-pink wall behind a row of tall cypresses.

Boris rubbed his hands. "*Mon cher*, you are a genius! It is a paradise—no one will ever find us here!"

The farmhouse, known as "Frabecchi," looked over the valley of the Arno. It consisted of two buildings of rough stone and yellow tiled roofs, joined by a patio under a vine-woven trellis. A second, lower patio overlooked the swimming pool, which was full of gray water speckled with dead insects. I explained to Boris that there was a decrepit generator that worked the pool's filter; but there was no hot water and no electric light, only oil lamps. The generator was turned on in the mornings for only an hour by the odd-job man, Signor Gochi, who looked after the place and tended the vines.

The whole of one house had been made into a large living room with arched doors to the upper terrace. There were two sofas along the walls on both sides of a great stone fireplace, each piled with expensively embroidered cushions; a couple of rocking chairs, some wooden stools, a handsome set of prints of Siena, and a stereo hi-fi set with three speakers but no electricity.

The kitchen, in what had been an adjoining outhouse, was equipped with a stove, refrigerator and deep-freeze, all run off gas *bombole*. The second building, which was on two floors, contained four bedrooms and two bathrooms. The bedrooms were bare except for unmade double beds; the bathrooms were each fitted with a marble bath and shower, marble bidet and a pair of marble basins.

The light was fading fast now. I lit a pair of lamps that gave off a steady yellow glare, and while Boris was busy in the kitchen, having opened himself a one-gallon wickerbound *fiasco* of Chianti, I found sheets and blankets in a dark hole under the steps and made up two of the beds, then had a cold bath and went downstairs to wait for Boris. I decided that while the weather was fine the best place to work would be out on a long table of pitted marble on the upper terrace under the vines.

I took one of the lamps and the two rocking chairs outside, where Boris presently joined me with his monstrous *fiasco;* and we sat rocking gently, watching the twilight grow like a blue mist out of the darkening wall of hills; and for the first time in many months I felt almost completely happy.

"Tom, *mon cher*, I am going to tell you something I have never told anyone in the West before." Boris' tone was hushed and circumspect. "You must promise never to repeat it—absolutely never." I nodded; and there was a moment's silence except for the creaking of our chairs.

"I once met Beria—for a whole evening. It was in September 1949, just after the first Russian atomic explosion. There had been a party in the Kremlin to celebrate, and my father was one of the guests of honor. Afterward he brought Beria back to our dacha outside Moscow. Beria came with his aide, Colonel Rafik Sarkisov, a handsome Armenian who used to procure women for Beria. They were both well oiled and in a good mood. Beria had brought half a kilo of beluga caviar, and although everyone had eaten, we finished the lot. I was only eighteen at the time, just back from reserve officer training, and wasn't much used to strong drink. Beria insisted we all drink pepper vodka, which he claimed made one's balls grow bigger. He struck me as a coarse man, very like Stalin, really. And like Stalin he had a strong Georgian accent, which can be very attractive, but Beria's had a wheedling sound like a spoiled woman. You see, he and Stalin were complete foreigners to us Russians—it was like Britain having two Pakistanis as Prime Minister and Home Secretary."

"What did he look like?" I asked.

"Repulsive. He always wore a tiny pince-nez, and his mouth was turned down in a look of disgust. He reminded me of a pediatrician I knew as a child. He was very well dressed—far better than the other Politburo members—in a dark-gray double-breasted suit which came from London, and an Italian silk tie. And I remember that he had very small hands and feet, with a mincing walk like a queer. Only he wasn't queer.

"Anyway, as soon as he met me, he said, 'Ah, I hear you are a budding genius!'—because before going into the Army I had won top entry to Moscow University. Then he asked me if I was going to be a scientist and help build the next Bomb, which would make Russia dominate the world. When I told him I was studying languages he sneered to my father, 'So your brat wants to study so he can be closer to these foreigners!'—as if Beria was not one himself—then added to me, 'The Army will soon knock that nonsense out of you!' I didn't dare say anything. Then he added, 'Do they give you lots of bull?' he used the Russian word meaning shit-cleaning. So I told him that a few weeks ago I had got into trouble with the sergeant for getting up late and was ordered to tidy a pine forest and to pick up all the pine cones. 'That's not a punishment,' Beria said, 'it's just a ramble in the forest.' 'Yes,' I said, 'but the forest went on for two thousand miles.' I must say they all roared with laughter, and Beria seemed quite friendly after that.

"Later that night, he insisted that we all play a game. He put a full bottle of pepper vodka on the table and each of us had to spin it around on its side, and whoever the label was pointing at had to drink a glass straight off. Several times Beria didn't spin the bottle at all, but just turned it toward himself. He got terribly drunk, but never lost his faculties. Then he wanted Sarkisov to call up some girls—he said the game was much better when there was an added penalty of having to take off a piece of clothing each time the label faced you.

"We only got rid of them both when it was getting light. Beria insisted on driving—he had a new bullet-proof Packard— and he almost crashed into the gate going out. Later we heard he'd had a bad accident on the new superhighway into Moscow —he nearly killed two people on a horse and cart. And after they came out of the hospital he had them put in prison because the highway was only supposed to be used by high-ranking Party members to get to their dachas."

Boris picked up the *fiasco* with both hands and refilled his glass.

"Didn't you even tell this to the Americans when they debriefed you?" I said.

"Holy Christ, no! You must understand that association with Beria is the kiss of death—both in Russia and outside. Just to have met him would have meant trouble. Anyway, Beria has been purged—he is of no interest to the Americans anymore."

"He might be, if it became known he was associated with present leadership," I murmured unthinkingly, and regretted it at once.

"Ah, that is something else."

It was dark now. The drive had left me exhausted, but Boris insisted that our first dinner at Frabecchi be a memorable one. He took a long time preparing it, and finally brought it out on a tray and laid it down before me with all the solemnity of an artist unveiling his latest masterpiece. "Coronation Chicken, as once served to the Queen of England," he told me. There was enough for at least four people; Boris had three helpings himself, and when we had finished I was too tired even to smoke a cigar.

That night I fell into a contented, dreamless sleep.

Boris was up by seven, brewing coffee, with liver sausage replaced by salami, followed by a tumbler of noxious Fernet Branca. "Never too early for a Ferny!" he said with a chortle, and stomped out of the kitchen into the big main room, where he began emptying his Revelation case and laying out his data bank, filling the empty bookshelves and a third of the floor with miscellaneous clippings and notes.

Meanwhile, I placed two stools at either end of the marble table under the vines and lugged out Kamenev's massive machine, which I laid between our two portable Olivettis, besides piles of foolscap, carbons, folders and felt-tipped pens. Then I settled into one of the rocking chairs, with a buff folder which Boris had just handed to me.

"Study this, *mon cher*. It is the biographical background to Beria. A lot of secret facts about his past that we will include in his reminiscences. But I have not put in any private stories, all the filthy sexual anecdotes and escapades, because there we will mix fact with fiction. These are just the facts."

They were four closely typed sheets of foolscap. The first was headed:

L. P. BERIA   CONFIDENTIAL DOSSIER

PROPERTY OF B. DROBNOV AND T. MALLORY

Asterisks denote:

* minor facts little or not at all known.
** important facts rumored but unsubstantiated.
*** very important facts known to a few privileged persons.

GENERAL BIOGRAPHY:

Born Merkheuli, Georgia, 1899—executed Moscow, 1953. Father a local government official under "liberal" czarist regime. Received good bourgeois education. Joined Bolshevik movement in 1917. Saw no active service in war. Held high rank in the Cheka and OGPU in Transcaucasia 1921–31. During the civil war (1919–22) is suspected of having been a

British agent working for the Azerbaijan nationalist movement. (Khrushchev accused him of this in his secret speech to the Twentieth Congress in 1956.) I happen to know*** that during this time B. had dealings with an Irish-German double agent called Dieter Ryan (also known by alias Reien), a former IRA gunman from Dublin who went to Russia as a soldier of fortune. He and B. are said to have handled large sums of money supplied by British Military Intelligence and by White Russian agents, in exchange for information leading to the arrest of top Bolsheviks.

Between 1928 and 1929 became Yagoda's chief agent in Geneva and Paris, in charge of a plan* to distribute forged U.S. dollars, using German Communist agents, many of whom were Jews—thus adding fuel to Nazi anti-Semitic campaign. (B. is said to have had this plan finally called off.)

Between 1929 and 1938 was in charge of subversion within Western countries, especially among leading universities. **Recruited, among many others, Guy Burgess, Donald Maclean and Harold (Kim) Philby.

Between 1932 and 1938 was First Sec. of Georgian and Transcaucasian Communist Party. On July 20 appointed Deputy Head of NKVD a week before July Massacre directed against Georgian Communists—probably to prove that, like Stalin, B. did not favor his own race over any other.

In December 1938 assumed total control of NKVD with title of People's Commissar for Internal Affairs.

In August 1940, the NKVD arranged the murder of Trotsky in Mexico —after one unsuccessful attempt which almost cost B. his job.*

In June 1941, following German invasion of Russia, became member of State Defense Committee. His record here was deplorable—only equaled in obstinacy and ineptitude by that of Voroshilov (whom Stalin later fired as People's Defense Commissar, calling him a "specialist in retreat").

B. himself almost lost the Russians the Battle of Moscow in October 1941, when he intercepted a message from a Soviet reconnaissance pilot who claimed to have seen a fifteen-mile-long column of Nazi tanks approaching Moscow along the Warsaw road. B. had the report destroyed as "unconvincing," and threatened the pilot with court-martial and execution for "pessimism."

During war was responsible for mass deportation and "resettlement" of national minorities—mostly Volga Germans and Tatars, most of whom were exterminated. Also in charge of POWs.

In May 1940 organized the massacre of 10,000 Polish officers at Katyn Wood. **Strongly rumored that Stalin, on hearing that so many Polish officers were concentrated in one camp, declared that it was a security risk and must be liquidated. (He used a Georgian word which means "disperse" as well as "liquidate.") B. presumed that Stalin was referring to the men and not the camp, and acted accordingly. He is also credited with killing—by execution, starvation and general ill-treatment—a total of 270,000 Polish POWs, captured during Soviet invasion of eastern Poland in Sept. 1939.

As head of GULAG (Labor Camp Administration) by 1945 is estimated to have been using fifteen million slave laborers.

***In July 1943 organized through SMERSH the murder of General Wladislaw Sikorski, head of the Provisional Polish Government in London, who had become increasingly troublesome to Stalin since the discovery by the Germans in April of Katyn Wood. Sikorski died in a plane crash while taking off from Gibraltar—described in the official inquiry as an accident. At this period the chief British Military Intelligence officer for the Gibraltar area was Kim Philby, one of B.'s recruits.

In 1943 made a Hero of the Soviet Union, and in 1945 Marshal of the Soviet Union. Also put in charge of Soviet A-bomb project which resulted in the first Russian nuclear explosion, probably sometime in August 1949—although not announced until Sept.—and known in the West as "Joe One." (Since most Western experts had predicted that the Russians would not have a nuclear device before the mid-fifties, at the earliest, this was an important triumph for B.)

During the next few years directed subversion and terrorism in the "liberated" countries of Eastern Europe, all of which, by 1949, had become 100 percent Communist satellites. ***In February 1948, following the Communist coup in Czechoslovakia, B. arranged, through the ingenious use of the new drug cortisone, the "suicide" of Jan Masaryk, the Czech liberal Foreign Minister.

In following years of growing Stalinist terror, B. either masterminded or turned to his own advantage the Leningrad Case, the Crimean Affair (directed at the Jews), and the Mingrelian Affair, believed to have been directed at B. himself.

Between 1952 and Stalin's death on March 5, 1953, B. came increasingly to realize that he was Stalin's prime target—protected only by his million-plus troops and police.

Arrested June 1953, four months after Stalin's death, and liquidated. There are three versions of his death:

1(the official and least likely). Arrested in the inner sanctum of the Kremlin, after being denounced at the Politburo meeting of June 27, 1953; tried before a secret military tribunal in December, accused of being "an imperialist agent and traitor to the Fatherland": and, together with the rest of his "Georgian Gang," was shot.

2. **Killed at his country estate outside Moscow while he and his Georgian guards were fighting troops commanded by Marshal Konev who had come to arrest him.

3(most likely version). **Shot in the Kremlin inner sanctum after the Politburo meeting by Marshal Konev and others who had been hiding in a back room. (Khrushchev told this version to a delegation of French Socialists in 1956, and later to Harold Wilson and others in 1964.) B. was the only member of the Politburo permitted to carry a gun into the sanctum, which he kept in his briefcase and which Malenkov (whom he trusted as an ally) is believed to have removed. The sanctum was forbidden to all except Politburo members; but B. kept his own elitist praetorian guard of 200 Georgians who loved him like a tribal chief and who all died defending his estate. At the Politburo meeting of June 27 Col. Nadoraya was commanding this detachment (about twenty men) outside the sanctum doors. I heard*** that when Konev shot B. he used a .22 pistol to conceal the noise, and had to fire five bullets before B. died. They then explained to Nadoraya outside that they had been letting off some firecrackers and were celebrating (not an uncommon event). They also said B. had drunk too much and was sick (*sic!*). But then they had the problem of smuggling the body past Nadoraya's praetorian guard, who would have murdered them all if they had found out. The body is said to have remained two days in the sanctum, where it began to stink, before they managed to get it out in a crate, pretending it was full of secret documents.

PERSONAL HABITS:

Liked good living. The only member of the leadership to enjoy real Western-style luxury, including a custom-built Packard, ordered at the end of the war through the Soviet Embassy, Washington. Had a mansion on Malaya Nikitskaya St., Moscow, which until recently* was the Tunisian Embassy. They left it after complaining it was haunted. (The cellars have been sealed up.) Also had his country estate, which had belonged to Count Orlov and was equipped with indoor heated swimming pools, tennis courts, billiard rooms, fields for volleyball, shooting ranges and a private cinema. B. prized himself as an amateur sportsman—especially at volleyball. Also had several dachas, including an enormous marble palace near Sochi. *Liked classical music, and had all the latest equipment, as well as one of the best collections of records in Russia. *Also very keen on fast cars and speedboats. *Owned large sartorial wardrobe and had all his clothes made in London and Rome. *A nonsmoker, but almost an alcoholic: drank mostly vodka, French brandy and Georgian wines. *Very fond of good food, and particularly partial to fruit. *Read only histories and biographies, and poetry of the romantic nineteenth century.

Worked in a well-furnished office in the Lubyanka Prison—in the part that was formerly the offices of an insurance company in czarist times— where he carried out many of his tortures and killings.

Often spoke Georgian with Stalin, which enraged the other Politburo members. *When Molotov tried to learn the language, B. had his teacher arrested, and Molotov took the hint.

SEXUAL INCLINATIONS:
Strongly heterosexual, with penchant for very young girls. Also liked mature women, particularly actresses and ballerinas, with some of whom he conducted long affairs. Always played a chivalrous, gentlemanly role with his "victims"—providing they were willing. If not, he used either drugs or force. Very generous with gifts and special favors to those he liked. Also very fond of girl athletes, whom his aide-de-camp, Col. Sarkisov, used to procure for him through the Chairman of the U.S.S.R. Sports Committee. And had a particular appetite for redheaded Svanetian girls—a tribe who are notoriously strict over the morale of their women— which presented B's aide with problems.

Married to Nina, reputed to have been the most beautiful woman in Georgia, and who is still alive. Had one son, Sergei, an engineer who is married to Maxim Gorki's granddaughter.

GENERAL OBSERVATIONS:
Of all Soviet police chiefs, B. was probably the cleverest, and certainly had most power over Stalin, who grew in his later years to fear B. Ideologically, was probably less of a fanatic than most Soviet leaders. Power and high living were his motivating influences. A great schemer. Hated by two prominent present-day Stalinists, Mikhail Suslov (leading Party theorist) and Aleksandr Shelepin, ex-head of KGB and Young Communist League—both of whom are strict puritans and disapproved of B's immoral conduct.

After Stalin's death is known to have planned a Soviet withdrawal from Berlin and East Germany, probably in order to pose as a "liberal" to the West. The plan was blocked by East German Stalinist leader Walter Ulbricht, who provoked the East Berlin uprising in June 1953, which had

99

to be put down by Soviet tanks. This plan of B's probably cost him his life.

* He is also rumored to have wanted to make up with Tito and abolish the collective farms. In order words, as Khrushchev suggests, he may not have been a real Communist at all—at least not in the ideological sense. (I think we make great play of this.)

The dossier ended here. I took it into the main room, where Boris had almost finished arranging his data bank.

"So! We are ready to start." He picked up a sheaf of Cyrillic notes from the confusion on the floor, then led me out to the terrace. It was not yet eight o'clock, but the sun was already warm and the sky clear.

"As you will have noticed," he said, "the précis deals mostly with Beria's background up to the end of the war. From then on, till his death, very little is known about him, except what I could dig out of the Radio Liberty archives." He opened another buff folder and showed me what looked like typed copies of a Russian railway guide, with columns of dates instead of times. "This, *mon cher,* will be the root plan of our entire work. It will be the skeleton around which I will supply the organs and the muscles of the book, and you will supply the flesh." He grinned beatifically. "Plenty of good young flesh—eh, comrade?" And he slapped me on the shoulder. "Now we will draw up our plan of campaign."

"This stuff about Sikorski and Philby," I began, "and Masaryk—"

He held up his hand. "Wait! We will go into the full details as we come to them. Beria will reminisce about his successful coups, including these political murders. But before we get down to the nitty-gritty, we must first get into the mood of the old killer. His diaries must be spontaneous—they must flow like the musings of a seasoned lecher, as well as of a self-confessed murderer. He would not have had time to polish or correct them, so the style is not so important—although, since he was a Georgian, you can allow him the occasional poetic flourish.

100

Only it must be reasonably consistent. Except when he is drunk, of course—and he is drunk quite a lot," he added.

"Now. We start with a few random thoughts on his position of power after 1945. How Russia has now swallowed half of Europe and Beria looks forward to consolidating that power. Liquidating the remaining bourgeois influences in Eastern Europe—tightening the noose around the necks of the old politicians who are still supported by Churchill. I think he makes some good provocative remarks about Churchill—things that will make your countrymen mad with rage!

"His thoughts are interrupted by Colonel Sarkisov, who comes to announce that he has found Beria a beautiful redhead —one of those from that mountain tribe who are really difficult to fuck. And Beria is really hot for her!"

We agreed that Boris would write out the opening entries, which would be highly technical, even boring—"If we make it too sensational at first, people will get suspicious. The publishers can always cut it down. But we must have some good factual meat for those goddam Kremlinologists to bite on, before we hook them!"

I was meanwhile to describe Beria's seduction of the young girl from Svanetia.

We worked steadily through the morning, interrupted only by the arrival of Signor Gochi—a small, primeval figure shaped like a stunted olive tree, who came sidling onto the terrace, grinning with one tooth in his head like a rusted nail. I introduced ourselves, and he bowed and jabbered a few words, while his feet, in a pair of laceless boots, did a shuffling two-step on the terrace floor. Boris disappeared into the kitchen and came back with two tumblers of *grappa*. He handed one to Signor Gochi, who downed it in one gulp, bowed again, and went off round the side of the house, presumably to attend to the generator and the housework.

For lunch Boris brought out plates of prosciutto, melon and cheese, drank a bottle of local wine, and a Strega with his cof-

101

fee, then read me what he'd written. As he'd promised, it was highly technical, full of names I'd never heard of, and a great many initials. These, he explained, were a nice trick because they would make it impossible for the experts to challenge them, yet gave authenticity to a busy man's nightly jottings.

I then showed him my work. He read it through with gleeful enthusiasm, while the sweat collected in the folds of his hairy belly, glistening like matted seaweed.

"Oh, this is splendid, *mon cher!* Holy Christ, if you go on like this, I will have to run upstairs and quickly masturbate!"

I was profoundly relieved. Collaborating with Boris was not going to prove so difficult after all, I thought.

The next few days passed without incident. The weather remained fine, our tempers good, the food impeccable, and the book was progressing at the rate of about four thousand words a day.

I soon decided that the reason we did not quarrel was that the roles we had assigned each other were so different that there was never any point of direct conflict. Indeed, while we each thought ourselves deeper into the character of Beria, we also assumed our own separate *personae*. Boris began each day by giving me a resumé of facts and dates, adopting the strict manner of a schoolmaster; then he would go on to attack his writing with a dogmatic venom, as though these "confessions" of Beria somehow expunged some furious, hidden guilt—perhaps the fact that his father had had closer ties with the Stalinist regime than he was prepared to admit.

At this stage I found the work surprisingly straightforward. I had no problems of plot, for all the facts were supplied by Boris—often without his even having to consult his data bank —and characterization was not difficult, for here again Boris came to the rescue, usually with a brief subjective description of one of Beria's cronies or enemies, such as "puffy-cheeked viper" or "sniveling bureaucrat with a runny nose." At the same time I found myself falling slowly, almost uneasily, into harmony with my subject, beginning to enjoy the cynical wickedness of our joint creation. I experienced, far more than with any character in my novels, a peculiar sense of identification with Beria: his ruthless opportunism tempered with earthy lust; his contempt for his fellow creatures and even the Party he served, and which often merely served him; his single-minded pursuit of power and pleasure. In fact, on rereading what I'd written, I felt that Beria would not have been wholly displeased with these "diaries": they would have gratified his arrogance.

On the other hand, as soon as I showed Boris one of my latest erotic episodes, his whole personality would change. The schoolmasterish manner was dropped and he adopted a passive, almost female role, and was soon making me read my pieces aloud while he sat in his striped Bermuda shorts, his huge thighs straddling the stool and his mouth lolling open, almost drooling at every word.

Only occasionally did he try to take over the dominant "male" role in what we'd come to call the "lech scenes"—but then only to offer suggestions. "Have him seduce a fat gypsy actress from the Romany Theater in Moscow," he said one morning over coffee. "He has slipped into the theater anonymously, because it was a slightly *avant-garde* place that started to fall into disfavor even before the Zhdanov Decrees came into force. Beria sends one of his NKVD boys to pick her up, then fucks her in his office in the Lubyanka. Make her big and juicy!" he added. "Her thighs and bottom are like satin cushions! And perhaps she smells a bit too—uses a lot of cheap perfume from the Mostorg store. After he has done with her, he throws all her clothes into the back office and tells her to get dressed and clear off. And if she breathes a word of her experiences, he will have her whole family arrested and deported."

Sometimes our combined enthusiasm carried the work on through our meals, which we ate in a confusion of foolscap and *fiaschi* of wine, carbons and coffee, piles of reference books and plates of scrambled eggs—planning, chewing, scribbling, dribbling, until the finished pages were often so smeared and stained that they had to be typed up again in the evening.

From time to time Boris would break off his noisy clatter on Kamenev's old typewriter and begin making notes in big Cyrillic handwriting that flowed across the sheets of foolscap in pencil, since ink would have smudged with the sweat that dripped steadily onto the pages from his nose and chin. When perhaps a dozen of these were covered he would hold up his hand for me to stop, then begin to read, translating as he went. He would read almost without pause, with a ferocity of concentration that was both infectious and perplexing: his mind racing along intersecting lines of thought like an express train crossing a network of points. Often he seemed to be talking to himself, even lapsing into Russian in excited undertones, or repeating several times the same name, date or event from the apparently endless convolutions of plot and counterplot, arrests, accusations, murders and executions, like some monotonous ecclesiastical dirge. I found this the most difficult part of the work: every detail had to be checked, verbally, since Boris' original notes were in Russian, and quite often—after an extended lunch, with plenty of *grappa* in the morning and wine with the food—Boris' words, though still articulate, were not always precise.

After lunch we would have a couple of hours' siesta, though too many black coffees in the morning usually kept me awake, and I spent the time working through Boris' data bank. In all these massive tomes I was struck by one common factor: the almost total lack of detailed information about Beria. Even the most definitive works by contemporary historians of the period included less than a few dozen mentions of him in their indices, and these were all perfunctory, almost incidental references. During the fifteen years of terror and conspiracy which Beria had personally initiated and supervised from 1938 until 1953,

104

he remained, from the chronicler's point of view, a cipher. There was even only one existing photograph of him: a balding, pince-nez'd face that might have been that of an international banker or hotel manager—cold, efficient, passionless.

Besides the Khrushchev memoirs, which we were treating as a special case, I had found only two works which offered any personal facts about him: Svetlana Alliluyeva's *Twenty Letters to a Friend,* and *Conversations with Stalin,* by the renegade Yugoslav Communist Milovan Djilas. In both English translations of these books the word "clouded" was used to describe Beria's eyes. "A magnificent specimen of the artful courtier," Svetlana wrote. "The embodiment of Oriental perfidy, flattery, and hypocrisy . . . His face, repulsive at the best of times, was now [at Stalin's deathbed] twisted by his passions—by ambition, cruelty, cunning and a lust for power and more power." While Djilas—perhaps a more sanguine and objective observer —describes a Kremlin dinner party in 1947 at which he noted Beria's "snickering vulgarity" and "coarse language," and how he fixed Djilas "with his clouded green, staring eyes, while a self-conscious sarcasm dripped from his square flabby mouth." But it was Khrushchev who supplied the most dramatic details, including Beria's womanizing, his heavy drinking and raping of young girls. However, despite Boris' conviction that these memoirs were genuine, we finally agreed to draw on the Khrushchev material with extreme caution—if only because he was the most obvious source of graphic material available to a forger. Khrushchev confirmed Beria's "arrogance" and "self-importance." "He was skillful at anything that was filthy and treacherous . . . a wolf in sheep's clothing who had sneaked into Stalin's confidence and been able to secure a high position by deceit and treachery." But throughout his rambling, folksy narrative, with his determination to blame all the crimes of Communism on Stalin and Beria, his "evil genius," Khrushchev's portrait of Beria still amounted to little more than that of an orthodox villain; there was no hint of the glamour of a Medici, the intellectual subtlety of a Machiavelli or a Savonarola. Beria remained a faceless intriguer behind the brutal bastion of Soviet power politics.

Of his private life I could find no mention. This seemed to offer two important advantages: not only would it render the "diaries" all the more valuable from an historical point of view; it also meant that we could indulge our fantasies about Beria's private habits almost with impunity. But it presented me an especial challenge. In the first few days I'd found the writing uncomplicated, almost easy; and my main concern had been that Boris would be doing most of the work while I played a sinecure role, typing up my pieces in English, only to have them translated back into Russian. But now I had come to realize that if the book was to prove truly convincing, it was going to demand a degree of creative writing; for while Boris supplied the background information, I not only was required to turn out lewd descriptions of the tyrant's sexual escapades, but must substantiate them with an imaginative insight into the man's character. He materialized as a cruel, cynical, selfish rogue who'd made it to the top and was determined to enjoy himself when he got there; and on rereading my material, I also discovered a certain disarming frankness, sometimes even a humorous humility in his confessions—as though he realized the kind of monster he was, and did not want to dissemble or try dishonestly to defend himself.

I even persuaded myself that this part of the "diaries" was not so much a hoax as a legitimate attempt to explain the character of a great villain. Boris' task was more specious: it involved the essence of the forger's art. For how many of the proven facts should be included? And how many of them should Beria inadvertently get wrong?

I remembered reading a powerful demolition of the Khrushchev memoirs by a leading Sovietologist who cited a number of factual errors. But then Khrushchev—if the official version was true—had been indulging himself in the rambling reminiscences of an old man in retirement. Beria, in the same way, had presumably not been writing for profit or posterity, but occupying his spare moments with random self-revelations. He would not have been likely—particularly after a heavy night's drinking, with the day's scheming ahead—to go back and revise his latest entries, checking every fact and date against the official records, such as they were.

Finally we decided on a compromise. While I worked at the man's private life—which, we agreed, was virtually impossible to check or challenge—Boris would not only assemble the bones of the book around the proven facts, he would also introduce a sprinkling of obscure details, some partially verifiable—or at least plausible—while others would simply be invented: memos of secret meetings; telephone conversations; a complex of fact, fiction, allusion and innuendo that would steadily pick loose, stitch by stitch, much of the fabric of academic theories, while leaving others not only intact, but reinforced; confirming some historians' *ad hoc* assumptions and refractory evidence, while distorting, contradicting or destroying others. No doubt many experts would be tempted to challenge the authenticity of the work on purely personal grounds; but others would hasten to welcome it as invaluable "proof" of what had hitherto been speculation.

It was Boris' idea to introduce throughout the narrative a string of fictitious characters to whom he would refer, in the traditional Slavic manner, by their Christian and paternal names only—of common Russian or Georgian origin—and which would be obscured still further by the abbreviations, initials and ingenious nicknames which, he claimed, would drive the Kremlinologists crazy with confusion and doubt.

These details, both true and fictitious, would be colored by casual references and observations by Beria—mostly concerning his accomplices and enemies—which would be impossible to confirm or refute on the basis of known fact. For example: Abakumov, Beria's chief henchman and former head of the coun-

107

terespionage organization SMERSH, using French colognes to keep down his body odor after playing volleyball with Beria; the habit of Rakosi, the Hungarian leader, of picking his nose after dinner; or Vlodzimirski, former head of the "Section for the Investigation of Specially Important Cases," always arranging to lose at billiards against Beria, even for sizeable sums of money.

Day by day Boris was also filling two fat notebooks, one red, the other black, their pages covered with columns of looping Cyrillic script and figures. These, he explained, formed the key to our entire labors; and each morning, as we laid out the manuscripts, books and typewriters in the shade of the vines, it was these two notebooks that he kept closest to hand, and which he sedulously gathered up and removed to his room when the day's work was done.

The black book contained the lists of all known members of "Beria's Gang," together with lesser associates and accomplices; and the figures against each name were the dates of their accession to grace and of their downfall or death—most of which had been by firing squad following Beria's own purge in 1953. The red books contained similar lists and dates, but this time of all leading Communists known to have opposed Beria or to have fallen foul of him—nearly all of whom had disappeared or been eliminated before 1953. However, the pattern was not always so simple, since a number of these names appeared in both lists. There was, for instance, the not untypical case of Rapava and Rukhadze, two notorious members of the Georgian Central Committee, each of whom had in turn had the other arrested and tortured for false confessions in 1951, ostensibly on Beria's own orders—each to be released and to retract his confession, only to be shot four years later as "devoted accomplices" of Beria. This kind of complication necessitated an elaborate system of cross-references which Boris had inscribed in both books with a kaleidoscope of stars, circles, crosses, queries, deletions, scribbles and scrawls, until, to my baffled eye, the pages now

108

began to look less like a railway timetable than the records of some diligent but chaotic accountant working in ciphered shorthand. I only hoped that when our work was finally done, these books would check, and that some tiny, vital flaw would not remain to expose the whole edifice of our fraud.

After two weeks of averaging about ten hours' work a day—which included detailed discussions over meals and through the evening—we had reached the beginning of 1948. In Moscow the dreaded drunken Zhdanov had just denounced a group of Jewish intellectuals as "cosmopolitans and anti-patriots, as dangerous to the Soviet Union as parasites on a plant." Beria, as founder of the wartime Jewish Anti-Fascist Committee, was not happy. But abroad things were going better. Most of Eastern Europe was now safely under the one-party system; the Marshall Plan had been blocked and Soviet administrators were managing these countries; Soviet generals commanded their armies, and Beria's security men controlled their police. Only Czechoslovakia, under President Beneš and Jan Masaryk, continued to cling to a precarious parliamentary coalition, which included the Czech Stalinist leader Otto Gottwald as Prime Minister.

Over the past few months Beria's men had been stealthily infiltrating the Czech police and armed forces, until Beneš's government resigned in protest on February 20; and in the political vacuum the Communist-dominated trade unions marched their armed militias into Prague and seized power. A few days later, Masaryk—known to have been deeply depressed by events —was found dead under the bathroom window of his ministry, having either jumped or been pushed.

"One of the great political whodunits of our time," said Boris. "Of course he was murdered—there are too many unanswered mysteries to explain a simple suicide. During the Dubček period in 1968 before the Soviet invasion in August, a number of

109

articles began appearing in the Czech press producing new evidence. The invasion prevented the full denouement, but there was enough to justify the worst suspicions. For instance, the presence in Prague of one of Beria's top field men in the NKVD, a major in civilian clothes, with several colleagues, all of whom disappeared immediately after Masaryk's death. Then the other known details—Masaryk found lying in his pajamas eight feet from the wall, with all the bones in his legs smashed. This did, in fact, suggest that he might have jumped; if he'd been pushed he'd have more likely landed on his head. But then there were traces of shit on the windowsill of the bathroom, which also had scratch marks on it, and there was tremendous chaos inside the flat. The medicine cabinet had been ransacked, there were smashed bottles all over the floor—and, strangest of all, a bed had been made up and lain in inside the bathtub."

"And you've got further evidence to explain all this?" I asked.

"Yes. From our old Hungarian friend, Laszlo Laszlo. At the time, as I told you, he was a high official in Rakosi's Communist government in Hungary. But a few years later, during the mass Stalinist terror directed at Jews and suspected Titoists, he took the unprecedented step of resigning from the Party. Of course it was madness, as well as bravery—but Laszlo Laszlo is like that. Later, under Khrushchev, and as a colonel of the Red Army, he was able to visit us in Moscow, where he told my father a very strange story.

"At the time of his resignation the Hungarian leadership had been so surprised by his action—which amounted almost to suicide in those days—that at first they didn't know what to do. Laszlo Laszlo wasn't on the official Moscow list for the mock show-trials, and, besides, he had been an old wartime buddy of Rakosi's in Moscow. In the end Rakosi demanded that he write out ten reasons for resigning. So old Laszlo Laszlo sat down with a bottle of *baratsk*, the local plum brandy, and wrote as his first reason that he found the police terror under Rakosi worse than that of the wartime fascist regime of Admiral Horthy. For the second he wrote that Stalin's anti-Semitic campaign was no better than the Nazi persecution of the Jews. Then for a long time he couldn't think of another reason. So he finished the *baratsk* and finally wrote: '*Three—Communism does not work.*' Then sealed it up and sent it to Rakosi personally."

"And then?"

"Well, for eight days nothing happened. It was a very hot summer, and he took his wife, who's dead now, and his son, who escaped to America in 1956, and they went down to Lake Balaton. Laszlo Laszlo says that he was hardly sober for more than a few hours during that whole week. Then on the morning of the eighth day he met a literary critic he knew from Budapest. An old Party hack, but Laszlo Laszlo had always thought him pretty harmless. They had a few drinks together, then suddenly he began to feel dizzy. He went for a swim, and an extraordinary sensation came over him. He wanted to drown himself. Of course, he was worried and depressed—he knew the AVH boys were going to pick him up at any moment—but he says this was quite a different feeling. Not an ordinary depression—this was a suicidal madness that came over him. It was only because he knew that *they* too wanted him to drown that he didn't just give up and sink into the water.

"When he got back to the shore, the critic had disappeared, but Laszlo's depression continued, and got even worse. For three days he could hardly speak or move, he just sat and wept. And every minute of those three days he had one desire—to do away with himself. It was only when he got back to Budapest and went to his doctor, who gave him some strong antidepressant drugs, that the feeling began to wear off. Then, two days later, they came and arrested him, and he was sentenced to ten years' hard labor for activities against the state.

"Now, Laszlo Laszlo had heard about drugs being used by the police. One of them was cortisone—or a very primitive form of it—which produced, as one of its many early side effects, acute suicidal depression. Laszlo Laszlo swears that not only

111

had this literary critic fed him a huge dose in his drink, but the same trick was played on Masaryk. In which case, *mon cher,* a lot of the mysteries of Masaryk's death are explained. He did jump, but not until he'd ransacked his medicine cupboard trying to find some pills—sedatives, perhaps—to ease his depression. Then the shit on the windowsill. Laszlo Laszlo told me that one of the effects of the drug was that he'd had to run to the toilet every ten minutes. Masaryk had had such acute diarrhea that he'd even made up a bed in the bathtub to be close to the toilet."

"And the scratch marks on the windowsill?"

Boris shrugged. "Perhaps at the last minute he tried to pull himself back. Or perhaps one of Beria's boys came in and gave him a helping shove."

"And Beria confirms all this?"

"Of course. It will create a small sensation—and it is again something that cannot be easily challenged."

"You're sure of your medical facts?"

"I'm sure of Laszlo Laszlo," Boris said defiantly. "He may be a strange character, but he does not invent stories!"

I didn't argue. I'd heard things myself about the early use of cortisone and its side effects—and anyway, we didn't have to specify exactly what the drug was. There were plenty on the market, even in those days, that could have induced a similar effect.

That day we wrote nearly five thousand words between us; and by sundown decided to treat ourselves to a little trip into Siena, where we sat in a café overlooking the floodlit bowl of the piazza with its tall Campanile pointing like a rust-red pencil into the black sky; and Boris insisted on ordering himself a "Buck's Fizz," which turned out to have been made out of Asti Spumante instead of champagne, and which he refused either to drink or to pay for. There was a furious argument, which I did not enter into, preferring to let Boris lose his temper with strange waiters rather than with his literary collaborator.

112

Things proceeded at this smooth pace for nearly a month before the first signs of trouble.

Summer was coming and the days grew hotter. We were both well sunburned—Boris a mottled brick-red and his nose flaking like a hunk of pink wax.

The book was now forty thousand words into the first draft, which we estimated would be between a quarter and a third of the total. We had covered Yugoslavia's split with Moscow—when Beria was frantically organizing Tito's assassination, first by infiltrating agents into the Marshal's offices in Belgrade, then by a planned assault force on his villa on the island of Brioni, and finally a desperate attempt to blow up his private yacht. But all failed. The Berlin Blockade was turning into a fiasco. The hopes of France and Italy turning Communist, on the same lines of Czechoslovakia, were now no more than a dim illusion. At home Stalin was growing old and mad, possessed by growing paranoia; and, like a drug addict, he not only craved ever larger doses of public adulation—*Pravda* was calling him "the Greatest Genius of History" and "the Shining Sun of Humanity"—but even larger quantities of blood. Jews and intellectuals were not enough. It was now the turn of loyal Party members. And in this poisonous atmosphere there now began what has been described as "the darkest chapter in postwar Soviet history"—the Leningrad Case.

Between the end of 1949 and the summer of 1950 more than one thousand leading Leningrad Communists were arrested and executed, while another one thousand still remain unaccounted for. Beria was entrusted with trumping up the necessary charges and making the arrests; and, thanks to Khrushchev's "secret" speech at the 1956 Twentieth Party Congress, as well as servile denunciations from Communist sources attacking "deviations from Socialist legality," we found the Leningrad Case fairly well documented.

Then the trouble began. All morning we had been writing up the background, through Beria's eyes: he'd been quite honest in admitting that he had used the case to settle old scores with Communists he either personally disliked or believed had too much dirt on him. At noon I broke off to drive down to Gaiole for fresh supplies before the shops closed. (Boris' combined greed and gastronomic imagination had led to a depletion of stores about every couple of days; and we were spending far more than I'd anticipated in our life of rustic husbandry—though Boris airily dismissed this, producing wads of 10,000-lire notes and again telling me that I could repay him as soon as my Swiss account was opened.)

When I returned I saw him squatting under an olive tree, naked except for a towel around his waist like some hairy Buddha, sharing bread and salami and a bottle of Chianti with Signor Gochi. He was waving his arms and shouting with his mouth full, not even looking up as I drove past and parked behind the house.

I eventually distracted him enough to get him to help me carry the provisions into the kitchen. "That fellow Gochi," he said, "is a charming old idiot. He is a Communist Party member."

"There are a few in Italy," I said, putting some chickens into the deep-freeze.

"At least he does not approve of the Soviet invasion of Czechoslovakia," Boris continued, "although that is only because the bosses in Rome tell him so." He rambled on until we had cleared the kitchen, then said, "We'll make some coffee. Then I want to discuss something with you, Tom. A matter of great interest."

He poured himself a *grappa*, then went out to the patio and collected a sheaf of notes. The sun was at its hottest, and he beckoned me toward the pool, where he sat down on the edge with his legs in the water, staring at his gargantuan reflection in the ripples.

114

"I have made an important discovery," he said at last, glancing around to make sure he wasn't being overheard. "It is a small detail, but it is highly significant in the context of what we are writing. Something I have suspected for some time, and this morning, while you were in town, I found the proof. In an old Soviet history published in Moscow in 1951." He rolled his bloodshot eyes at me, and continued in a low voice, his breath thick with garlic and *grappa*.

"The present Soviet Prime Minister, Alexi Kosygin"—he spoke the name in a whisper—"has a daughter married to the son of General Gvishiani, who is one of the only survivors of 'Beria's Gang,' as it was called, and one of his worst henchmen." He paused; I waited, saying nothing.

"It is a completely unknown fact," said Boris. "These Soviet leaders keep their lives very secret—few people in the West probably know the Prime Minister even has a daughter. But this man Gvishiani is a monster. He is retired now, but his record is one of the most terrible in Russian history—after Stalin and Beria. Yet he is still alive. And you know, they have a son called Dzermen. For a long time I was puzzled by this, because it is not a Russian name—or any name at all, for that matter. Then I found out. It was an invented name. They had made it up from the prefixes *Dzer* and *Men,* from Dzerzhinsky and Menzhinsky—the founders of the Cheka, and two of the first really big killers of Communism. Just imagine naming your child after men like that!"

"It's hardly a crime," I said casually, "even in Soviet Russia?"

"Crime!" Boris bawled. "But you miss the whole goddam point! Kosygin is supposed to be a 'liberal' by Communist standards—he is a sort of counterbalance to the conservative hard-liners in the Presidium. But if it ever got out that he was involved with one of Beria's Gang he would be finished overnight."

This time I spoke a good deal less casually. "You're not thinking of bringing this into the diaries?"

Boris grinned cunningly. "Oh, I intend to do more than that, *mon cher*. What I ask myself is, why are Gvishiani and Kosygin still *alive*? An old Stalinist killer and a revisionist liberal? It is because they have each, at different times, had too much dirt on the other! Take the Prime Minister, who is an old Leningrad Party member. In 1949 Stalin decides that the Leningrad leaders are getting too fresh—they were more intellectual and honest than the Georgian gang—and Stalin has them rounded up and shot. But there were some big names among them, and in spite of the usual forced confessions, Stalin needed more positive 'proof.' Now, Kosygin was certainly no friend of Stalin's. I happen to know that after the war he was talking to Maisky, the former Soviet ambassador to Britain, and referred to Stalin as 'that pockmarked butcher.' Yet Kosygin is not only alive, but in power. Now, why? Because—"and he thumped the marble paving with each new word—"because he *supplied just that proof that Stalin needed*! Kosygin ratted on his comrades. He was ordered to spill the dirt on the other Leningrad leaders—or else!" He splashed his legs in the pool and laughed. "And that, *mon cher*, is what Lavrenti Pavlovich is going to say in his diaries!"

I stood up. "Now, listen, Boris. Conning an American publisher is one thing. Trying to destroy a leader of the Soviet government is another game altogether."

"You think it is immoral?"

"I think it's dangerous," I said, trying to avoid the jovial contempt in Boris' eyes. "Besides, you've said yourself the man's a liberal—or at least better than the rest of the bunch. Why destroy him?"

"Bah! They are all the same! All out of the same stable. When you say 'liberal,' you are not talking of good old chaps in the British Labour Party—these present boys in the Kremlin weren't picking strawberries during Stalin's last purges. And anyway, if one goes, another comes. It makes no difference."

"Then why bother at all?"

116

"It will make the book far more sensational. With all the sex and the political scandal we have a tremendous best seller! I think perhaps we ask for *three* million dollars?" he added, kicking the water and rubbing his hands together as though he were washing them.

"At this rate we could probably sell it to both the CIA and the KGB for twenty million dollars," I said, standing up. "Play our cards right, and perhaps we don't have to bring in a publisher at all." I was sweating and went into the kitchen for some iced mineral water.

The trouble was, I didn't know how to handle Boris in this situation. Usually when he became cantankerous or moody, I either went for a swim or drove down to Gaiole for some shopping, and by the time I got back he'd have forgotten what he wanted to argue about. But this was different. Boris had got his teeth into what he considered a succulent scoop, and it was going to take more than a shopping trip to make him forget it. Nor did I think that reasoned persuasion would do much good. I decided that my best course would be to distract his attention with another, equally outrageous scandal—only less perilous.

When I got back to the pool I said, "Listen, Boris, about the time that Beria was in charge of subversion in the West—his Paris-Geneva period—he was responsible for recruiting agents in the universities, wasn't he? Well, how about bringing in the famous mystery of the Fourth Man? The one who finally tipped off Philby to tip off Burgess and Maclean? That would stir things up a bit!"

The trick seemed to work. That afternoon we backtracked several chapters, and I was soon busy with Beria reminiscing about his experiences in the West, indulging a few of my own incipient right-wing prejudices at the expense of those intellectuals of the thirties: the silliness and gullibility of the Shaws, the Webbs, Gide—well-intentioned men and women who traveled through the Soviet Union on the eve of the great purges and came away with radiant accounts of its "vigor" and "the youthful purity of its efforts toward true Socialism." Beria would have been the first to laugh at such idiocy.

Finally, and not without some prick of conscience, I introduced the name of a rare man of letters, now dead, who had been a resident fellow of one of the leading Cambridge colleges, and was known to have been a friend of both Burgess and Maclean. Boris was thrilled; but as a precaution—or perhaps for added authenticity—we had Beria spell the man's name slightly wrong, translating it letter by letter from the Russian.

From then till the time we finished the day's work, the little matter of Kosygin's family relations seemed forgotten.

PART
THREE

It is not the lie that passeth through the mind, but the lie that sinketh in and settleth in it, that doth the hurt.

—Francis Bacon

Paper Three

Moscow, January 1950

Another irritating day, with Vlodzimirski[1] whining at me about
the pneumonia schedules, and begging me yet again to prevail
on the Boss to bring back the death penalty—at least for the
more common crimes.[2] But I know the Old Man is adamant about
this. He insists that the Western Socialist intelligentsia must not
be awakened from their dreams!

But privately I agree with V. This constant discretion, which
is being insisted on by the Ministry of Justice (again to impress
the stupid foreigners, no doubt!) just bungs up the service with
still more red tape. One of V's deputies even called last week to
suggest we open private files of fictitious jobs to justify our extra

---

[1] L. E. Vlodzimirski, head of the Section for the Investigation of Specially
Important Cases, part of the NKVD (People's Commissariat for Internal Af-
fairs). He was executed in December 1953, along with the rest of "Beria's
Gang."

[2] In 1945 Stalin abolished the death penalty, allegedly as a sop to Western
"liberal" opinion, and thereafter victims of the secret police were often stated
to have died of pneumonia. The penalty was reintroduced, under pressure from
Beria, early in 1950.

121

expenses—paying executioners, disposal of corpses, etc. Such bureaucracy becomes a farce!

And on top of it all I had a most tiresome experience on Friday night, and although I had the last word, the whole incident has soured my week.

On Thursday night I had been to a big reception in the Museum of the Revolution to celebrate some trashy film, *The Kuban Cossacks*. (Apparently the film industry feels in some need of my protection—or perhaps they are just anxious to be seen to have the right social connections!)

These film people can be very tiresome, always trying to impress me and catch my eye, and their gatherings are only made tolerable by the female supporting cast, which in my experience is usually good. On Thursday night there was one particularly striking girl—a young blonde called Natasha Z., a Moscow girl who plays a small role in the film, but who Rafik told me was quite promising. Besides her long blond hair, which she wore modestly in a bun, she had a perfect complexion, and was also plump and amply built.

I introduced myself and we got talking very pleasantly—although I was disappointed to see she was only drinking fruit juice. I tried to make her try some Caucasian wine, but she refused firmly. (She was obviously from a good family, though probably not influential, and I made a note for Rafik to pursue the usual inquiries.)

Our conversation continued very nicely, and again I was impressed by her modesty. To draw her out a little I informed her that I was not without influence myself in the film industry! At the same time I decided to tread gently, in accordance with her general demeanor, and just before I took my leave (which Rafik arranged with considerable ceremony) I invited her to a dinner party next night. She blushed to her neck, and her big blue eyes were shining with excitement as she accepted.

On Friday evening at 7:30 sharp my driver collected her from an address in the District, where she lives with her family. (Rafik

122

informed me that her father is a minor official with the Ministry of Transport.) But the moment she arrived at Malaya Nikitskaya[3] I saw she was ill at ease, clearly disconcerted to find me alone. She had obviously been expecting some grand banquet—another opportunity to meet more influential people, no doubt!

However, I was very correct with her, and when we went in to eat, with the table laid for just the two of us, I was relieved that she at least did not refuse a glass of French champagne—although she sipped it as though it might poison her. I found the conversation much more heavy going than the night before, and began to get impatient. I asked her about her family, but she did not seem disposed to talk about them, and I guessed that she was perhaps ashamed of their position—which was a pity, since I could be very helpful to a humble railwayman!

We reached the coffee and dessert—fresh strawberries from Africa—and I had almost to force her to accept one glass of green chartreuse. Suddenly I lost patience. I had made a pointed observation about her dress (a really chic evening gown which confirmed my most optimistic anticipations about her figure), but although my remark was not unseemly, she seemed to take it almost as an insult. I could see I was going to have to maneuver with care. I got up, refreshed my liqueur glass, and invited her to the couch. She was clearly reluctant to leave the table, and when she did so I grabbed her from behind. I could feel the delicious contours of her body under her dress—and my senses were so inflamed that for a moment I could hardly believe what happened next. The bitch slapped my face!

I must be quite frank here. I cannot remember, since my early days in the Georgian Party, anyone—let alone a girl—actually striking me. I was so taken aback that my reactions were not spontaneous, or I would have certainly dealt with her there and then. But something restrained me. Instead, I faced her with my coldest, most commanding stare—a look that has made far greater mortals than her tremble and fall on their knees in suppli-

[3] A central street in Moscow where Beria had his private mansion.

cation. But this bitch was either very courageous or just simple-minded. She turned to me and said she was a "proper girl" who did not respect the advances of older men.

I'm afraid at this I lost my nerve, my whole air of stern restraint. I could have countered by telling her that we Georgians are in our prime at the age of seventy—that Georgian men have lived to be 150 and sired children when they were within a score of those years! But I was no longer in a conversational mood. Instead I just dismissed her.

I followed her to the stairs and watched her make the long descent, which she did with an exasperating dignity. Then at the last moment I went out onto the balcony of the reception room above the street. (I felt it more appropriate to see the little fool off from above, rather than at street level, for she was quite tall.) I leaned on the balustrade and watched her reach the car. The driver was holding the door open for her. She bent down to climb in, then noticed the roses I'd left for her on the seat. She looked back at the house and saw me.

"Thank you for the bouquet," she called.

And I called back, "That's not a bouquet, little girl—that's a wreath."

I could see her turn pale, and the driver, who had not missed my little joke, either, bundled her into the back and drove away.

I did not wait for my rage to subside, but called Headquarters at once and gave instructions for her to be taken straight to the Lubyanka. In the morning I made the necessary dispositions to ensure she receives the proper sentence.

Meanwhile, I must be philosophical and consider the whole incident as further insight into the oddities of human nature!

Moscow, November 1951

A tiring week, since the traditional celebrations[4] coincide this year with the Tenth Anniversary of the Battle of Moscow, and

[4] The November 7 anniversary of the 1917 Bolshevik Revolution.

124

the Boss has made sure the whole works are laid on—not only for the common people, but for the foreigners too.

Apart from the rounds of parties and receptions for the military and the arse-licking diplomatic circle, our Service last night had its own "do" at the Hotel Moskva. (I must mention here that it is a really disgraceful establishment—a blight on our capital—whose architects should be summarily punished! The heating is irregular, the plaster walls are crumbling or covered in blotches of mold; bunches of wiring hang out of them like entrails; the plumbing makes a noise like a railway station; half the bathroom doors do not close properly and the toilets often won't flush. Yet this is supposed to be one of the finest hotels in the city—not only for Western bourgeois visitors, but for important delegates from the fraternal countries! The impression it must make on them is really shameful.)

The party was held in the banqueting rooms on the third floor. I arrived late, and in ill humor, since there have been yet more repercussions from the miserable business of the two British defectors.[5] Both are disgusting homosexuals, and alcoholics to boot, so that I continue to treat their material with the greatest caution. But news has reached me that not only has their disappearance continued to alert the bourgeois powers to the dangers in their midst, and so made them more vigilant, it has also led to the dismissal of H. A. R. Philby from his official post—a loss that cannot be underestimated. But, worse, it has also threatened ——[6]

The British, of course, are so law-abiding and mealymouthed that they have not arrested P. But his dismissal from the British Foreign Service is not only a grave setback, but if inquiries are pursued with the correct diligence, they may lead to the unmasking of ——, which could prove highly embarrassing for me. For the moment, I can only thank God that P. has not followed the other two to Moscow.

[5] Burgess and Maclean.
[6] Name deleted by ed. on security grounds.

Anyway, when I arrived at the hotel last night the party was already well under way—the tables crammed with bottles and sweetmeats, of which at least half had already been consumed. But a special corner of supplies had been reserved for me, and the crowd fell back to make a path for me through the middle of the floor.

All the Old Gang were there to greet me: besides Abakumov,[7] there was Dekanasov, Gvishiani, Bagirov, Merkulov, Bakradze,[8] as well as a number of junior district officials from outside town, who stood around, all scrubbed and shiny-faced, squinting obsequiously in my direction. I must say their expressions sickened me: for here I was, looking at the Flower of the Security Service— the hand-picked guardians of Socialism and of the Soviet people —and what did I see but a band of fawning flunkeys, all scented and sweating, in their creaking new shoes and well-pressed suits, like a lot of schoolboys getting tipsy at their first dance.

As was usual, the few wives of the senior officials had departed after the first toasts, and the rest were now waiting for me to set the pace. I accepted a glass of Osoboya vodka and glanced around, watching how these devoted vigilantes cringed and reddened at my gaze, and only wished for some relaxing female company, but this was against all protocol.

Instead, I inevitably found myself surrounded by Abakumov and his circle of acolytes. He was one of the few guests in full uniform—his thick black hair combed back with oil, his coarse dark features stinking of perfume—preening himself like some loutish master of ceremonies. He was drinking cautiously, as he always does in my company, and at once began to indulge me with his small talk—discussing the various blood levels to be found in a man's urine after a kidney-beating.

[7] Viktor Semyonovich Abakumov, a Georgian and Beria's right-hand man, who was first in charge of the counterintelligence organ SMERSH (Death to Spies), and became Minister of the Interior in 1946. He was dismissed at the end of 1951 and executed in 1954.

[8] All Georgian members of "Beria's Gang." With the exception of General Gvishiani, who is still alive, they were all executed in December 1953.

As the Boss is fond of saying, "Out of shit, princes are made." Well, this Viktor Semyonovich is certainly such a prince! When the Boss talks of "intellectual saboteurs and rootless cosmopolitans" one can be sure he is not referring to our beloved Abakumov!

I endured him with patience, but he began to sicken me—for I know that although he appears so loyal and earnest, he is really a scavenger and bully-boy from the back alleys who'd sell his sister's virginity for some new promotion or medal. I left him finally, in mid-sentence—watching him redden to the ears—then turned to the circle around us and lifted my glass. "To the patriotic members of the State Security Services!" I cried, and they all bayed the words back at me like a pack of hounds.

"So!" I went on, with my glass still raised. "Let us test your initiative, comrades! We'll play Hunt the Mike." (It is a familiar game, to find the hidden microphone in the room, and the signal that the festivities could at last run wild.) I must say I always enjoy the spectacle of these eager little men ripping up the carpets; standing on each other's shoulders to reach the chandeliers, which they dismantle bulb by bulb; tapping the walls; sticking penknives behind the wainscoting—tearing the rooms apart like a gang of happy professional vandals.

But last night we had a special joke. Perhaps there had been more drinking than usual—but my men really went to work with a will on that rotten hotel. There was so much loose wiring that we often had false leads, and the boys would come back, all flushed and sweating, to refill their glasses for the next go.

Soon the rooms were half in darkness, the air heavy with plaster dust, and still no luck. (Usually on these occasions the operating agent for the area knows the spot and bides his time before he makes the discovery; but last night I think the men responsible for the hotel either were too drunk or had genuinely forgotten.)

The game was in danger of turning sour, when three burly fellows began to haul a great gilt sofa away from the wall—one of those real monstrosities, in the eighteenth-century style, that must have weighed fifty kilos. Suddenly, with a bellow of excitement, they called me over, while several others had gone down on their hands and knees and were setting to work with their knives.

I strolled over and saw, on the dusty patch where the sofa had stood, a metal grille about the size of a pocketbook. The ones with penknives were using the tips of the blades as screwdrivers, trying to keep their hands steady, and I watched each screw come out—twelve in all. As the last one came away, something dropped out of the bottom of the grille, and the next moment we heard a terrific crash from below.

The men looked puzzled for a moment, until one of them came rushing back to announce that the chandelier in the room underneath us had fallen out of the ceiling, smashing into the floor! (The joke was only slightly spoiled by the fact that the room had been empty at the time.) But I must say I was bent up with laughter until tears were running down my cheeks!

MALLORY'S REPORT

The days dragged on; it was now high summer; the first draft of the typescript, in English and Russian, was more than three-quarters finished and Boris and I were still on speaking terms.

The progress of this scriptural marriage had been bumpy, sometimes bitter; yet it had retained a certain rhythm, dictated by Boris—whether he was assuming the passive "female" role during the creation of Beria's lascivious escapades, or the dominating male *persona* as we waded through the political revelations.

Then came the crunch. Like all marriages where one partner works with desperate patience to keep the relationship stable, the moment arrives when the patience flags: a mistaken word, a lapse into rhetoric, and the whole edifice comes crashing down. And as in such marriages the crisis between Boris and me was reached suddenly, without warning.

It was still early when it began. Boris was already out at the table on the terrace, stripped down to his Bermuda shorts, his shoulders and the crown of his head gleaming like fresh-cooked prawns. He heard my sandals on the steps and looked round from his pile of notes.

"Ah, comrade. Today we are going to make some real mischief!"

"Mischief?" I approached him cautiously. As usual the work in front of him meant nothing to me—a mass of Cyrillic scrawls, circles, underlinings and crossings-out. He gave me a lewd wink and reached for his statutory glass of Fernet Branca.

"A really big mischief," he said, nodding, and tossed back the drink without a wince.

"What sort of mischief?" I said, sitting down on the little wall in front of him.

"Ah!" He brought his hands down with a loud smack on his thighs. "We are going to take the whole Soviet leadership, every single bastard one of them, and we are going to put them right up there under the spotlight, on the best-seller lists of the world, and then we are going to shit on them from a terrific height!" He broke off with a laugh like a dog barking.

"We are going to shit on them, *mon cher*, until they are completely buried. We will destroy them!"

"You mean the present leadership?"

"Of course. Every murdering one of them! We take them with great cunning, you see—nothing obvious, because most of them were pretty small fry when old Beria was at the top. But we mention them—a word here, a word there—you see, it will be done with the most beautiful expertise. And when we have finished they will each stink like an old corpse!"

He sat back, grinning hugely. I watched him with a wave of weariness. It was going to be a long hot day.

"We've already shat on them," I said at last. "On the Prime Minister, at any rate—with the Leningrad Case."

"Ah, that was a mere bagatelle! You see, I have decided that in this game, this blackening of reputations, we have got to remember always whom we are dealing with. The Leningrad Case is old history. Beria can give his own version of the story, but then it is only *his* version. And he is a proven liar, everybody knows that—it was his great genius!"

130

"Then if everyone knows it, they're not going to believe him anyway." But I felt no relief at this curious cross-reasoning, sensing that it must conceal some devilish inner motive.

"That is true," he said slowly, "but only to a degree. You see, if we are really to incriminate the present leadership in the crimes of Beria and Stalin, then we must approach it not just from the *political* angle. Politically the present leadership all know each other's faults—their crimes and weaknesses. They will know, for instance, whether old Alexei Kosygin really was implicated in the Leningrad Case, and, if so, how deeply. When it appears in our book it will certainly be highly embarrassing for him, but not incriminating. And even if the book goes into *samizdat*, it will only reach a few thousand people in Russia. Besides, something like the Leningrad Case is old history by now."

"That's not what you were saying a few weeks ago."

"No, perhaps not. But I have had time to do some thinking. And what I have been thinking is that it is no good just smearing the leaders with old political stories. What we need is something more subtle, more personal—something that will get between the breaks in their armor and stick like tar!"

I said nothing. Boris shifted his rump with a crackle of wicker, and resumed his argument:

"So you see, *mon cher*, in order to do a really good smear job we must find something that is not generally known to the rest of the leadership. Not something that they will immediately say is just another propaganda lie from the CIA files, and which they know isn't true anyway, but something they *will* believe—something that is both simple and shocking. Something that people cannot easily refute—even coming from Beria himself—for the excellent reason that it could very easily be true!"

He sat back and beamed at me with bloodshot delight. "You see what I am getting at, *mon cher*?"

"Vividly."

He rubbed his hands together and chuckled. "In Russia we

131

have a proverb: 'The best lies are like margarine—they must contain at least ten percent butter.' Butter is the truth, and all our lies will contain at least ten percent of the truth. Okay?"

"No. You talk about us having to do a really good smear job. I thought we were supposed to be doing a con job—a con on the great Western reading public, and on the Soviet experts in particular. Right?"

"Right. But what is the good of a con job unless we do a little smearing too?"

"Why the hell do we have to do any smearing at all?"

"Why the hell do we write the goddam book at all!" he yelled. "You tell me—what's the goddam point?"

"Money, Boris." I got up and turned toward the steps. "Money and security. So I can pay off my overdraft and buy a new car and lie on an empty beach with a beautiful girl, and not have to worry where my next paycheck's coming from—or have to sweat every time I open a newspaper or sign a hotel register, all ready to pack and do a midnight flit on the soonest plane to the farthest place, with perhaps half a dozen Interpol agents half an hour behind me." I paused at the top of the steps. "That's the goddam point, Boris."

He began to bellow. "What has Interpol got to do with it?" But I didn't answer. I didn't for the good reason that there was only one answer to give, and Boris knew it, with all its ugly permutations, even better than I did. He was merely provoking me into a senseless argument. His voice followed me into the house, bouncing around the stone kitchen with a shrill echo: "You are just frightened like a goddam schoolboy!"

I boiled up a saucepan of strong black coffee, poured it into an earthenware jug, put it on a tray with two soup bowls, and carried it outside. Boris had fallen silent and was hunched again over his notes, scribbling rapidly. He waited till I'd put the tray down on the wall, then looked at me with his sly grin. "What do you know about Aleksandr Shelepin?"

"Shelepin?" I shrugged. "Not much, except from his photographs. Handsome, cold, hard-liner. Used to be head of the KGB—now chairman of what they laughingly call their Trade Union Movement." I sipped my coffee, holding the bowl in both hands. "Why? We haven't brought him in yet," I added carefully, and watched his smile break into a broad grin.

"Not yet, *mon cher*. But there is still time." And he drew a messy circle around one of the names on the foolscap. "Shelepin is a real Number One baddie—neo-Stalinist of the purest water. Old enough to have helped in the purges, but not important enough to have got the chop himself. From 1952—at the height of the second Stalinist terror—he was head of the Komsomol, the Young Communist League, as well as a member of the 'World Federation of Democratic Youth,' in which he was in charge of countering bourgeois subversion. In 1958 he took over the KGB, until old Nikita had him knocked down a peg or two in 1961. Now considered one of the Kremlin's most ambitious and dangerous Young Turks—and no doubt planning a comeback."

He sat for a moment chewing the knuckles of his thumbs. "I think we will play a few games with Comrade Shelepin. He would have been old enough for Beria to have seen him in action as head of the Komsomol. Perhaps young Aleksandr Shelepin was rather fond of his Young Communists? Even young boys, perhaps?" He leaned forward, breathing the rancid fumes of Fernet Branca. "You like the idea?"

"No." I shifted a couple of feet away from him and poured another bowl of coffee. I knew the next few minutes were going to be critical.

"It's an amusing idea," I said finally, "but it won't work."

"Why not? Because nobody will believe it? Bah! Once they have swallowed the book as genuine, they will believe anything, particularly details about the leaders' sex lives."

"You're contradicting yourself again," I said. "You were saying just now that people wouldn't believe Beria because he was a proven liar."

"Ah, but only in the political field, *mon cher!* In the sexual context people are far more credulous—particularly puritanical people. And at heart the Russians have always been a very puritanical race, not least among the top Communists."

"Whom are we trying to convince, Boris—the reading public of the Free World or the Kremlin bosses?"

"Ah, there you have it, in a nutshell. As you would say, six of one and half a dozen of the other. But you sound unhappy?"

"I'm worried, Boris, that you're going to wreck our whole enterprise."

"Wreck?"

"Wreck. Absolutely." I put down my empty coffee bowl and leaned forward, spelling out the reasons on my fingers:

"Point one. We agree that whoever is shown this typescript is going to be disposed, from the start, to see it as a fake? Right. And smearing the present leadership with dirty tittle-tattle about their sex lives is just the kind of crude nonsense worthy of some grade-B hack in the CIA—or, more likely, some crackpot emigré outfit. No, Boris. It's cheap, it's easy, and it's too bloody obvious.

"Point two. Supposing someone falls for it—then we're going to raise a whole nest of agencies against us. First, the State Department. For a start, they don't like people rocking the boat— other people, that is. And some unknown individual or gang of individuals who begin spreading slanderous filth against the established Soviet government is going to be asking for the works. Governments tend to gang up in this sort of situation— not to mention publishers. After all, next time around it might be the turn of some big shot close to the White House or Number Ten—scurrilous pillow talk from an anonymous aide or secretary. I tell you, Boris, we may be starting a whole new art form in political assassination—if that's what you really want?" And to my despair I saw that fat grin spread across his face again.

"Point three," I went on. "The Soviet authorities themselves are going to take an interest. A very keen interest, Boris—which means the KGB. At which point we're going to find out ourselves in the embarrassing position of being hunted down by the best-equipped intelligence services in the world. And that's not all. Because if the pressure's put on—and put on it will be!—we're probably going to find it difficult to move our money around. Even those Swiss banks aren't sacrosanct anymore, as Clifford Irving and his wife discovered. All of which leaves you and me, Boris, hot-footing it through some South American swamp, scattering dollar bills as sweeteners to every gun-happy government official who happens to ask for our papers. No nice empty beach, Boris. No cool blondes or iced cham-pagne—" and I saw him gulp as his imagination stirred into first gear—"in fact, no peace and security for the rest of our lives, until we're either terminated with extreme prejudice, as the CIA puts it, or dispatched by a cyanide bullet from a silencer, which I think is one of your people's specialities, isn't it?"

He sat watching me with a mournful stare, and for a moment I thought I'd got through to him. I stood up to refill my coffee, when I heard him chuckling, "Poor old Tom! That is what comes of being a creator of pure fiction—you become the victim of your own fantasies."

"You think the KGB is a fantasy?" I asked.

He shook his head. "If you want to write fiction, *mon cher*, you write it. But you write it with me. And if some of the details are not to your delicate English sense of good taste, then you can just piss off. Write your own book. I am going to write ours." He turned back to his notes, then said, as though there had been no argument or even disagreement between us, "I think we start with Shelepin. Nothing too startling—on the surface. Just a little snippet here and there: a disapproving refer-ence by Beria, who finds young Shelepin's tastes somewhat re-volting to his high standards of Georgian virility. For we must remember that apart from the age of consent, Beria was quite a *straight* old bastard. He would certainly have disapproved of any hanky-panky with healthy Young Communists.

"Then we have Brezhnev—that vain arrogant rapist of

135

Czechoslovakia! We take him and skewer him really good and proper. Young *apparatchik* in the thirties, learning his trade under Beria and his gang, and working his way up by doing them little favors on the side. For in Stalin's last days, young Brezhnev arrived in Moscow and was taken up by Georgi Alexandrov, a Stalinist toady who later became Minister of Culture. He now works at the Institute of Philosophy in Minsk—but I don't suppose he'll give us any trouble!"

"Why should he?"

Boris squeezed his hands together with a little grunt of pleasure. "Alexandrov used to give famous orgies in his house in Moscow—orgies laid on specially for Beria and his friends. Young actresses would be invited, and after a good dinner they'd be stripped nude and covered with sour cream, which the guests would then lick off! And, besides Beria, some of these guests were very big names in the Soviet cultural world. For instance, Sergei Mikhalkov, a famous writer of children's books and morality poems, whose works still sell in millions and who is today the Party Secretary of the Moscow branch of the Union of Writers. "Then there was Vadim Kozhevnikov, the author of hack war novels, and Boris Chirkov, a great star in prewar Soviet films, whose wife, Stepanida, was one of Beria's mistresses. Both not only were great buddies of Alexandrov, but also knew young Brezhnev during his formative years." He nodded as drops of sweat splashed onto the notes in front of him.

"Yes, *mon cher*, I think we can have some good sport with these boys!" He laid both hands on the table and heaved himself to his feet. "Make the whole Politburo sweat—every goddam one of them!"

"Boris, how do you know about all this?"

"Ah!" He smiled and started toward the kitchen. "I have my sources, comrade. My father, as I told you, was at one time very close to the leadership. Though of course," he added quickly, "he never attended any of Alexandrov's orgies."

136

"Of course not." It was my turn to smile now—though I still found the situation far from funny.

Boris paused on the steps. "My father was a scientist," he said, frowning. "Strictly nonpolitical. He kept his nose clean."

I nodded. "I suppose helping to build Uncle Joe's A-bombs was strictly political?"

I saw a muscle jump in his jowls, and the sweat streamed down his face like an unwiped windscreen.

"That is slander," he muttered, "goddam slander!" And his fists clenched into the size of two coconuts. "Repeat that and I will sue you."

"Better call Signor Gochi as a witness," I said.

Boris took a step forward. His eyes rolled, his belly wobbled; he belched, then suddenly laughed. "Tom, you old bastard. I am going to get a bottle of wine and then we are going to get down to some real good work!"

I knew it was hopeless. What had begun as a taunting joust had now become a serious venture. Boris was soon seated under the vines, a great medicine bottle of local wine at his elbow, busily writing—this time in English. Far from having been discouraged by my little homily on the dangers of international intelligence organizations, he seemed to have drawn fresh stimulus from it; and his illegible scrawl was this time for my benefit—a long list of Soviet leaders, most of them of world renown, the rest with significant positions behind the diplomatic scenes.

He now began reading off the list like a roll call, bracketing each name with the man's credentials, potted biography, and the least detail that might tenuously associate him with Stalin's reign of terror. It was an impressively clinical, even scholarly performance; and as I listened, I wondered what others would make of it: those crisp liberated females high above Madison and Fifth, enameling their nails and passing their opinions up to their editors in chief; or those flint-eyed boys at CIA headquarters, Langley, Virginia, scramblers ringing, routing out every Soviet specialist and academic hack, studying every name,

137

date and detail against a battery of archives and records, leaving long faces and piles of pink confetti memos.

I didn't get around to working out what they'd be doing in that six-story building in Dzerzhinsky Square; for I was more immediately worried about losing my temper with Boris. All the old tricks—going for a swim, down to the town, distracting him with other spicy tidbits—would be clearly useless now. He was enjoying himself too much.

"I think it an especially delicate touch," he was saying, "to have Comrade Brezhnev learning his pious views about Socialist literature at the feet of Alexandrov and Mikhalkov—so that today he can attack Solzhenitsyn for being a traitor—while at the same time he was sticking his big snout between some girl's thighs and rolling his tongue around . . ."

"You're talking about a head of state," I said primly.

"Podgorny is head of state, *mon cher*. Brezhnev is First Secretary of the Party."

I knew I should have broken with him then: told him that this was not the sort of book I had set out to help him to write; paid him back what I owed him; packed and left.

Instead I stripped off and plunged into the pool. I began to swim my regular six lengths, and at the end of the fifth was still wondering whether Soviet citizens could sue for libel in British and American courts, when I put my head up and heard the clatter of Boris' Russian typewriter. It continued while I dried off and dressed; and he did not even look up as I came back down the steps to the terrace. He paused only to take a gulp of wine, between stabbing at the machine with two stubby fingers, crouching over it and breathing hard. As I stopped opposite him he began intoning the name of Marshal Grechko, Soviet Minister of Defense. "Another arch-rapist of Czechoslovakia," he said. "In 1945 Grechko was with a Red Army unit in Germany that liaised with British and American occupation forces. Beria had a particular interest in Germany, and could have had dealings with Grechko—or rather, his superiors. I suggest that

138

the future Minister of Defense also had had private ambitions—perhaps to earn some illicit Western currency by trading military secrets? Beria found out and made a deal with him. Young Grechko would have paid in part with secrets from the Western side, which he passed on to Beria personally. We will say that his contact was a man called Harvey—there is always someone called Harvey in the middle ranks of the American Army. We don't have to be too specific—just a casual reference. But if there is even a whiff of truth about it, the man will be ruined."

"Why didn't Beria have him shot?"

Boris drank some wine and mused for a moment. "He was still useful to him. Beria liked to keep lackeys who were useful —he tended to shoot only loyal men with principles. Or men without principles who were in the pocket of some rival."

"He'd have had him shot in the end," I said, pulling at my cigar, while Boris stared out at the hills, which had grown smoky in the heat. Even the tall cypresses were blurred against the ash-gray olive trees.

"We will assume the future Minister was lucky. Or perhaps Beria just liked him?" He turned at last, smiling. "To have been liked by Beria is the ultimate damnation!"

I strolled away, round the back of the house to where I kept the Citroën parked next to Gochi's toolshed; got in and slammed the door. The hydraulic suspension had just finished lifting the car high enough to negotiate the steep track when I saw Boris bounding toward me in the mirror.

"We have enough food for lunch!" he panted, pushing his face through the passenger window. "But get some good veal. Tonight we have *escalope à la crème!*"

I took my foot off the brake, and the car rolled forward. Behind me I left a cloud of dust snaking up the hillside like a yellow smokescreen; and behind the dust, a hidebound, heavy-drinking Russian fanatic who seemed impervious to reason or balanced judgment. But perhaps the most invidious problem I faced, after several weeks of collaboration with Boris, was having no clear criteria by which to determine the value of our work. Unlike a novel, it did not depend on pace or plot, elegance of style, or precision of characterization; nor was it a straight work of nonfiction, relying on diligent research and an accurate appraisal of facts. Instead, our labor had so far amounted to a mass of truths, half-truths, fantasies, lies and imponderables, each like the separate part of a space rocket for which failure in one would cause instant catastrophe for the rest.

Boris and I were engaged in literary fraud—a specious but relatively rare art form whose rules were still ambiguous. At what precise point, I wondered, did authorship of the faked diary of a dead murderer become a criminal act? And could the work, once unmasked, be claimed as a literary achievement in its own right? Or did success merely augment the scale of the crime in legal terms? But then what were these terms, by the standards of international law?

I was trying to recall the details of the legal tangle over the Hughes–Irving episode, as I drove into Gaiole. It was very quiet and hot in the main street. Few tourists ever ventured into this corner of Tuscany, even in summer. I sat on a chair outside the only café, in the shade of the wall, and ordered coffee from an unshaven old man in a white apron. A cat came out and blinked at me, then crept away with its scrawny belly almost brushing the dust. I thought of our bulky typescript, in English and Russian, and of Boris banging away at his typewriter, sweating and boozing and ruining our whole joint creation. Or, if he didn't ruin it, he was going to turn it into something so dangerous that it would explode in our faces before we even had the chance to cash one Swiss check.

In this new game of political smearing I realized I was helpless: Boris held not only all the aces—his extensive data bank which I could scarcely understand, let alone challenge—but also the joker: language. For when it came to typing out the final draft, he could include in his Russian extracts all the ven-

140

omous details he liked—pimping, child rape, sodomy, treason—
slipping them into the flesh of the work like a lethal injection;
and, without the least knowledge of Russian, and barely of the
alphabet, I wouldn't even be able to see if the skin was broken.

If only Boris were just interested in money. But, for all his
wanton extravagance, his greed and gambling and erratic generosity, he seemed to have completely abandoned the main ambition of our work. He was no longer writing for an indiscriminate
public, but to spite a small clique of academics, and even smaller
gang of *apparatchiki* who ruled the second most powerful nation on earth. I could already hear his motto as he put the final
touches to the book: "I've built the clock—now I want to hear
it tick!"

In the dusty heat I shuddered. I'd drunk too much coffee, and
my hands were shaking.

Boris was eating in the kitchen when I got back. He ate standing, using his fingers, and his bare feet had left wet marks on the
stone floor. I noticed that the cuticles of his forefingers were
scraped raw from the steel-rimmed keys of Kamenev's typewriter.

I picked up a fork, speared a chunk of melon, and said, "You
know that the British still keep a file on every Englishman who
fought in Spain? And we're not even a police state."

He laughed with his mouth full of Parma ham. "The same
idiots who hired Philby and sent Guy Burgess to Washington,
huh?"

"The Americans keep their records in fireproof tunnels," I
went on, "several miles of them, six hundred feet deep and outside the radius of a medium-megaton bomb on the center of
Washington. A Polaroid eye photographs you as you go into the
lifts, and the picture is fed into a computer which sanctions it
before you reach the bottom. I met an American in Saigon

141

who'd been down there—said they didn't even have guards. If the computer doesn't like your face, the steel doors just don't open, an alarm goes off, and the lift whips you straight back to the surface."

Boris folded a strip of ham into his mouth, wiped his fingers on his Bermuda shorts, and turned to the door. Outside on the table a pile of typed foolscap lay splayed out like a broken fan. He sat down, examined the half-written sheet still in the typewriter, punched out a couple of Cyrillic letters, then slammed the carriage back with a noise like a badly oiled ratchet.

"Let me tell you something, *mon cher*. For you English and Americans the efficiency of your secret services depends mostly on which spy novels you read. Whether your hero drinks Polish vodka or the villain orders red wine with his fish. Pure fantasy! The real details you know nothing about—whatever your friend in Saigon may have told you."

"But you *do* know? About the KGB, for instance." I sat down once again on the terrace wall opposite him. "Tell me about the KGB, Boris."

He gave me a quick suspicious look, then poured himself the last of the wine, cloudy-yellow like a urine sample. "I am not an expert—I have no personal experience," he said defensively. "But I can tell you they are not so goddam efficient as most people in the West think. A typical example, for instance, took place just after the Soviet invasion of Czechoslovakia in 1968. The Czech Foreign Minister at the time was Jiři Hayek, who happened to be in Yugoslavia when the news broke, and he flew straight to New York, where he attacked the Russians at the U.N. This was slightly embarrassing for Moscow, where the KGB ran around in circles trying to dig up some dirt on the Minister. They thought they were lucky, because their files showed that Jiři Hayek was the pseudonym of a Jewish Czech author whose real name was Karpeles, and who had come to fame during the 'Dubček Spring' for his so-called 'liberal' views. The Soviet press immediately denounced him as a Zionist impostor, and backed up their charges with quotations from his 'anti-Soviet attitudes.' Everything seemed to be going fine—particularly the anti-Semitic angle, which always goes over big in Russia—until the Foreign Minister pointed out that Karpeles was somebody quite different, who had in fact emigrated to Israel before the Russians invaded. The KGB boys had simply got their files muddled. And they actually apologized to the Minister—something unheard of in Beria's day."

"You're trying to tell me that the KGB are not only incompetent but courteous?"

"I am telling you simply that, like all big organizations, they become victims of their own bureaucracy. They think that if something is not in their files it does not exist. And once something *is* in their files, it is gospel. They are incapable of flexibility or imagination—they grow to be more like clerks than secret agents. The CIA is the same. You must have met CIA men in Vietnam?"

I nodded. "They usually wore either Che Guevara beards or white socks with brown shoes. But what made the KGB so civilized all of a sudden?"

"Not civilized, *mon cher*. Careful. There is an important distinction. Under Beria the KGB operated like a separate government—a kind of Mafia, responsible only to the Boss. Sometimes the executioners were executed, the torturers got tortured, but basically they never had anyone to answer to outside the organization. Then up gets Nikita at the Twentieth Congress with his famous attack on 'deviations from Socialist Legality,' and after that nothing was ever quite the same again. The Soviet Penal Code is a pretty comprehensive document, and there's at least one article—Number Seventy, about spreading anti-Soviet propaganda—that can be bent to mean practically anything the regime wants. But at the same time the boys have to be careful. If they slip up on a case there's no longer any guarantee that at some future date it won't be held against them. It spoils a lot of their fun."

143

"I bet it does. And I suppose you're now going to tell me that maybe they muddled up their files on Comrades Shelepin and Grechko and Brezhnev? Or are you just counting on them thinking their records are incomplete? That they never kept files on homosexuals and pederasts in the Young Communist League? That Red Army Intelligence or SMERSH missed any details about Grechko's activities in Germany in '45? That they don't have whole vaults of films taken at Alexandrov's parties—probably taken on Beria's own instructions? And what about poor old Alexei Kosygin? You said yourself they'd know all the details about his part in the Leningrad Case. So why not the others? Taking pot luck? Hoping some American publisher just won't be able to resist the temptation—or is too scared someone else will beat him to it?" I paused in the breathless heat. "Come on, Boris, you know the score. We're writing a serious book. Let's get on with it."

He smiled. "What are you so frightened of, *mon cher?*"

"Frightened?" I could hear myself echoing the word—mocking, taunting, goading me into losing my temper. But whatever I did I must remain under control. Calm but unyielding. Never show fear or anger—like dealing with a child, or a dangerous animal. I tried to look blankly back at him, but the sun was too strong and my eyelids were sticky with sweat. Too hot to argue; too hot to think.

"What the hell are you frightened of?" he cried again.

I tried to answer, but my mouth was parched, and when I blinked, my eyes stung with sweat. "Go screw yourself!" I muttered. "You want to ruin the whole project and get us charged with fraud . . ." But I was not even sure he heard me—whether I was shouting or just mouthing the words in dumb rage. For all he did was laugh.

"You're just frightened of upsetting those murdering gangsters in the Kremlin. You think because they wear suits and ties and drink toasts with your Western diplomats under chandeliers, that they're nice guys? Bah! You don't imagine any of those swine survived Stalin and are in power today if they don't have quarts of blood on their hands!"

Again I knew it was no use. He looked as though he were enjoying a huge joke.

"The trouble with you, *mon cher*, is you are at heart a playboy. All you want from this is a big boring check. So you can buy girls and champagne and a Citroën-Ferrari."

"Maserati," I corrected him. "And what do you want?" I added; I didn't like being called a playboy.

"To screw those Kremlin bastards," he said. "Screw them with the biggest political scandal the world has ever seen!"

"They won't believe you. You know that. You said yourself the KGB have probably got specimens of Beria's handwriting —perhaps some of his secret papers, even a genuine diary. So what's the point of just concentrating on a crude smear job?"

Boris chuckled. "You forget about the ten percent butter. The old totalitarian maxim—the big lie is more effective than the whole truth."

I turned wearily away and stumbled up the steps to the house. "You don't need me anymore, Boris. I've done my porn stint. Now you can put in all the political shit you want. Only you'll have to get yourself a new chauffeur to do the shopping."

I heard his chair scrape back as I reached the door, and his voice bellowed, with an unusually thick accent, "You're not running out now! We made a pact—fifty-fifty! Anyway, I've been doing all the cooking. Without me you would have starved."

I hurried up to the bathroom and stood under the tepid shower, trying to reason calmly. To argue with Boris would only consolidate his obstinacy. The time had come to make a break for it. I walked, still wet from the shower, into the bedroom and began to pack. I threw in my things at random, too hot and exhausted to care about anything except getting away.

I was almost finished before he appeared. I still don't know what it was that worried him most: the prospect of losing the car? My share of expenses? My collaboration? Or just the humiliation of not winning an argument? He stood there in the door, fists clenched, his spongy face gray.

"Running home, are you? Running home to your doctor? To your bloody head-shrinker? To get yourself plugged in again, huh? Plugged in . . . !"

It was then that I hit him. His features had become blurred and felt soft and damp under my knuckles. He gave a yelp, and I lunged out again and caught him on the shoulder. The next few seconds were confused. He lurched forward and pushed me backward, still naked, onto the bed. Instinctively I kicked out, first with one leg, then the other, and one foot made contact. I heard him grunt as I climbed back to my feet, and saw there was blood on his face. He said something in Russian, and I stepped quickly round him, grabbed my clothes in a bundle off the bed, and was reaching down for my suitcase when something hard collided with the back of my head.

I was lying face down in a pool of water, the tiles covered with wild daisies and the shattered remains of an earthenware jug—a gift from Boris to cheer the starkness of my room.

I picked myself up and touched a large lump on the crown of my head. I felt dizzy and sick. There was no sign or sound of Boris. I went back into the bathroom and bathed my head; dressed and carried my luggage out to the car. The bruise was throbbing painfully. I switched on the engine and crunched softly across the gravel toward the dirt track. Still Boris did not appear. At the last bend before the farmhouse disappeared from sight, I thought I caught the flash of his striped shorts in the driving mirror; and remembered, with some relish, that I'd been due to make a trip down to Gaiole that afternoon, and was leaving him with scarcely enough food for a snack. He was on his own now, abandoned to a three-mile walk into town.

This cheered me as far as the *autostrada*, where I turned north toward Florence. I drove slowly, without any plan. The city was stifling, jammed with coaches and tourists with bare arms and legs burned the color of raw ham. For a moment they reminded me bitterly of Boris, and I cursed all Russians.

I parked outside the Excelsior Hotel. It was cool and quiet inside, and I sat in a deep leather chair and ordered a cocktail called Monseigneur, the mildest of whose ingredients was champagne. It was the first drink I'd touched in eight months, and I felt the perverse pleasure of sin. It tasted deliciously innocent. I finished it and ordered another; it had left me lulled and listless. The afternoon was passing peacefully. I no longer cared: the past became blurred, the future a blank; I ordered a third Monseigneur, and the chandeliers were turned on. Later I paid by traveler's check a sum that would have kept me for a week at Frabecchi. Not trusting myself with the Citroën, I took a taxi to Sabatini's restaurant.

It was very crowded, and I was kept waiting several minutes. Then the head waiter led me across the paneled room to a far corner. At the next table Boris was snouting at a hunk of *ossobucco*.

⚑

"Sit down, comrade." He nodded at the chair opposite, signaling at the same time for a fresh bottle of Frascati. He looked composed and contented; the only traces of the afternoon's fracas were a slight contusion on his left cheek and a cut, clumsily stanched with a clot of cotton wool, on his upper lip.

"How did you get here?" I asked finally.

"By taxi. Gochi took me to Gaiole on his motor scooter." He obviously knew I'd been drinking and poured the last of his wine into my glass. "So you are in a happier mood, *mon cher?* Happy enough to talk seriously."

"About what?"

He called a passing waiter and without consulting me ordered shrimp cocktail and *ossobucco*. He leaned across the table. "The murder of Stalin."

"Murder?"

"That's right. As a direct result of the Doctors' Plot."

"Who murdered him?"

"Beria, of course—to save his own skin. You remember Stalin's great motto—'Members of the Politburo must be changed frequently'? Well, it was Beria's turn and he reacted accordingly."

"Where did you find this out?"

"From Beria himself. From his diaries—where else?" He chuckled and jabbed his knife at my glass. "Drink some wine, *mon cher*. It will make you more receptive to the delicacy of my plan." He devoured what was left on his plate, then drew out a wad of his typed Russian notes.

"First you must understand the full details of the Doctors' Plot. It was the last spasm of Stalin's second reign of terror, cut short by his death on March 5, 1953. All his life he had distrusted doctors, especially if they were Jewish, and—like Hitler —preferred self-medication and patent drugs. In fact, in his last days he was as crazy as the Hitler dog—only perhaps cleverer." He sat back now and began translating from the typed foolscap:

"The scenario of the Doctors' Plot was as follows: In the autumn of 1952 a woman doctor denounced fifteen of her most distinguished colleagues in an open letter to the authorities. Among other crimes, she accused them of poisoning Shcherbakov and Zhdanov, both of whom were known to have died of heart attacks induced by alcoholism. All fifteen doctors confessed to having been working for the British, American and Israeli intelligence services.

"After they had confessed under torture, Stalin unleashed a full-scale campaign against the Jews, claiming in an unsigned editorial in *Pravda* that Zionist agents were undermining the country and "destroying the leading cadres of the state." This was the opening shot in what Stalin intended as a massive anti-Semitic purge in which Jews were to be deported to North Kazakhstan—supposedly at their own request for protection against the 'wrath of the masses.'

"But the fabrication of the Doctors' Plot had more subtle

148

aims. For instance, among those leaders whom the doctors were accused of planning to murder, a number of senior Politburo members were conspicuously absent: Molotov, Mikoyan, Voroshilov—and Beria. The implication was that the accused doctors had received orders from their foreign masters to spare these members, so that Stalin would eventually be able to accuse them of being imperialist agents themselves. Stalin also emphasized that the plotters had been attempting to undermine the health of the leading Soviet military personnel—an indication that the plot was not directed against the Red Army, but would actually benefit them by the removal of some of the most powerful Party leaders.

"As for Comrade Beria, the officials entrusted with concocting the plot were all stooges chosen by Stalin personally from outside Beria's NKVD. Only a few days after Stalin's death, thirteen of the surviving doctors—two had died during interrogation —were released and the whole thing was publicly repudiated as 'a deviation from Socialist Legality.' "

He glanced carefully around him and folded the sheets back inside his jacket.

"So you see how convenient it was that Old Leatherface died when he did? We can forget about the other members of the Politburo. Once Stalin turned against them they would have been quite helpless. But with Beria it was a different story. At the time of Stalin's death he had more than a million armed men under his personal command—and seventy-five thousand of these were in Moscow alone, complete with tanks and flamethrowers. I remember them myself, in their special blue uniforms, standing guard at every street corner with machine guns at the ready. Beria's private army."

"So why didn't he move? Instead of waiting four months, then getting knocked off himself?"

Boris tilted his head with a wistful grin. "Ah, *mon cher*, that is one of the mysteries of modern history! Maybe we can lay a few clues—suggest, as was probably true, that the Red Army, who feared Beria as much as any group, acted in the nick of time and murdered him in the inner sanctum of the Kremlin." He broke off to refresh my glass from the new bottle of Frascati that had just arrived. I ignored it.

"And how did Beria kill Stalin?"

Boris took several seconds to reply, like an actor timing his cue. "As a writer of novels, you will appreciate the subtlety. It will be the *coup de théâtre* of the whole book!" He leaned across the table.

"I am going to claim that the Doctors' Plot was *true*! Not the one engineered by Stalin, but another—this time by Beria himself. After all, we know from several sources, including Khrushchev and Svetlana, that old Stalin was suffering from blood pressure and phlebitis. And we know from Svetlana that at his deathbed he was surrounded by strange doctors who finished up by applying leeches to his neck and giving him all kinds of injections until he finally choked to death. And we know, too, that when in the end he died, Beria was the only one who showed no sign of grief, but actually laughed, summoned his car and drove away.

"So. We know that at this time every member of the medical profession attending the leadership was quaking in his shoes. So what does Beria do? He calls in one of these doctors and tells him straight out, 'Doctor, either you work for me or you get beaten to a powder by Stalin's men!' And what could have been simpler than to have persuaded him to slip Old Leatherface a dose of poison—perhaps even through one of the leeches on his neck?"

He snapped his fingers and ordered *marrons glacés* and two Stregas.

"You think we can make it stick?" I said.

"Stick! It will stick like a leech, *mon cher*—and make us both a fortune. Three million, I suggest. It will be cheap at the price."

"Bloody cheap," I repeated. I was drunk and I believed him. And why not? For, as he kept emphasizing, the proven facts all fitted; and the rest, although conjecture, amounted to a theory so plausible that historians would have to treat it seriously. After all, it was no more preposterous than the fashionable conspiracy theories about the assassination of President Kennedy.

By the end of the meal I had become enthusiastic about what Boris went on calling his *"coup de théâtre."* I helped him finish the wine, drank my Strega, and allowed him to settle the bill. I had surrendered unconditionally.

Fifteen days later the first draft was finished, and another week saw the final version. Now a second letter arrived from King's College, this time addressed to us both, confirming our appointment to meet Mrs. Tatana Bernstein in Cambridge ten days later.

Since our punch-up, Boris and I had been in a state of uneasy peace. He was in high spirits, battering Kamenev's machine from sunrise until often well after dark, while I was left with the laborious revision, touching up or toning down the ribald and odious sexual escapades in Beria's postwar career. The political smear campaign was not mentioned again: it was safely typed in Russian, for the eyes of Mrs. Bernstein only. Besides, I had little inclination to reopen the argument. It was as though the hangover I'd suffered after our night in Florence pursued me through the following two weeks with a dogged sense of doom. I was still badly worried. Once I even woke in the night, sweating with the image of that balding fish-eyed face with its pince-nez rising from some unmarked grave to claim Boris and me as his ultimate victims.

On our last morning, as the two bulky typescripts were packed into the boot of the Citroën and we set off for the last time down the track to Gaiole, I experienced none of the elation I usually felt on finishing a novel. Boris insisted on a call at Harry's Bar in Florence to celebrate, and I joined him reluctantly, drinking orange juice.

We took five days to reach Boulogne, stopping at six two-star Michelin restaurants and a couple with three stars. Whenever we left the car Boris hauled out the suitcase containing the typescripts and kept it between his knees under the table, or beneath his bed in each hotel, for fear of it being stolen or mislaid.

Cambridge lay under a midsummer drizzle. May Week was over, the marquees were dismantled, the waterlogged punts moored by the Mill like rows of barges. Our appointment with Mrs. Bernstein was for five o'clock. I parked the Citroën down by one of the side gates of King's leading into Webb's Court.

"If it wasn't raining," said Boris, "we could carry out our negotiations on a punt—someplace where we wouldn't be seen."

"For God's sake, who's going to see us, anyway? And don't begin by scaring the girl," I added, as we entered the court and started round the entrances to the staircases, marked in alphabetical order. "She may prefer being a bye-fellow of King's to breaking the law." We reached E staircase, where Miss T. Shumara appeared third down a list of six names.

"This will be her!" Boris cried. "Shumara is a Georgian name —her virgin name." And as he led the way into the familiar dark passage, I found myself pondering on how the college authorities, faced with this sudden intrusion of women, coped with the problem of bisexual ablutions.

Mrs. Bernstein called to us to come in. She was lying curled up on an unmade bed that filled most of one wall, smoking and reading a French paperback.

"Mr. Mallory? Mr. Drobnov? Ah, yes." Her only movement

was to stub out her cigarette and light a fresh one from a packet of Corporals on the pillow. "I can't offer you tea or coffee—the stove outside is broken. Would you like whisky? Or cherry brandy?" Her English was deliberate and assured, her accent more French than Russian.

Boris opted for whisky, and she pointed to a half-empty bottle on a shelf by the gas fire. I chose the armchair. Boris poured his drink and remained standing. Our hostess still did not move.

Even from her position on the bed I could see that she was a tall, big-boned woman, striking rather than immediately pretty, dressed in jeans and a black sweater which showed she was wearing no bra. She was barefoot, with blood-red toenails; her features were wide and bold, with a straight nose, and her hair was heavy, the color of polished chestnuts. She must have been somewhere between thirty and thirty-five.

"If you want water," she said to Boris, "there's a tap outside." He shook his head. "You can give me one, too," she added.

While he poured it I looked around the room. It was a tiny bed-sitter overlooking the court, so dark that the light was on. There was nothing in the least feminine about it, and for a moment I was reminded of a small replica of Boris' apartment in Munich: the desk piled with papers, the bookshelves crammed with editions in French and Russian.

"So you've written a book together," she said, stretching her hands behind her head. "Half in English, half in Russian, and you want me to translate it into Georgian?"

"In the Mingrelian dialect," said Boris.

"So you know I am Mingrelian?"

"It was in the papers," I said.

She looked at me with sleepy black eyes. "This isn't an interview, is it? An official interview?" But before I could answer, she said something in Russian to Boris, who was now moving from one foot to the other like a restless animal in a cage. He replied with what sounded like a flow of Russian invective.

She shrugged and turned back to me. "Let us understand one

another, Mr. Mallory. You are an old Kingsman, as they say, and you write to me—a complete stranger—from West Germany, suggesting I do some special translating work. Now you come to tell me that you want the book translated, not into Georgian, but into the Mingrelian dialect. Is that correct?"

I nodded. Boris took a gulp of whisky.

"Very well. Now, there are perhaps a few thousand Georgians living outside the Soviet Union, most of them in Paris. Only a few of them speak Mingrelian. So I ask myself, what is it all about? Unless, of course, you intend to smuggle the book into the Soviet Union?"

Boris, who had begun pacing the cramped floor, stopped and opened his mouth; but she held up her hand. "Please, let me finish. Because even this does not make sense. All Mingrelians in the Soviet Union speak Georgian, and most of them know Russian. So why does it have to be in Mingrelian?"

Boris finished his whisky and without asking poured himself another. He had gone very red in the face. "You ask too many questions!" he cried. "We have not even discussed terms yet." And he broke again into a stream of Russian.

She said something that made him go even redder and turned to me. "Mr. Mallory, your friend is not being very helpful. I am not a member of any intelligence agency—and I am not particularly offended by the suggestion that I might be. On the other hand, I have no way of knowing who you might be. After all, when it comes to smuggling manuscripts into the Soviet Union, it is being done all the time. The idea does not worry me. But I do have a thesis to finish for a Ph.D., and if you want me to help you with some undercover work involving the Mingrelian dialect, you must at least be honest from the beginning. As well as pay me a decent rate—not a miserable three pounds a thousand words."

"It's not so much being honest," I said, "as discreet. For your sake as much as ours. But I can tell you right away that it is not going to be smuggled into the Soviet Union. Not by us, anyway.

What we've done is write one hundred thousand words which we want you to translate into Mingrelian, and then we're going to try and sell them to an American publisher."

She sat very still, staring at her toes; then lit another cigarette, slowly unfolded her legs and went over to the shelf by the gas fire and refilled her glass, returned to the bed and lay for some time inhaling deeply and sipping her whisky. Finally she sat up and nodded. She was not looking at either of us when she spoke.

"We Georgians haven't played a very big part in Russian history—most of the time we've spent hiding under Mother Russia's skirt to save ourselves from the Persians. It was only about fifty years ago that we began to come into our own, producing a gang of rulers of whom Ivan the Terrible would have been proud. The worst was the son of a drunken cobbler, Joseph Djugashvili, better known as Stalin. But he wasn't a Mingrelian, although he did have a few around him. The most notorious was 'unpersonned,' as they say, in 1953." She smiled. "Am I on the right track?"

Neither of us spoke. Even Boris had stopped still.

"How much do you expect to get for it?" she asked.

"Three million dollars," said Boris. "You will get a percentage —if the project is successful."

Her lips parted and blew smoke across the room. "Three million dollars," she repeated softly. "I shall want it in writing, of course."

"Of course," I said. "On the understanding that not a word of this conversation—not even the fact that you've met us—is ever mentioned to anyone, now or later."

She gave a gentle laugh. "You think I'll go into hall and gossip to a lot of long-haired research students and senile dons? I don't suppose they'd even know whom I was talking about, most of them—if it's the man I think it is. Ber-y-a." She pronounced it in the Mingrelian way, with the long *i*. "They'd probably think he was a flower, or perhaps some tropical disease." She laughed again, then added seriously, "I'm not a fool, you know."

"I can see that," I said, while Boris finished the whisky.

"Beria has relatives alive," she went on, "living in Russia. Which one have you chosen?"

"Beria himself," I said. "His diaries from 1945 till his death."

"You are an expert on Beria?"

"Boris is. I just helped with the writing."

She nodded. "I only asked because very few people know anything about him. He's a very good subject—if you can get an American publisher to fall for it. But it seems they fall for almost anything these days." She looked at her watch. "We had better meet later, for dinner. I have to go and see my supervisor —an old fool who calls himself a professor of Russian literature. He's very sweet, but I find I have to teach him more than he does me." She stood up.

"I've already booked a table," I told her.

"We will meet you somewhere discreet at seven-thirty," Boris said.

"Make it the bar in the Blue Boar. And you can buy me another half bottle of whisky." She opened the door with a smile. "I must say you're both very trusting. Or perhaps just optimists? Still, for three million dollars . . ." She let the words trail away into the passage. She closed the door behind her and shook hands with us both.

"See you at seven-thirty." She waved and disappeared into the main court.

"A good, strong-willed Georgian girl," said Boris, nodding to himself. "And smart too."

"Smart isn't the word. But if she's rumbled us that quick, God knows how soon it'll take the professionals!"

"Don't worry, *mon cher*," he said, as we got into the car. "I tell you—she is okay."

"Well, if she isn't, it's too late now to do anything about it." We turned toward King's Parade.

The restaurant was on a lawn overlooking the Cam. Boris spent the first quarter of an hour studying the menu, while Tatana—as I was now calling her—talked to me about her life in Paris, where she'd taught Russian at a *lycée*, and how she'd studied for three years as a child at the Bolshoi Junior Ballet School in Moscow.

Boris sent back a bottle of burgundy on the grounds that it was corked; ordered for us all, then changed his mind; changed it back again and ordered the same, all in a voice that could be heard across the room. Tatana showed no surprise at his behavior and chain-smoked French cigarettes, drinking glass for glass with Boris.

The dinner went well. Boris soon took the lead in confiding everything—or as much as could be imparted without letting her read the whole typescript. As for the contract, it was agreed that my London solicitor—a competent lawyer with little imagination—should draw up a formal contract, guaranteeing our translator ten percent of everything we earned.

On reflection, such an agreement seemed dubious, even futile, since a prosecution for fraud would surely take into account any accomplices; but Tatana took a sturdy, philosophical view of these matters. Her only purpose was to ensure that if the fraud were a success, she would at least have some legal document with which to threaten us in case we defaulted. Indeed, she actually used the word "blackmail"—shamelessly, if not with pride. Nor did the threat in the least disturb Boris, who merely accepted such criminal insinuations as further evidence of the seriousness of our conspiracy.

It was only toward the end of the meal that we broached the matter of her producing evidence to support the authenticity of the book. "A little incident at the Bolshoi Junior Ballet School," Boris began.

157

"Don't talk about that school. They threw me out because I was too tall and my feet were too big!"

"Before you read the typescript," I said, "I think I should explain a couple of things. The book really falls into two parts—the political section, which is mostly written in Russian by Boris, and the English one, by me."

"The English one is disgusting—pure pornography!" Boris howled.

I ignored him. "What we really want from you, Tatana, is some hard proof for the publishers that these papers are genuine."

"American publishers don't need proof," she said. "Just the hope of a big profit on their sales."

"I doubt if it will be quite the same with this book. Boris has included material about the present Kremlin leaders which could have serious political repercussions. In Russia, I mean."

"Good for Boris. The more trouble you make for them, the better. Unless, of course, you do it by making out that Beria was a misunderstood man, and that it was really all Stalin's fault?"

"Absolutely not," I said. "He's extremely frank throughout—particularly in his appetite for very young girls."

"How young?"

"About twelve."

"Ah, yes. It's not so uncommon among the southern races in the Soviet Union. But where do I come in?"

"You were one of his victims."

"*Me?*"

"Beria sees you walking in the street and has you picked up by one of his aides. He takes you back to his house in Moscow and rapes you."

"When I was twelve?"

I nodded, and she sat thinking for a moment, her expression grave. "Yes, I suppose I'd have been about the right age. Did I enjoy it?" she added, quite seriously.

"Certainly not."

"And do we go into all the details?"

"We do. And later—either before the book comes out, if the publishers are being troublesome, or later, if there's a lot of legal controversy—you are persuaded by me to come forward, very reluctantly, and give an interview to the press, confirming that this episode at least is genuine."

Boris broke in: "We say your father was shot by Beria personally—because he refused to keep quiet, even after he'd been offered five thousand rubles a year and a dacha by the sea."

She looked at him curiously. "How did you know that my father was killed by Beria?"

"Killed—by Beria?" Boris repeated, gaping at her.

She nodded. "In the so-called Mingrelian Affair in 1951. He was a schoolmaster at the time, and was accused of associating with nationalist intellectuals. He was arrested and I never saw him again."

Boris clapped his hands. "This is excellent news—really superb!"

His tactlessness left her unmoved. "This is all part of the deal, I suppose?" she asked.

"For three hundred thousand dollars," said Boris, "you cannot expect to do just six weeks' translation work."

She nodded again. "Always supposing you get away with it—even with my help. There are a hundred ways you could be caught out. What about the paper and the typing, for instance?"

Boris explained about the paper and his arrangements for borrowing an old Georgian typewriter from his friend in Paris.

She seemed impressed. "I like it. It is so beautifully simple."

"And what about your thesis?" I asked.

She laughed. "What thesis do you think is worth three hundred thousand dollars?"

"So when can you start?"

"At once—tomorrow."

159

"Not here," said Boris. "In a university, even in vacation time, there is too much gossip. We go to a little hotel I know in northern France, near Abbeville. It has one star in *Michelin*. But very quiet, even in summer."

"Then I'll need a few days," she said. "I will tell them here that I have to do some research in Paris."

"Will anyone be able to check on you, after the story gets out?" I asked.

"Are you anticipating that I will have to disappear?"

"It's possible."

"Then I can disappear," she said. "I have done it before. I am what they used to call the Jews in Stalin's day—a 'rootless cosmopolitan.' "

"Do you still hold an Israeli passport?"

"Yes. But it is no problem, except that I cannot visit the Arab or Communist countries—but we won't want to disappear to them, anyway."

"So it seems everything's settled?" I said. "Except for the contract, of course."

She gave a small secret smile. "I have a better idea. Let us forget about the contract and just trust each other. After all, these poor American publishers are going to have to. If we cannot even trust ourselves—" She broke off and stretched across the table toward me. We shook hands all round, in solemn rotation; then Boris called for two large brandies. I drank the toast in ginger beer.

🐦

Tatana cut short her studies, and five days later we left on the car ferry for Boulogne. We arrived at the little town of Le Crotoy in time for lunch, which Boris organized with his usual aggressive panache. The *patronne* of the Hotel de La Baie, Madame Mado Poncelet, was a massive bejeweled woman in a blue wig and dark glasses, who was accompanied at every step by two morose Alsatians. She proved a formidable challenge even for Boris, but their gastronomic tastes coincided and the first meal at our new place of work was a success.

That afternoon Boris took the train to Paris, where he'd made arrangements to meet the old Georgian restaurateur and collect the typewriter. Tatana had settled herself on her balcony in the late sun and began reading the typescript.

We seemed to be the only foreigners in the town—a quiet jumble of houses gathered around the wooden fishing jetty on the edge of the broad estuary of the Somme. Most of the other guests in the hotel were Parisians who had come down for the duck shooting on the mud flats, or for a quiet weekend *à deux*. That evening a young man was sitting at the bar with his girl friend when Madame Mado, with her two Alsatians at her heels, passed them with a pat on the man's shoulder, saying, "*Ça va, l'amour?*" and waddled on without waiting for a reply.

Providing her clients were contented and well fed, she seemed totally disinterested in them. When we'd first arrived and filled in the registration *fiches*, she had shown no interest in Boris' or Tatana's passports—his giving his place of birth as Moscow, hers as Zugdidi, Georgia, U.S.S.R. However, I'd have been happier if we hadn't had to fill them in at all, for somehow they seemed to constitute our first real act of complicity; and I wondered what happened to those *fiches* after they were sent to the local *préfecture*. Over the summer they must amount to more than a million in France alone. Were they destroyed at the end of the season? Or did they molder in some monstrous filing system, to be dug out months later and land on an inspector's desk?

At seven o'clock I went up to Tatana's room. She was lying on the bed finishing the first typescript. The ashtray on the side-table was full of dead cigarettes, the air hazy with tobacco smoke.

"Would you get me a drink?" she said. "A large Pernod with a lot of ice." When I came back with it, she laid the typescript aside, and I noticed with relief that she was in the middle of

161

one of the Russian passages. I wondered how she was taking the rest.

"I'm enjoying it very much," she said at last. "My only real criticism is that at times you make Beria almost amusing—a sort of jolly, sexy old blackguard who used his position simply to enjoy himself, drinking and wenching and occasionally shooting people, and proud of boasting about it afterward. Of course, the clever thing is, there might have been some truth in that. Certainly you have captured a lot of atmosphere. And, my God, you're right when you say that some of the present leaders are not going to be happy when they read it. I just hope Boris has enough facts right."

"Do you think it'll convince a publisher?"

She lit another cigarette. "I'm prejudiced. I know the truth. But from what I've read, I don't see why not—providing you can plant a good enough story about where the stuff came from."

I then told her about our plan for me to go to Budapest and make contact with the courier. At first she looked doubtful. "You only have Boris' word that the man will do it?"

"His word is usually sound," I said. She didn't press the matter.

"You'll have to be very careful," she said finally. "We're all going to have to be careful. If we leave even the smallest trail, the slightest clue . . ." She drank some Pernod. "This isn't just fraud," she added, nodding at the typescript on the bed. "In Soviet eyes it's high treason."

"You think we'll be in danger? From the Russians, I mean?"

"Well, of course we will. You don't think they're going to let these slanders go? They can't afford to. The reputations of half the leadership will be at stake. But by then they'll have to find us first."

I sat listening to the roar of the tide racing in over the mud flats. The irony of it was that when I'd come up to her room my only real concern had been her reaction to the pornographic

162

passages in the book; and these she hadn't even mentioned. Instead, she had now awakened all my original fears, confirming my lost stand against Boris and his wild vengeful motives. She too had been a Soviet citizen, and she knew the score; but what worried me more was her lack of anxiety, her simple acceptance of the danger as no more than part of the general deal. For, as Boris had said, a girl didn't get paid $300,000 for a straight translation work.

At dinner that night she talked about her life in Russia and Israel. After she was rejected as a ballerina she became a film actress for a short time, though of what standing she would only say, "I played waitresses and barmaids—the films were all propaganda rubbish." At twenty she married a regular officer in the Red Army, and was divorced after three years. "He was a conceited fool—very fond of strutting about in his uniform. I was surprised he even took it off in bed, he was so proud of it." There were no children. Later she became a teacher, first in an infants' school, then at a polytechnic in Moscow, and there met an elderly Jew who'd managed to get permission to emigrate to Israel during the more liberal years of the Khrushchev era.

"I felt completely suffocated by Russia—I wanted to get out, anywhere—so I married him. He was far too old for me. The only amusing thing about him was that he started a restaurant on Lake Tiberias where he sold pork to tourists, pretending it was charolais steak!"

"I heard he was killed in the Six-Day War?"

She laughed brutally. "He was—and you know how? He drove a mobile canteen into a tank. The crew were all doctors—five of them. But there was nothing they could do. He was killed outright."

She chain-smoked as she talked, and drank steadily, both wine and black coffee. She also had a strong appetite. I found her amusing and attractive, but not relaxed. It was difficult to tell whether she was worried, thoughtful or just bored. I did not understand her at all.

163

When the meal was over we stayed at the table while she drank cognac and more coffee, and talked about Cambridge. Her comments were characteristically terse. "It is a delightful backwater—but everyone is either too old or too young. Most of the undergraduates are just idealistic juveniles. They think it is revolutionary to smoke pot and have pinups in their rooms of Jane Fonda and that Stalinist bitch, Angela Davis. Yet at heart they are all so innocently bourgeois."

She ordered another cognac, then suggested that I sit with her upstairs on her balcony while she drank it. I followed her up, and as soon as the door closed she put her glass down on the bedside table, grabbed my head in her hands and kissed me on the mouth. I spilled half my coffee.

"Get undressed," she said; and a moment later she was naked. Her body, which she'd kept successfully concealed beneath her dull clothes, was magnificent, and her lovemaking ferocious, but also considerate and imaginative. It ended with her twisting her head round and biting the pillow to prevent herself from screaming. When it was over she kissed me affectionately behind the ear, then got up and washed. When she returned to the bed she said, "I'm going to read for a little—you don't mind?"—and climbed under the sheets with her back to me. I didn't mind, but I felt that it should somehow have been the other way round. I had nothing to read myself and, looking over her shoulder, saw she was starting on one of my passages in the typescript. She read steadily in silence. Soon I fell asleep.

I woke late, and found her outside on the terrace drinking Pernod and reading the second typescript. She made no reference to the night before, not even a hint; yet it was not as though she were embarrassed or wanted to forget—rather, that it had been a natural episode that called for no comment. She was a perplexing girl.

Boris did not telephone from Paris till late that afternoon, and when I met him off the train at Abbeville he complained of a hangover—something unique in my experience of him.

164

"Those old Georgians are fantastic," he muttered. "The food was not of this world—better than I have tasted for years. And at the end of dinner the proprietor presented me a free bottle of vodka, on the house."

He was carrying what looked like a small battered suitcase, which he told me was the typewriter, vintage 1938.

"The owner didn't ask too many questions?" I said.

"He didn't ask any questions at all. He was drunk. All he did was sing. He even said I could have it as a present. They are wonderful people, these Georgians!"

I silently agreed: wonderful and weird; but I was anxious about how Boris would take it when he found out about me and Tatana. During dinner they both talked a lot in Russian, which I found very irritating, although I was careful not to show it. Boris' hangover was soon washed away, and he and Tatana ordered balloon glasses of liqueur brandy which they drank outside on the terrace overlooking the estuary. I felt awkward, almost in the way, sitting there with my mineral water while they chattered away about the eccentricities of the Georgian community in Paris. I got up to leave. Tatana smiled and said good night. Boris just nodded.

Sometime after midnight I heard their voices, and as Tatana passed my door she laughed. I couldn't get to sleep, and several times was sure I heard sounds from her room. Finally I got up and tried her door. It was locked. I called to her, and after a moment her voice came back, sleepy but impatient: "What do you want? It's late."

Confused rather than angry, I returned to my room. Next morning it was almost noon when she appeared, although this was to be our first working day. I mentioned this while she was drinking her coffee on the terrace.

"You are angry?" she said. "Why? You are not jealous, are you?"

"Jealous? What do you mean?"

She shrugged. "You men are so difficult to please."

I stared at her dumbly, and realized that it had been the memory of her body, as much as the sound of voices, which had kept me awake, taunting me till the small hours. I was now tired and ill-tempered.

"Not Boris?" I said at last.

"Why not Boris? Just because he's not as nice-looking as you doesn't mean he has no passion. You must not be intolerant—please. I don't belong to anyone."

"Where is Boris?" I said at last.

"I think he went for a walk. You're not going to be difficult, are you?"

"You propose sharing us, then?"

"Why not? You are such different characters. Anyway, have you never had an affair with two girls at the same time?"

I stood up. "This has got absolutely nothing to do with what we're here for. As long as you get on with the work . . ." I looked at my watch. "I don't know how Boris is going to take it."

"Boris is very understanding."

"More likely he's just grateful," I said spitefully, and was turning away when she caught my arm.

"Please don't be angry, Tom. It would spoil it all—and it was so good."

"You'd better get on with your work," I said and walked quickly away past the fishing port and along the sea wall. Perhaps I should accept the situation, just as Boris had accepted the free bottle of vodka in the Georgian restaurant. The Georgians had spawned Stalin and Beria; they had also produced Tatana Shumara, who was a bye-fellow of King's and whose body I wanted.

That night I made love to her again, savagely and several times. She told me she liked being pinched and smacked. I thrashed her till my hand was sore and she was beginning to squeal, when I heard Boris pounding on the door. At once she called out something in Russian, and I heard him go away.

"He thinks you were hurting me!" she said with a giggle, and pulled me down inside her and began to heave and moan and bite the pillow all over again.

Afterward, as I lay listening to the crack of the guns out on the mud flats, I realized that I'd rather lose face than lose her. The trouble was, Boris had evidently decided the same.

The next few weeks were not easy. Tatana's working habits were perhaps even more chaotic than Boris', and the combination of the two called for a labor of patience and tact on my part which I found far more exhausting than the work itself. This consisted mostly of a second revision of the typescript as it was translated, with Boris haggling over details and Tatana arguing over niceties of language. She worked slowly, in her own time, and resented the least hint of haste. Their discussions would often drop into Russian, which enraged me, while I struggled to prevent Boris from adding still more inflammatory material.

He had become a changed man. He went to the barber once a week, shaved punctiliously every morning—and sometimes at night too—always smelling of an expensive eau de cologne, and his fingernails were snipped to the quick like pink teeth. At the end of the first week I asked him casually what he thought of Tatana. "I love her," he said, "like a sister. I also love her body —it is the perfect *instrument d'amour*." Then he added, without rancor, "But I must warn you, *mon cher*, do not chase her. These Georgians are a very passionate people, but they are also very independent. If you chase them and try to hunt them down, they take to the hills and disappear. You know that Tbilisi has been rebuilt more times than any other capital city in the world?"

I didn't see how this last detail helped explain Tatana's habits, except that Boris assured me that no one had ever succeeded in subduing Georgia for more than a generation.

We made love to her on alternate nights, and her passion and proficiency seemed never to slacken or change. I also fell in love with her. It was a lonely, unsatisfactory love which I could confide neither to her nor to Boris; it became a secret sickness, relieved at regular intervals by spasms of pleasure, followed by the bitter hours of anticipation until it was my turn again.

Meanwhile, slowly and painfully, the personal papers of Lavrenti Pavlovitch Beria were translated into his native dialect that was as remote and foreign as Tatana herself.

☙

Seven weeks later the translation was finished—revised, corrected, cut and polished—its two volumes of coarse yellow paper carefully wrapped and sealed in anonymous cardboard folders.

Boris and Tatana drank between them three bottles of Madame Mado's best champagne, then persuaded me to drive them to the Casino de la Forêt in Le Touquet, where I feared the worst: Boris insisting on betting solely on red—"Beria's favorite color"—while Tatana jokingly played black; yet after only half an hour they had both won. I lost two hundred francs playing a laborious system that fell victim to zero.

The two of them continued their celebrations with Dom Perignon, and this time forced me to share a glass with them; but again I had that uncomfortable feeling of being alone and somehow in the way. On the drive back Tatana taught us Georgian songs which Boris bellowed in an ear-cracking bass, grossly out of tune. It was after three when we reached the hotel, and we had to knock up the headwaiter, to the ferocious barking of the Alsatians. Upstairs Tatana kissed us both on the cheeks and disappeared into her room. It was as though she wanted to establish on this night of rejoicing that neither of us stood any higher in her affection than the other. Boris went to his room, where I heard him bumping about, trying to find the light. He accepted what he was given and no more. He was lucky.

The next night, my last before leaving for Hungary, Tatana invited me to her room, although strictly it was Boris' turn. Perhaps because I was apprehensive of the future, our lovemaking was not a success. As we lay together vaguely caressing each other, I tried to talk to her, to fathom her intentions; but she gave away nothing. "We will have to see what happens with the Americans," she said. "If we all become rich, then perhaps we can make plans."

"If you become rich you may want to go your own way."

"If the Americans buy the book," she said gravely, "we are going to have bigger problems than deciding what to do with our money." She kissed me and turned away.

I thought of that fatuous fight with Boris in Tuscany and how I had tried to reason with him about smearing the Soviet hierarchy. I wondered whether she'd tried to dissuade him as well; but when I asked her, she replied sleepily, "I am just the translator, Tom. That is up to you and Boris."

At first light I woke her and we made love, and this time it was as good as it had ever been. I had an early breakfast with them both, finished my packing, and left on the road east, across the ripening champagne country, through Nancy and Strasbourg and on to Stuttgart, where I picked up the *Autobahn* for Munich and Vienna.

PART
FOUR

"Tell me what you think of Hungary, and I will tell you what you are."
> —From a leading article in the Polish Communist Party newspaper *Trybuna Ludu*, October 1956

Paper Four

Moscow, August 1952

This morning Rafik brought me news of fresh disturbing developments. The Boss had been gathering in more dossiers. Of the seventeen confirmed names, six are leading Moscow physicians, the rest intellectuals close to the Party leadership—and at least five of these are Jews.

The news becomes the more sinister when I learn that the matter is not to be handled through the usual channels, but that instead the Old Man has delegated the whole affair to that stooge Ignatiev,[1] which means that for the moment I have no control over the business.

In normal times I would bring the matter up with the Boss face to face; but something warns me to act here with extreme caution. His moods are becoming increasingly unpredictable, and last night at Kuntsevo was a particularly grueling one. He was again full of his sly taunts, which in recent weeks have been directed at Molotov, who bears them with a stolid, sickly grin; and

---

[1] Semyon Denisovich Ignatiev, a minister for State Security, who was delegated by Stalin to fabricate evidence in the so-called Doctors' Plot. He died of natural causes in the late 1960s.

173

at one point he lost his temper and spat burning pipe tobacco all over that toady Voroshilov.

Then, in the small hours, he started on me—a thing he has almost never done before.

He was discussing Israel—"that Zionist nest of microbes planted by the Americans right on our Asian doorstep"—then turned to me across the table and said, "But of course some of us cannot be as alert to this danger as others—especially those who have worked for such organizations as the Jewish Anti-Fascist Committee!"

I could sense the rest of them smirking in their sleeves at my supposed discomfort. But I was not to be outfaced so easily. I looked the old fox straight in the eye and spoke in Georgian (which as usual enrages the others).

"Master," I said, "it is just as well we cleared up that Mingrelian Affair when we did, or we might have another little nest of microbes breeding in our midst!"

For a second I thought he was going to lose his temper. But he laughed loudly, and turning to the others, with a twinkle in his eye, said, "The Prosecutor is right! As usual he is alive to every danger. You mark my words—he is cleverer than all of you put together!" And he gave me a friendly cuff on the ear.

I could sense their hatred for me all around. They know I am the only one of them who dares to answer the Old Man back, and that this does not displease him. Nevertheless, I remain uneasy. His growing preoccupation with Zionism becomes all too reminiscent of the old troubles. It is certain we have a long and difficult winter ahead of us.

Moscow, September 1952

The heat wave continues. The city is baked dry like a barracks. Even the young saplings inside the Kremlin wall are shriveled and dying, although they are watered regularly twice a day.

My spirits are low, my nerves bad. My doctor—who is himself

deeply concerned by the growing rumors—blames my condition on too much drinking, and has prescribed a disagreeable diet of fruit, yoghurt and bitter cordials.

Nina and Sergei are still at Sochi. It is better they remain away from Moscow. The business of Ignatiev and the Jewish doctors has not yet come to a head; but I have decided to broach the matter with Nikita Sergeyevich[2] personally, for he and Ignatiev are as close as two mice in a larder.

Meanwhile, yesterday saw the beginnings of a nasty incident. I was returning in the Packard to Malaya Nikitskaya when we were held up at the junction of Arbat. At that moment a crocodile of young girls was crossing the street, very smart and pretty in their dark blue tunics, short dresses and white socks. Rafik, who was beside me, read my thoughts at once and told me they were pupils from the Junior School of the Bolshoi Ballet.

One girl struck me in particular. She was taller than the rest, very dark with a fine olive complexion and that slightly aquiline profile that is so common among the Mingrelian people. She excited me greatly, and at the corner of the next block I ordered Rafik to make the usual approach.

An hour later he called me at Malaya Nikitskaya and informed me that the girl is as I guessed—a Georgian from Zugdidi. Her father is a schoolteacher there. The daughter is twelve—although she looked older.

I could see Rafik was not happy about the affair, but he carried out my instructions to the letter. I had Anna prepare dinner for two in the small upstairs study with the French couch. It was a simple meal, with a young wine as befitted the occasion, and a box of liqueur chocolates from Switzerland.

Rafik arrived with the girl at 7 P.M. in the unofficial Volga sedan. Her father had been informed I was an official with the Ministry of Culture and that our meeting would be in his daughter's interest. Fortunately my liking for music should make the going smoother.

[2] Khrushchev.

175

Her name is Tatana—a cultivated Georgian name which fits her appearance, which was really enchanting: a plain white frock which showed the slight pubescent mounds of her breasts, and her hair arranged in two dark pigtails down to her shoulders.

When we met she seemed far less nervous than Rafik, which amused me and put me in a good mood for the evening. She was very polite, with a pleasant restrained manner that was quite grown-up; and I could tell she was brimming over with excitement at meeting such an important person.

The house obviously impressed her, although I am sure she did not guess who the real owner was—even if she was politically conscious—for as usual Rafik had approached it from a roundabout route, driving up to the back entrance.

I took her straight up to the study, where I offered her the orange cordial with two grains of sedative. Then I showed her my Grundig record player with the two built-in speakers and my library full of long-playing records, which impressed her greatly since she had never seen them before. And I was soon chatting to her like an old family friend. I played her pieces by Tchaikovsky, Borodin, and Rachmaninov's Second Piano Prelude, which I told her had made me cry when I first heard it.

She sat and listened very correctly on the couch. Then I offered her a little wine, which she accepted only after some coaxing. Later, while we ate dinner, she told me how she wanted to become a great ballerina like Pavlova and Ulanova, and became very excited when I told her that I could arrange for her to meet Ulanova. This girlish enthusiasm, combined with her virginal beauty, began really to entrance me; and I compared her to some of the eager, overblown harlots that Abakumov is constantly flouting under my eyes. Beside them Tatana was a little saint, as pure as fresh snow.

By the time we reached the liqueur chocolates I could see she was becoming drowsy. But she obviously still felt completely safe with me, and I was relieved that she did not clamor to go home. She was entirely in my power.

I played her more music, and after a while she dozed off. I lifted her slim legs onto the couch, removed her shoes, then slid my hand under her dress. Her thighs were narrow and very soft, setting my senses on fire. She half woke when my hand touched her little pubic mound, but I was careful not to run too fast too soon. I went back and turned down the lights. Then I undressed quickly and sat down beside her. The combination of the sedatives, the wine and chocolates had rendered her only half conscious of my tentative caresses. I put on the Rachmaninov prelude again, which lulled her further, while I began unbuttoning her clothes. Her brassiere was one of those new ones that have just come on the market, with a little hook at the back that gave me no trouble. Soon she was naked except for her pants. I caressed her all over, rubbing her shallow breasts.

Perhaps it was on account of the music, but I experienced a curious mixed sensation: my lust, which was communicated through the rush of blood to my prick, seemed mellowed by a strange reverence for her beauty—a sensation that I have known only when contemplating a great work of art or listening to a fine piece of music. I felt almost ashamed when I surrendered to the animal within me.

I mounted her, resting my weight on my knees and elbows, and carefully parted her soft vaginal lips with my fingers. It was then that she came wide awake and gave a sharp scream of terror. It was the signal for me to change my tactics. I became stern, almost angry. I was obliged to put my hand across her mouth and threaten her. I told her I would beat her if she did not stop her noise. It had no effect. As soon as I removed my hand she started screaming again.

This made me angry. I jumped up, with my prick swinging like a militiaman's truncheon, and seized the leather strap I keep handy in the drawer next to the couch. Then I lifted her bodily— she was very light—and turned her over, pushing her face firmly down into the cushion. Then I administered four quick lashes across her buttocks, not hard enough to break the skin, but sufficient to bring up red weals across the peachlike surface.

She had been screaming all the while, but when I released her she was suddenly quiet, and her whole body began to shake from head to foot. I turned her over again and adjusted a cushion under her buttocks. Her eyes were wide open, staring at me, and I recognized the symptoms of hysteria.

By now I was fully aroused, although sufficiently in control to cover my prick with petroleum jelly. Then I flung myself down, no longer caring about hurting her, and plunged myself deep beneath the little clump of childish hair. She screamed again—a gurgling sound from far back in her throat—and I could feel her little haunches tensing helplessly against my savage thrusts. At the same time I became aware that the cushion under her was soaked warm with urine—which added to the pleasure of the moment.

My one regret was that it was finished so soon. I had been like a rampant bull and had not felt her hymen break, but when I finally withdrew, I saw that my greasy prick was all crimson, and there were stains on the cushion and along the inside of her thighs.

I went next door and washed myself, then brought in a basin of warm water and a towel. She had lost consciousness and had turned as white as a corpse. I washed her down and forced some water between her lips, and she began to revive.

She began crying like a baby and trembling so that her teeth chattered in her head. And her nose ran disgustingly. I was now eager to be finished with her. I gave her a drink with two more grains of sedative and put her in a spare bedroom.

I felt tired and drank some of the 1906 cognac which Balmadze got for me through the French Embassy in Teheran.

Moscow, September 1952

Things are at last coming to a head—I am convinced of it. I had Khrushchev in this morning, but the meeting was not satis-

178

factory. He is a solid brute of a man, with all the stubborn cunning of the Ukrainian peasant, combined with tenacious ambition. Yet he has played the faithful drayhorse for so long now that one has scarcely noticed him, until he appears in our foremost ranks.

But what I disliked most was his self-confidence. It amounted almost to insolence. With that creature of his, Ignatiev, safe in his pocket, and the Boss's apparent benediction for his being privy to these new investigations, he can no doubt feel smug even in my presence!

I was frank with him right from the start—perhaps too frank. "You know it is the Jews he is after?" I said, bearing in mind that Khrushchev has a good record where the Jews are concerned, especially in opposing the worst excesses of anti-Semitism in the Ukraine before the war. But he was not to be tricked into even the smallest admission. He is a poker player who holds his cards close to his chest, and his bright little pig's eyes give away nothing. He replied that the Jews are not sacred in Russia, that the investigations cannot discriminate between one race of citizens and another. Of course he knows what is afoot as well as anyone, but so long as he remains on the right side of the Boss he will not utter a bleat.

Afterward I had lunch with Nadoraya and we drank heavily. Later in the afternoon a nasty problem arose—a complication ensuing from the affair with the Bolshoi girl. Rafik brought her father to my office in the Lubyanka. He had been summoned overnight from Georgia: a fine-looking man, tall and straight as a czarist officer. I could see that he was not going to be easy. Of course, my presence in that place had the usual sobering effect, but I read in his eyes an anger that was stronger than any fear.

I offered him cognac and coffee, and spoke to him man to man: my standard offer of a pension of five thousand rubles a month and a dacha on the Black Sea. And of course I would use my influence to see that his little Tatana received the best opportunities in her career. But I saw almost at once that my generosity was wasted. He heard me out with a cold arrogance that was positively offensive and when I had finished he exploded with venom. For a moment I thought he was going to attack me, for his fury was like nothing I have ever encountered before in this situation. He poured out a torrent of vile insults. Fortunately Nadoraya was in the next office and came in before he got out of hand. I was shaking with anger, but was determined not to give myself away. I told him that such personal invective amounted to criminal slander against a leading member of the state; and that he was therefore insulting the Party itself, and that such behavior would not be tolerated.

Nadoraya then seized him, but he offered no resistance. I noticed then that he had a game leg; but I had no sympathy for the pigheaded fool. I gave Nadoraya the signal and the old man was taken outside. My anger was now so great that I decided to finish him off myself. I took my pistol from the desk drawer and followed along to the execution room. Nadoraya told him to stand with his back to the wall, his head level with the little window.

Still the old man gave no resistance. He must have known what was in store for him and was going to play the martyr to the end. His obstinacy and arrogance maddened me. Nadoraya struck him in the stomach, then beat him to the floor; but only when he had placed a firm kick in his testicles did the old fool cry out and begin to whine like a dog. We got him to his feet again, but he would not stand straight, so it was no good trying to use the little window.[3] I shot him twice in the head, but my aim was not as good as usual. My first bullet shattered his cheek, the second went through his neck, and the blood was pumping out all over the floor. I used the butt of my gun to smash in his skull, but even then his stubborn spirit did not leave him easily.

I gave myself a strong cognac when it was all over. Nadoraya called two of my Georgians to take the body down and bury it

[3] The traditional method of execution by the NKVD was to stand the victim with his back to a small window, through which he would be shot in the back of the neck.

under the cellar. I considered issuing the necessary instructions to have the girl picked up at her home, but at the last minute relented. She probably still has no idea who I am; and, besides, it might create complications with the widowed mother. I have enough to worry about, without these extra domestic crises.

MALLORY'S REPORT

I reached the Austro–Hungarian border by midmorning next day: over a mile of plowed mine fields with electrified fencing and rows of tank traps that reached across the brow of the horizon like giant concrete teeth.

The Hungarian frontier post at Hegyeshalom was an anticlimax. I remembered it from October 1956, full of haggard students in fur caps and tricolor cockades, and girls in greatcoats with captured Russian submachine guns. Instead, a couple of smart, smiling guards who bowed me into a freshly painted room with easy chairs and posters of the Danube and Lake Balaton. It was more like a travel agency than a door through the Iron Curtain.

My visa was a formality, valid for thirty days. One of the guards glanced in the boot and back seat of the Citroën, saluted and waved me through, with the envelope containing the ten hundred-dollar bills safely in my breast pocket.

I drove east across the dull plain of Hungary, through towns whose names had sounded across the world in 1956—now neat and drab, with no trace of Russian troops. I reached the suburbs of Budapest by noon. Gray stretches of tenement blocks, cheerless even under a clear sky; queues in lumpy clothes; trucks and antique trams and ugly little cars of East German or Czech design; the odd red star on an official building; a few slogans.

The Danube swept into sight—a shimmering breadth of water between the heights of Buda, dominated by the pale-yellow palace of the Hapsburgs, and the Gothic dome of the Parliament building on the opposite bank of Pest. The streets here were of lusterless baroque, with the occasional modern structure that looked like a prewar wireless set. It was all quiet and tidy. I last remembered the streets choked with rubble and the charred carcasses of armored vehicles, walls pitted with bullets and gaping shell holes. The few concessions to Western affluence were a number of Coca-Cola signs and the huge new Duna Intercontinental Hotel, like an upturned mouth organ. This was where Boris had arranged for me to meet Laszlo Laszlo in the downstairs bar at one o'clock.

As I drew into the forecourt I was surprised to see rows of opulent cars with Western number plates, including several Rolls-Royces and *gran turismos*. At the doors a porter hurried up and said, "Sir, you are for the party?"

For a confused moment I thought he meant the Communist Party. The glass-walled foyer was crowded with a very unproletarian range of faces. It was only at the desk that I understood. A large printed notice in English read: WILL ALL GUESTS OF MR. SEAN FLANAGAN PLEASE CONTACT MR. WALTERS, SUITE 527.

Sean Flanagan, the actor, married to the much-wed beauty Vicki Byrd, was celebrating his fortieth birthday in Budapest, where he was making a film, and they had invited a few hundred guests. I had interviewed him once, some years ago, when I'd been working in Fleet Street and he was still in rep. We'd got agreeably drunk together, and later he'd written to thank me for my piece. He had since risen to stardom, and his ultimate

183

union with Vicki Byrd had entered the romantic folklore of show biz. They now led a nomadic, tax-free life between continents; and wherever they moved, with a caravan of retainers—secretaries, and secretaries-to-the-secretaries, agents, lawyers, hairdressers, chauffeurs and masseurs and bodyguards—they were stalked and harassed by journalists. I wondered if this would affect or endanger my encounter with Laszlo Laszlo, or whether we should not establish our relationship, and thus sow the rumor that it was at this celebrated birthday party that the Beria papers had passed into the hands of a Western courier.

I rode up to my room, the usual air-conditioned cell with sealed windows, bedside radio and television, push-button service and American plumbing. I took a bath, shaved, then went down to the bar. Although it was crowded, I had no trouble recognizing Laszlo Laszlo: his was the only face that did not have the self-consciously relaxed look of famous people who expect to be recognized.

Laszlo was a thin man with what Boris had described as "labor-camp eyes"—dark sockets above mushroom pouches—and teeth like broken piano keys. His suit hung on him as though made for someone much broader. He was sitting alone on a bar stool in front of a vodka bottle. I introduced myself, and his response was immediate: his eyes gleamed deep in his skull as he wrung my hand with a grip that made me almost shout with pain, at the same time calling to the barman.

I explained that I did not drink, and he told me he had many friends who had ruined their livers in service to the Red Army and Party banquets. His English was fluent and fast. He talked avidly, about Boris, the 1956 Uprising, oppression, the state of world literature; until gradually, as the level of the vodka bottle fell and I was on my fifth Coke, we approached matters more immediate.

"A thousand dollars," I said finally, "in dollar bills. And a further payment of ten thousand dollars if and when the work is published."

"Listen, my friend. Money does not interest me. It is not important. It is the book that is important. Boris has written to me and explained that it is a difficult book—a book that might have come from outside Hungary. From Russia, for instance? And I think it is a book that will not please certain people in Russia?"

I told him everything, including all the libelous passages about the Soviet leaders which Boris had included against my better judgment, and as I talked he smiled into his glass. "It is good," he muttered. "It is very good. It must succeed! Those butchers have been on their horses long enough. It is time they fell off!"

I then explained what he needed to do: a signed statement describing in detail how he had brought the typescript out of Russia. He did not have to be too explicit as to who had given it to him: there were certain secrets that an American publisher, even at the cost of three million dollars, would have to forfeit. The mechanics were all that mattered.

Laszlo seemed satisfied; he also seemed sober. Later, we went to a restaurant in a wine cellar on the hills of Buda, full of young couples—men with shoulder-length hair and girls in miniskirts and what I took to be homemade caftans. There was an atmosphere of gaiety and relaxation.

"Do not think it has always been like this," he said, as though reading my thoughts. "Freedom, as Lenin said, is a precious thing, and must therefore be rationed. We are today enjoying our ration. But tomorrow Moscow may decide to pass the ration on to Poland, or even Czechoslovakia. Moscow still holds the strings, like a puppet master, and we jump as she pulls them."

I detected a note of alcoholic gloom, and changed the subject. I asked him about his little trouble with the Dean of Canterbury, and he cheered up at once, with a rasping laugh. "Ah, that old idiot! Yes, it was while I was one of the Party's errand boys. One night I looked in the Party newspaper, *Nepszabadsag*, and saw this old, half-bald, white-haired fool all dressed up in his church costume, and I was sure he was the Bishop of Györ,

185

who had been a leading collaborator. So I called my boys and said, 'Boys, I want this fascist pig dead or alive!' Fortunately they took him alive. At four o'clock in the morning they telephoned me and said, 'We have the bishop, but he says he is English and pretends he cannot speak Hungarian.' And I said, 'Ah, boys, we've heard that one before!' Half an hour later they telephoned me again and said, 'We are worried, comrade—the Bishop of Györ died in 1943.' Then I remembered that our leader, Rakosi, had invited this English idiot as his guest of honor, and I leaped out of bed, called my car, and arrived at police headquarters here in Andrassy Utca, where the old Dean was in the cells, looking pretty miserable. Next day I had to write personal letters of apology, not only to the Dean, but to Rakosi himself."

Before we left, I said, "Listen, Laszlo. You are taking a big risk in all this."

He shrugged. "I am getting old. I have no more wife. My son is in America. What do I care?"

"All right. Well, let's enjoy ourselves. You know there's a big party tonight at the Duna? Well, there'll be journalists there. And photographers. Would you mind risking being seen there with me? Even having our pictures taken together?"

He gave a low laugh. "Pictures? With actresses? I see you there at what time?"

We arranged to meet in the bar of the Duna at 7:30. I paid the bill, and he thanked me with his bone-crushing handshake, then walked quite steadily up the stone stairs to the street.

🦋

Just after seven o'clock Sean Flanagan came into the Duna bar. There was at once that wave of hushed expectation, the artificial excitement generated by minor royalty, which greeted him wherever he went. Behind him came his bodyguard, a dark-yellow Chingro from Martinique.

Flanagan crossed the bar and cast an experienced glance

around. The guests watched greedily to see which of them he would acknowledge. Suddenly he looked straight at me. He was very tall, dressed in clothes that would have suited him as well on a beach as in a hotel bar; and his hair, which was a sun-bleached blond, was fastened at the nape of his neck by a chunky gold ring the size of a child's fist, giving his features a piratical look.

I smiled back, trying to conceal my astonishment that he should remember me. A secretary arrived with a beer, which he took without looking.

"Now, about your last book, Mallory. I liked it. You've sold the film rights, of course?"

"No."

"No! Then we'd better have a talk about it. I'm having a party tonight. Come along."

I looked at my watch. "I'm meeting a Hungarian friend for the evening. Did a few years in a labor camp, and now writes poetry. You might like to meet him?"

"Surely. Have a word with my secretary over there," and he waved toward a small man standing by the door. "He'll fix you up with a pass—we have to be careful about gate-crashers."

I went across to the secretary by the door. "Mr. Walters?" He nodded. I explained who I was and what I wanted.

"You say Mr. Flanagan has sanctioned this?" He was an American, his accent quiet and cultured. "Mr. Flanagan hasn't mentioned you to me," he added.

"I told you—he's invited us. But if you have any doubts you can always check with him yourself." I nodded back down the bar.

"I know my job," the little man said quietly. He took out a wallet and a platinum pen, and produced two stiff cards with the words in embossed italics, *Passport to the Flanagan Party. Not transferable.* "Your names," he said.

I told him, spelling out Laszlo Laszlo's name, took the cards and returned to my seat.

"Tom Mallory, you old bastard!"

I turned and looked into a pair of pink eyes, familiar from many a liquid lunch in El Vino during my newspaper days. Frank Smollett, now an almost legendary figure in Fleet Street, had worked his way steadily through most newspapers, usually getting the sack for some act of drunkenness. I was always surprised to find him alive, let alone working; but somehow he survived—this time as an aggressive Sunday columnist.

He had sat down beside me, holding a large dark drink. "You're not here for this fucking jamboree, I hope?"

"I'm here on business," I replied, keeping an eye open for Laszlo Laszlo. A plan was now forming in my mind. Smollett could be relied upon for two qualities: despite his heavy drinking, he was a highly professional journalist, a man who could scoop a good story and might keep a secret.

"Working on a new book?" he asked.

"Yes and no," I said, and added quickly, "but I can probably help you out as an old friend. I suppose you haven't got an invitation for tonight?"

"From those two megalomaniac clowns? You must be joking! I can't get a full list of the guests—not even the walking wounded of show biz, let alone the stars." He took a hefty drink. "Don't tell me *you've* got an invitation?"

I handed him my embossed pass. He nodded and slid it back across the table.

"Okay, so tell old Uncle Frank what it's all about?"

"Just good friends," I said smiling. "Sean Flanagan and myself—from way back when I was working on the Street. We got sloshed together and I did an interview he liked."

"Did he pay your fare?"

"He only invited me this afternoon."

"Just like that?" He caught the waiter's eye.

"He says he's interested in buying the film rights of my last book."

"I can use that?"

"Be my guest—I can certainly do with a bit of publicity, even if Flanagan can't." I was still watching the door for Laszlo, trying to decide whether it would be wise at this stage for him and Smollett to meet. For myself everything seemed to be falling perfectly into place.

"I'll tell you what I'll do," I said. "I'll go to the party tonight and pass on to you any scandal for your column."

"It'll have to be a news story—and not later than eleven," he said, "or the paper'll have gone to bed."

"Not later than eleven," I repeated, as I saw Laszlo Laszlo approaching across the crowded floor. I introduced him to Smollett, formally, as a poet. The Hungarian began by being garrulously secretive, since he knew he was talking to a Western journalist. I didn't think Smollett missed much. He had a practical knowledge of world affairs, including the Communist sphere, from firsthand experience. There was a story about him during the Soviet invasion of Czechoslovakia in 1968, which I now got him to tell Laszlo. Smollett and a group of fellow journalists had been arrested by Russian troops in Prague for breaking the curfew. The showing of press cards had cut no ice with their captors, and things had begun to look ugly for them, when Smollett found a colonel who spoke some English. He'd fixed the Russian with his bloodshot eyes and said, "Colonel, if one hair of my head is touched—just one—the London correspondents of *Pravda* and *Izvestia* will be hanging in Hyde Park tomorrow morning." He had added a few phrases about "the Thames running with Russian blood," and the colonel had finished by apologizing and had ordered them to be driven back to their hotel in an Army vehicle.

After this the conversation became a good deal easier. The three of us dined together in the hotel restaurant, and I signed the bill. "I'll meet you down in the bar at a quarter to eleven— if anything happens," I told Smollett.

He gave us both a crooked wave. "Have fun in the holy of holies!" Then he lurched away across the silent carpet.

189

"A strange man," said Laszlo. "He drinks like that always?"

"Always."

"It is like all journalists? Is he to be trusted?"

"Absolutely. He's an old friend."

Laszlo consulted a watch with a faded yellow face. "It is nearly nine o'clock," he said. "Perhaps we should join your friends?"

The party was being held in the hotel vaults, the stairs guarded by three of Flanagan's security men in dinner jackets. The first checked our passes; the second handed us a giant orange candle in a wax-coated vase, together with a choice of champagne glass or stone beer mug; and the third just nodded.

The party was already packed and stifling, with a stench of perfume, after-shave, Havana cigars and a hint of cannabis. Laszlo's glass was charged several times before we managed to find a corner of a table in an alcove draped with artificial cobwebs.

What the hell was I doing here, I thought, except that a fat film contract would be a welcome bonus if our project collapsed. I was thinking of Tatana and wondering how she'd have made out here, and of her and Boris, alone together in the Hotel de La Baie, when the Flanagans paused by our table.

"Everyone happy?" Sean asked.

A starlet slid forward and cried, "It's a fabulous party, Sean!"

They all smiled except Mrs. Flanagan. She was a small woman with a spectacular bosom encased in skin-clinging green silk, her hair elaborately arranged, her eyes hooded with lashes like miniature iron railings. She reminded me of a beautiful doughnut covered in paint and precious stones. I introduced her to Laszlo Laszlo, whose rose and kissed her hand. Her smile flashed on like an electric light, then went out.

Her husband, however, seemed at ease. He was showing us his wife's present to him: a fulvous diamond set in a coral of

190

rubies—the whole thing the size of a plum, attached to a heavy gold chain.

"She wanted to buy me the Tutankhamen treasure!" he cried, giving her a smacking kiss on the cheek, while the starlet squeezed up to make room for them.

Laszlo sat very still. "You are making a film here—yes?" he said gently.

Sean Flanagan nodded, while his wife arranged the jewel around his neck.

"I know many film people here," said Laszlo. "Have you met any?"

"Quite enough of them!" Flanagan said cheerily. "No offense meant, but we're working with a Hungarian crew. Not to worry, though—the film's strictly for external consumption. Orgies in old castles, historical porn. Or at least, knowing how puritanical you Communists are, no doubt you'd call it porn!"

"I am no longer a Communist," Laszlo said.

"Of course not. No one in Hungary is. Like all good Germans, eh?" Flanagan laughed and drank some champagne. "Cheers, Laszlo!" He raised his glass again, but the Hungarian did not move.

"Have you invited any Hungarians?" I asked.

"I've invited my friends," said Flanagan.

It was then that I lost my temper. "For Christ's sake!" I shouted. "You're not in Beverly Hills now! Haven't you any tact at all? The Hungarians are your hosts."

Flanagan sat with his mouth turned down. "Get fucked," he said quietly, and I was aware of the bodyguard's huge frame behind me. "I don't want to see these two creeps again," Flanagan added, "and that includes Living Skull over there."

All this time Laszlo sat sipping his champagne as though nothing had happened. I had got to my feet. The bodyguard pushed me aside, then leaned over and took hold of Laszlo Laszlo's shoulder. There was a mild struggle.

A few seconds later we were standing in the hotel foyer. A

couple of flashbulbs went off, as Laszlo was pitched forward beside me onto his hands and knees. He straightened up and grinned wearily.

"You okay?" I asked.

"If I wasn't okay after that I'd have been dead many years ago," he said.

"Come on," I said, "let's find some civilized company!" I pushed aside a couple of photographers and hurried Laszlo toward the bar. It was just 10:40. Smollett was drinking with a group of journalists, but broke away from them as soon as he saw me. "Up to your room, Frank! You've got your story." I led Laszlo quickly back toward the lift.

"British author and Hungarian poet ejected from Flanagan party," I said as the bedroom door closed. Smollett had a notebook out and seemed almost sober.

"Right. Let's have it."

Ten minutes later his call to London came through.

![decorative flag icon]

I was shaving when the phone rang. It was Smollett.

"That was a great story last night! I'm downstairs having breakfast. Why don't you join me?"

The restaurant was almost deserted. It was clearly going to be some time before last night's revelers roused themselves. Frank Smollett was sitting by himself eating a beefsteak tartare with a raw egg on top, washed down by black coffee and a glass of *baratsk*. It was only eight o'clock.

"I don't have to file again for five days," he said as I sat down. "Now, I don't suppose you can give me a hint of what you're up to here? Apart from peddling your film rights, of course."

"You can forget about the film rights," I said, accepting a cup of coffee. "The rest's a little delicate at the moment."

"To do with Laszlo Laszlo?" Smollett had taken his fork and was mashing the meat into an odious pâté.

192

I looked away and said, "You and I have known each other for a long time, Frank. And I gave you a good scoop last night . . ."

"Front page, old boy. Front page," and he shoveled the egg-and-meat into his mouth.

"Right. I want to tell you something strictly off the record."

He picked up a napkin and wiped some sweat from his upper lip. "You don't suppose this place is bugged, do you?"

"Not in Hungary today. Unless they want to record a few hundred thousand hours of package-tour chat. Now, listen," I said, "if you sit on what I've got to tell you for a couple of months, perhaps less, I may be able to give you a really big story. World news."

Smollett peered at me with his small red eyes. "Off the record, eh?"

"Strictly. You've got egg on your chin."

He nodded. "I know the rules."

"You'd better. Because if you break this confidence, you don't only screw me up, and a lot of other people too, you ruin the best story you've had in years."

"Okay, okay, you don't have to give me a bloody lecture, Tom. Just the facts."

I tasted the muddy black coffee. "That Hungarian, Laszlo Laszlo—it's not his correct name, by the way."

"Thanks. I used it in the story last night. I just hope my editor's got a little East European sense of humor."

"Last autumn Laszlo went to Russia, where he came into possession of a certain manuscript."

"Next year's Nobel Prize winner for literature?"

I shook my head. "The guy who wrote this isn't going to get any Nobel Prize—even if he was alive, which he's not. Nor is it exactly literature. It's a diary—the secret memoirs of a top Soviet official."

Smollett had stopped eating. "Who?"

"I can't tell you that, not at this stage. All I'm promising is that if you play ball now, I'll be able to give an exclusive in about a couple of months' time."

"There have been a hell of a lot of memoirs coming out of Russia recently," Smollett said thoughtfully. "Penkovsky, Svetlana, Khrushchev. And apart from Svetlana I understand that not all of them have been exactly genuine?"

"That'll be the publishers' problem, not yours."

"You've read it?"

"I haven't seen it yet. I'm collecting it today from Laszlo."

"And then going to smuggle it into Austria? Right?"

"Right. I wish you'd get rid of that egg on your face."

"Supposing you're caught," he said, dabbing the napkin at his chin.

"I'll just have to be damned careful I'm not."

There was a pause. "So why does the story have to wait a couple of months?" Smollett said finally.

"Because certain people have to be protected—Laszlo Laszlo among them. Also, these diaries may involve people in the West, witnesses who may have to come forward and authenticate the work. So it's absolutely vital that we don't do anything premature. You'll just have to trust me and wait till I give you the word."

Smollett downed his *baratsk*. "What I don't understand is why you're giving the whole story to me. Why the hell don't you just sit on it, then write it up yourself?"

I smiled. Frank Smollett might be a drunk, but he was no fool. "Look, I'm not just the courier and contact man, Frank. I'm the person who's got to convince the publishers—particularly the Americans, because that's where the money is—that the manuscript is genuine. I can't implicate Laszlo unless he defects, which he's unlikely to do. So I've got to have at least one independent witness. And that witness is going to be you."

Smollett nodded slowly. "There's just one thing that puzzles me, Tom. Last night you went out of your way to catch the limelight, you and Laszlo. You've established the fact that you're in Budapest and friendly with this Hungarian, so why come down and spill the beans to me as well?"

"Because apart from trusting you, I want you to be fully in the picture when the story breaks. As I said, there may be a few witnesses in the West who'll have to be interviewed."

"You'd rather it was me than you?"

"I told you, I've got to do the convincing. It would be too damned facile for me to dig up the witnesses and interview them myself. It wouldn't ring true."

Smollett nodded again, chuckling this time. "You're taking one hell of a chance with me—you know that? I mean, I can do a little amateur guesswork as well as the next man. And you and Laszlo Laszlo certainly aren't the only people in the world who must know about this manuscript."

I stood up and held out my hand. "You blow this, Frank, and you blow the best scoop you've had in years. Thanks for the coffee. I'll see you around later."

I turned to go, but he called after me, "Since I'm in the know, any chance of my being there when Laszlo hands the thing over?"

"Not a chance. If he knows a journalist's within half a mile of him, that's the end."

"You certainly seem to be taking a few liberties with this poor bastard. Especially if he doesn't know about me."

"I told you—I'm trusting you, Frank."

"Oh, piss off," he said, grinning. As I left the restaurant I saw him waving his empty glass at the waiter.

That afternoon I met Laszlo Laszlo at the entrance to the thermal baths of the Gellert Hotel in Buda, on a pinnacle of rock high above the Danube. He was looking a lot fresher than yesterday, almost spruce, in an open white shirt, flannel trousers and sandals.

"We go in your car," he said, "to the Margaret Island. It is

195

quiet there, and we can talk in safety." It was obvious that he did not share my confidence in the laxity of Hungarian security methods, but I put this down to habit more than design.

It was a hot, cloudless Sunday and the streets were crowded, the trams grinding and sparking down the broad avenues, with people hanging out of the doors like bunches of grapes. When we reached the island, he told me to park under some trees just beyond the bridge. The lawns round us were full of couples strolling or lying in the sun. He watched them for a moment, then pulled from his hip pocket some papers which he smoothed out on his knee; there were four sheets covered with single-spaced typing in Hungarian. At the end of the last one was an illegible flourish of ink which I took to be his signature.

"This is what you want," he said, and handed them to me. "When you have them translated you will know everything that is necessary. I have not written a single word that is not true."

I put them carefully inside my jacket pocket, next to the envelope with the thousand dollars which Boris had given me. Laszlo made no move to get out of the car. "Our friend Drobnov told you something of the affair?" he said at last.

"He told me that you helped bring some banned literature out of Russia," I replied, but did not tell him that Boris had also given me the name of the author. He nodded. "Let's take a stroll," I said.

He seemed to hesitate before opening the door. "I will not tire you with the unimportant details," he began. "Just the essential facts."

We got out and started to walk along a path between the flower beds.

"Last summer," he went on, "I met an old friend, a Hungarian journalist, who had just returned from Russia after three months with an official delegation. During this visit he had made contact with a man living about thirty miles outside Moscow, a leading dissident intellectual who has so far escaped

196

prison. He told me that this man had certain documents that he wanted to reach the West, but my friend did not try to bring them out himself because he was afraid that the KGB already suspected him. So he asked me if I could help.

"I made my visa application to the Soviet Embassy here in Budapest, but after two months nothing happened, so I telephoned them and said I had received no reply." He grinned. " 'Comrade Laszlo,' they said, 'no reply is a reply!' Well, I was expecting this, so I then wrote to the Red Army Veterans' Association and told them I wanted to attend the November the Seventh anniversary parade in Moscow as a member of the Hungarian Anti-Fascist Brigade. The officer in charge of the Association is now a very important man, a Marshal of the Soviet Union, and he wrote back at once enclosing a Red Army invitation to the Veterans' stand at the parade, and a first-class return air ticket from Budapest to Moscow. Of course, the KGB were crazy with anger, but there was nothing they could do. The Red Army are the only people they are perhaps a little frightened of—just like cats and dogs. So I flew to Moscow and was met by an official Army delegation and treated for ten days like a prince. Of course, I was under constant surveillance. But here you must understand something about the Soviet system. These days the KGB technically can arrest anyone on suspicion, but with us citizens from the 'fraternal Socialist countries' they have to check first with the authorities back home, which gives us a certain immunity. I know it does not seem logical, but then nothing in Russia is logical. And a citizen from a Socialist country who is also an official guest of the Red Army is almost untouchable.

"Anyway, on my last day in Moscow I got on a train to visit this dissident writer. I knew the KGB were following me, and I think they had a pretty good idea where I was going. But they could not stop me personally, so instead they stopped the train from stopping at the station where the man lived!" He broke off with a hoarse laugh.

"Of course, it didn't worry me. I got a lift with a truck back to the town where we should have stopped, and went and visited my friend without any trouble."

"Were you still followed?"

"Oh, yes. The KGB boys commandeered a car from a local Party member, but there was still nothing they could do—legally. They just sat outside the house and waited. I stayed to dinner and caught the last train back to Moscow. He hadn't given me the documents at his house, but had told me an address where I could collect them in the city. So next day I sent one of my old Army friends to pick them up, and that afternoon I went along with my luggage—with the documents inside—to the offices of Malev, the Hungarian airline, to check in for my flight back here. But as soon as the girl saw my name she told me the plane was full. I knew it was a lie—those Moscow flights are never full, especially the first class. So I went to a hotel around the corner, taking the documents with me, and telephoned my old friend the Marshal and explained what had happened, and that I might have a little trouble with my luggage. I didn't have to explain anything more—he just told me to stay there in the hotel, have a bottle of vodka, and he would sort things out. And in exactly one hour a young lieutenant appeared and asked me to accompany him back to the airline offices. As soon as we appeared, the same girl said, 'Ah, Comrade Laszlo, you are lucky! A seat has just fallen vacant in the first class on your flight to Budapest.'

"At the same time the young lieutenant said, without the girl being able to hear, that he understood I had some overweight luggage. Of course there is no such thing on first class, and anyway I had only this one case. But he explained that he would take the case and arrange for it to go next day on one of the Warsaw Pact military flights to Hungary, and that I could collect it from the Red Army depot at Szeged in southern Hungary, about fifty miles from here. Then I just checked in and boarded the bus to the airport. Although I now didn't have any luggage at all, the Customs weren't taking any chances. Usually they don't bother with us 'fraternal' visitors, but with me they made a real exception. They pulled my shoes to pieces, stuck their fingers up my arse, even X-rayed my stomach! Altogether they kept the plane waiting nearly an hour. But they didn't find any-thing, of course, and I could even see the KGB men at the bar-rier as I went through—and they looked ready to burst their blood vessels, they were so angry! And I just flew back to Buda-pest, and next day went down to Szeged, gave my name to the duty officer at the depot, and he handed me my suitcase with-out any more trouble." He paused at a bench and sat down. He was out of breath and his face had lost its color.

"In spite of your Army comrades, you were surely taking a very big risk?" I said.

He smiled. "My friend, I have an old philosophy: 'The string of life is so long that when I pull it I cannot feel the end.'"

"And what happened to the documents?"

"Oh, a tourist took them to Vienna. As you know, the border with Austria is not very closely guarded—unless it is someone they suspect."

"And you've written all this down?" I said, tapping my breast pocket.

"Everything, except the names of the Marshal and the intel-lectual concerned."

I nodded, and we sat on the bench and watched the girls strolling past in the sun. "So the Red Army helped you bring it out?" I said at last.

"Old soldiers will always help their comrades—especially where the KGB is concerned."

Tentatively I took the sealed envelope from my pocket and gave it to him. He broke it open and peered down at the jovial features of Ben Franklin looking up at him from the fresh hundred dollar bills. Very calmly he closed it and handed it back to me. "I have told you, my friend, I do not do these things for money. Not even for good American dollars."

"A few dollars can be very useful," I said meekly, holding the envelope between my knees. "If you ever came to the West . . ." I added; and, obviously sensing my discomfort, he patted my shoulder.

"If I ever come to the West, my friend, you will give me the best of everything—champagne and roast beef and as many beautiful English girls as I can love in my whole life!"

I tried to laugh, and found I couldn't even smile. His refusal of the money, although not unexpected, had left me both embarrassed and faintly uneasy. Such idealism was strangely out of tune with our mercenary motives. I reminded myself again that Boris had promised me I could trust my life to this man; yet somehow I had felt happier dealing with the boozy self-interest of Frank Smollett.

After a few moments he stood up. "I must go, my friend. I will walk, you will go by car. But we will meet again—here perhaps. Perhaps in England."

I flexed my muscles against his crushing handshake, and we embraced each other on both cheeks. "Good luck," I said. He gave a little wave and began to walk away in the direction of the Danube. I never saw him again.

I left Budapest next morning and reached Vienna by noon. Boris was in the café of the Hotel Sacher, as arranged, sitting by himself in an electric-blue suit and brand-new alligator shoes, devouring a vast Sachertorte—three layers of crisp pastry between almond-flavored chocolate and whipped cream.

He greeted me with his fork raised and his mouth full. "So! You have the papers?" He swallowed luxuriously and pointed with his laden fork to the chair opposite.

I handed him the envelope containing Laszlo Laszlo's statement and the thousand dollars; I'd carried it across the border concealed in a two-day-old copy of *The Times* bought in the Duna Intercontinental before I left. "Everything was fine," I said, "except that he refused the money."

Boris shrugged. "He is very proud. There are not many like him—a man in a million. How is his health?"

"He seemed pretty fit, considering the amount of vodka he put away. You read about our little trouble at the Flanagan party, I suppose?"

Boris frowned. "Of course. It was in all the Austrian newspapers. I admire your sentiments, but you were crazy to make such an exhibition of yourself—particularly as you involved Laszlo Laszlo."

"At least it proves beyond doubt that I was in Budapest with him."

"Exactly. That is what worries me. Perhaps you have proved it too well." He sat for a moment, sucking his fingers. "Have a torte," he said suddenly. "They have the best cakes here in the whole world."

"I'd prefer a coffee. Where's Tatana?"

"Sleeping. But she is fine. Absolutely top-notch. And I think we're in luck too. There's a big book fair in Montreux at the beginning of next month. All the leading international publishers will be represented, and I've got my eye on a New York firm called Burn, Hirsch. They specialize in nonfiction, and they've landed a couple of big best sellers in the last year, so they should be in the chips—as well as being less likely to get scared off by the possibility of another Irving–Hughes foul-up."

"And who makes the approach?"

Boris dug his fork into another hunk of cake. "I will. Better a Russian than an Englishman. It will add to the general air of mystery, and the Americans appreciate that. I shall wear a slight disguise—a false beard, perhaps—and operate under a pseudonym."

"You think you're up to negotiating with an American publisher?" I asked dubiously. "They can be pretty tough boys, you know. And for the kind of money we're going to be asking, they'll probably send in a battalion of top-line lawyers who'll really put the squeeze on."

"I can deal with them," Boris said, munching confidently. "The Slavic temperament is more suited to this kind of bargaining than the Anglo-Saxon. One must not be too smooth—better ruthless and cunning, like Stalin with Roosevelt. Just leave it to me. I understand these Americans."

I then told him about my arrangements with Frank Smollett. As soon as the publishers had agreed on a contract, they would issue a statement that they were in possession of the private diaries of L. P. Beria. At this point I would arrange a meeting between Tatana and Smollett, to whom she would blurt out her experience of having been raped by Beria as a child of twelve. Then she would have to disappear. That would leave altogether five possible leads: myself, Boris, Tatana, Laszlo Laszlo, and Smollett—although the latter knew only part of the story.

The risks would remain, but so would the evidence—Laszlo Laszlo's signed testament and Tatana's public statement. Neither would be conclusive proof in law, but I was calculating that without firm evidence to the contrary the publishers would be sufficiently satisfied to take their chance. For the moment the most obvious hazard was the unpredictable nature of Boris' negotiating abilities. Would his volatile temperament be an advantage over those dry legal minds, or a catastrophe? But I conceded his point that a Russian would be a more plausible negotiator than myself.

Although it was almost lunchtime, I left him ordering another torte and went up to find Tatana. Her room was still in darkness when she finally opened the door; she was clutching a thin nightdress across her breasts and blinked into the light. When she saw it was me she pulled me inside, pushed the door shut with her foot, kissed me and dragged me down onto the bed. "The walls are very thick," she said. "You can do what you like to me—tear me to pieces!" Her legs rose and gripped my waist, her fists beating the bed and her head writhing, half crying, half laughing until she gave a howl that must have carried down the whole corridor, and with a shudder fell still.

"That was the best ever," she gasped. "You must think I am a terrible whore—but that was the best of all."

I had never heard her talk like this before, and I wondered if things between her and Boris had not been quite so glamorous as he'd made out.

"You *do* think I am a whore, don't you?" she said again, but before I could think of a strategic reply, she giggled in the dark. "Better be a good whore than a bored housewife!"

"Not only good, but expensive," I said; and on an impulse I got up and fetched the envelope with the ten hundred-dollar bills and dropped it on the pillow. "*Un petit cadeau, chérie.* Our Hungarian friend was too proud to accept it."

She turned on the bedside light and examined it, and her eyes opened wide. "You mean I can have all this?"

"Providing you buy us dinner tonight. Boris will choose the restaurant."

"Ah-h!" Her fingers closed round the envelope. "Even if I am a whore, will you stay with me tonight, Tom? Please."

"I'll stay with you," I said; but I felt no nearer to understanding her than before.

It was another half hour before I could coax her downstairs, where Boris was hacking up yet another torte, this time a *rhumbaba* with maraschino cherries, walnuts and pineapple.

PART
FIVE

A man cannot be too careful in the choice of his enemies.

—OSCAR WILDE

Paper Five

Barvikha,[1] Moscow District. October 1952
I have taken to keeping away from the Congress, since the signs
are unmistakable. The Politburo has been abolished, and replaced by a Party Presidium which includes at least sixteen no-
bodies—lackeys of the Boss who will no doubt echo his merest
whim. In fact, it is clear he intends to make a clean sweep of all
of us—a fresh start with a new Party, perhaps even a whole new
political philosophy.

But the most ominous development of the Congress is its constant theme: vigilance—or rather, the lack of it. Every simpering
Party hack who mounts the rostrum has the word framed on his
lips like part of a catechism. Vigilance—and terror. And of
course, the Jews. For the Jews are everywhere—the microbes of
society, the rootless cosmopolitans, the economic saboteurs and
cultural vermin whose loyalties are to Israel and her Zionist-
American backers. And who is it who has allowed these vermin
to breed—to infiltrate every precious nook and cranny of Soviet
life—but the Security Forces? Indeed, I hear it is being whis-

---

[1] Formerly the country home of the Counts Orlov, dating back to Catherine
the Great; one of Beria's private residences.

pered not only that I am the Jew's Protector, but that I am Jewish myself!

And there is another thing—a real thorn in my side. For that abominable Poskrebyshev has reappeared, this time stepping into the full limelight and dominating the whole Congress, while the Boss sits demurely in the third or fourth row, modestly acknowledging the applause. As for P., I thought I had taught him a lesson three years ago, or perhaps it is the Boss's little joke that this hunchbacked hireling of his should be sent up to accuse me of sloth—even treachery. For P. is too much of a coward ever to turn on his own master, but he would no doubt gladly wreak upon me every vengeance of which he is capable!

However, I take pride that I am not beaten yet. The old fox has tried many times—particularly in the Mingrelian Affair, and the replacement of my trusted Abakumov with this sickly worm Ignatiev—but I am still breathing and far from idle!

Vigilance and terror. So let them spell the words out in every speech at the Congress. They are not unknown to me. In fact, their meaning is probably better understood by me than by any other Soviet citizen alive—including even the Boss himself!

Barvikha, Moscow. November 1952

The news from Prague this morning is very bad.[2] Indeed, if I did not have my sweet, faithful Nina at my side I might have broken down. Even old Rudolf[3] seems to have collapsed utterly and confessed in public to the most outrageous fabrications—and all this in a country which used to pride itself on having been a so-called civilized Western-style democracy, where there is not even a single unit of Soviet troops!

---

[2] In November 1952, the last and most notorious of the postwar show trials in Eastern Europe was held in Prague, in which fourteen leading Czech Communists, eleven of them Jews, confessed to being paid agents of the West. Eleven were hanged, including Rudolf Slansky and Bedric Geminder, both Jews and close friends and protégés of Beria.

[3] Slansky.

Though perhaps I am not the one to weep too freely over these events, but to take their lessons to heart, and learn from them. I count myself an old and practiced hand at the Boss's tricks, but this Czech business is perhaps the biggest trick of all—and accomplished without my having been allowed to lift a finger!

Of course, that crafty Armenian Mikoyan laid the groundwork, and this fellow Likhachev[4]—whom I have not even set eyes on, and seems to live in the Boss's pocket—did the rest. For God knows these Czechs are not made of such stern stuff as old Kostov —or that accursed Josip Broz, the so-called "troubadour of Wall Street"![5]

Even so, the Old Man seems to be outreaching himself—obviously planning a second Yezhovchina[6]—a fearful, final joke, at the expense not only of the Party, but of history itself. For I see that in Prague they even got this wretched youth Frejka, son of one of the accused, to write an open letter to *Rude Pravo* and demand the death sentence for his father—"my greatest and bitterest enemy." I must say, such crude personal tactics are not to my liking, particularly in a civilized country like Czechoslovakia, for in doing so we are surely overplaying our hand. Terror is one thing, absurdity another. Yet absurdity seems the rule of the day, and I am taking no chances.

Meanwhile, I am laying contingency plans. Had Rafik prepare a full breakdown of our resources. The Special Purpose Forces are at a strength of around 300,000, and I think I can count on their commanders' complete loyalty—if only because they know that the moment I go, they go, too!

There are also 250,000 Convoy and Railway Troops, more

[4] Mikhail Likhachev, deputy head of the Section for the Investigation of Specially Important Cases, the control of which Stalin had taken away from Beria and placed under his own supervision late in 1952, prior to the Doctors' Plot. Likhachev was executed with Abakumov in 1954.

[5] Stalin's name for Tito.

[6] Name given to the Great Terror of 1936–38, after Nikolai Yezhov, Beria's predecessor as head of the NKVD.

209

than 300,000 Frontier Troops, and another 200,000 miscellaneous guards, agents and plainclothesmen scattered about the country, answerable to the various MVD commanders. We also have seven full armored divisions in the Moscow area, another two around Leningrad, and four in the Ukraine.

But against this I must calculate on more than five million Army, Air and Naval forces whose commanders will remain loyal to the official leadership. (I have considered calling in as many marshals and generals as possible, and arresting them as they arrive; but have decided that this would be premature while the Boss still breathes.)

I have also had Rafik call up a total of 250 medium tanks and 300 APCs, with heavy cannon and flamethrowers, with double this figure within a day's march of the capital.

Have also considered, as a last extreme, taking sanctuary in the West. While I still control the Frontier Troops, this should not be too difficult. An aircraft is the obvious choice, and I have been studying the various points within immediate range: Finland, West Germany, the Western-occupied zones of Austria—even Turkey or Persia. The main problem will be the frontier forces on the other side, as I dare not try to get a message across.

However, I would be playing the hare running even before the hounds have been let loose. I am not a coward. For the moment I prefer to stand and fight.

Moscow. January 1953

The storm has broken at last. The dogs of war have been unleashed.

Yesterday *Pravda* carried a full list of the doctors—nine professors of medicine and house physician to the Kremlin, of whom five are Jews—describing them as "assassins in white blouses," a phrase that can only have come from the paranoiac pen of the Boss himself. They are accused of having poisoned those two drunken pisspots, Zhdanov[7] and his smarmy parasite, Shcherba-kov,[8] as well as half the General Staff—all on orders from the British and American intelligence services!

All nine have confessed, of course. Ignatiev, supported by Ry-umin,[9] has made sure of that—if only to save their own skins. (I am told that Ignatiev has been under heavy sedation since the Boss spelled out his orders to him in plain language: "Beat, beat, and beat again, Ignatiev—get their confessions, or I will shorten you by a head!")

But the really astounding thing is that the Boss seems to be getting away with it. Not only with the Soviet people, who are now numbed by these outbursts of hatred and national panic, but even our comrades in the West seem ready to swallow every crazy new lie the moment the Boss feeds it to them.

Each morning I am brought a full resumé of the Western So-cialist press, and I am sometimes close to weeping at the morbid humor of it all! The French are the worst—not only the old Party faithfuls, who will dance to every tune we play them, but also some of that great Parisian intelligentsia who seem to be lapping up these fantasies as greedily as blind kittens at a saucer of milk! What kind of people can they be? Whipped by Hitler, and now groveling in front of the Boss!

In normal times I would be out at Kuntsevo, enjoying this little joke with the Old Man himself, for there is nothing that tickles him more than seeing these Western bourgeois scum nodding and

[7] Andrei Zhdanov, Stalin's brother-in-law, whose son was married to Svet-lana. He was the author of the "Zhdanov Decrees on Socialist Realism," under which many writers, painters and musicians disappeared into camps between 1946 and 1948. He died of alcoholic poisoning in August 1948—his death cer-tificate being signed by Professor V. N. Vinogradov, a top heart specialist in the U.S.S.R. and later to be one of the leading accused in the Doctors' Plot.

[8] Colonel General Shcherbakov, wartime political commissar to the Red Army, a close friend of Zhdanov, who died in 1945, also of alcoholic poisoning.

[9] M. D. Ryumin, General of State Security, Ignatiev's deputy, entrusted with fabricating the Doctors' Plot. He disappeared, believed executed in 1954.

capering to his vaguest whim. But alas! the joke seems to have turned sour. Unless I watch my footing carefully, it will be me whom they will be reviling next in their puppet press, mouthing in chorus that I am the greatest traitor of them all—for God only knows what crimes the Boss would concoct against me!

Barvikha, January 1953

Pravda continues to be full of praise for the contemptible Timashuk woman,[10] who has now been awarded the Order of Lenin. And the Boss's pen is everywhere, spitting venom and hatred across the whole nation, ranting against "the thrice-accursed murdering doctors."

But worse—there are now daily diatribes against "vile spies and murderers, and hidden enemies who must be squashed like disgusting vermin," and these articles always end with a call for "an end to the lack of vigilance in our ranks." It would take a simpleton not to be able to read between the lines!

Meanwhile, the roundup of the wretched Jews goes on. They are winkling them out of the ministries, the universities and schools, the Academy of Science—even pouncing on them in the cafés and dance halls.[11] Even Georgi Maximilianovich,[12] who alone seems to enjoy the Boss's favor, is losing his nerve. He is an intelligent man, cold as a fish, but is proving a loyal ally in whom I have come to have great trust. He strongly suggests that I break my silence and put in an appearance at Kuntsevo—show my mettle by bragging with the Boss over a few bottles of wine. For Georgi even goes so far as to claim the Old Man is lonely and longs for honest company.

[10] Dr. Lydia Timashuk, an elderly Moscow cardiographer, who is alleged to have written to Stalin personally, denouncing nine of her fellow doctors, thus setting in motion the Doctors' Plot. Her award of the Order of Lenin was revoked after Stalin's death. Her fate is unknown.

[11] Probably a reference to the popular Jewish bandleader Utesov, who disappeared at this time.

[12] Malenkov.

But yesterday, when I did call him—on a routine matter concerning the new GULAG schedules—all I got was the soft sneering voice of Poskrebyshev, gloating down the phone that the Boss was busy, too busy to talk to his old fellow countryman and Keeper of the Socialist Security, as he has so often called me in the past.

Well, I must continue to lie low and bide my time. My moment will come—I am sure of it, sure as I am that spring will follow this long and painful winter.

Barvikha, February 1953.

Fear and panic have seized the nation like a cancer.

Moscow is grown deathly silent, under deep snow. Half the ministries lie in darkness, and the gates of the Kremlin are like entrances to a sepulcher. Even the old fox out at Kuntsevo seems to be lying low—for he almost never leaves his lair now, except to put in an occasional appearance at the cinema.[13]

Georgi, who is a constant visitor these days, irritated me last night by suggesting that I am scared of the Boss. As if we were not *all* scared of him!—most of the mob mesmerized like rabbits before a snake.

He also told me that that stone-arsed Molotov and the hapless Voroshilov are both as good as dead. The Boss is apparently quite convinced that they really are—and have been for years—agents of the Western powers. So he has come to believe even his own fantasies!—while the largest and second most powerful nation on earth is ruled by a senile maniac.

At the estate I have trebled the guard, and sent Nina and Sergei back to Gagra. It is better they keep out of Moscow.

I have the sweats again and my hands shake. No doubt I

---

[13] A private cinema in the Kremlin where Stalin was fond of watching foreign films captured during World War II—his favorites being American Westerns, which had no subtitles and for which the Minister of Cinematography, Bolshakov, supplied a running commentary.

should cut down on my drinking; but as for medical attention, it used to be easier to get a thousand abortions performed[14] than it is to have one of these luckless Moscow physicians come to treat us. (There is even a joke that of those doctors who are still at large, their hands tremble so much that they cannot even hold a stethoscope steady! And Georgi tells me he had great difficulty getting a dentist to attend to his daughter's toothache.)

And while all this is going on, the wretched Dekanosov[15] comes whining to me, complaining that he'd been held up for over an hour by the guards at the Spasskye Gate.[16] The man is more of a fool than I imagined! For he dares not go within a mile of the Kremlin while the Boss is there—but as soon as he's away, all the idiot thinks about is his petty pride! Sometimes I wish I had men about me of stronger fiber with whom to share these difficult times. Thank God for Nadoraya and his faithful Georgian boys!

Barvikha, February 1953

Things are looking up. This morning Rafik reported that a unit of the Special Purpose Forces penetrated the Kremlin and shot Kosnykin[17]—allegedly for resisting arrest—and disarmed all his men. It means that the Moscow area, with the exception of Kuntsevo, is reasonably secure. I only wish I could count on a few of those marshals and the General Staff, and remind them of 1938—at least enough for them not to lose their heads in love and admiration for the Old Man. But these soldiers are dullards —they have poor memories and no imagination, and they follow

[14] Under Stalin, abortions were illegal in the U.S.S.R. since they offended against "Socialist standards of decency." After his death they were legalized in one of the first acts of liberalism.

[15] Vladimir Dekanosov, another of Beria's right-hand men, executed with the rest of his "gang" in December 1953.

[16] One of two gates kept open in the Kremlin, manned by Stalin's personal bodyguard.

[17] Major General Kosnykin, head of the Kremlin Guard. The circumstances of his death have always been a mystery.

like sheep. Still, I may yet prove a match for them, in which case I shall treat them like sheep!

Meanwhile the press campaign has died down in the last forty-eight hours. (Perhaps those obedient hacks are beginning to smell blood on the wind, and are looking to see which way it is blowing!) Nor has the Boss stirred from his den. Sometimes I wonder if, after more than thirty years of arse-licking servility he has grown careless in his old age. But no! Suspicion is too much a second nature to him—and, like the rest of us, he is awaiting his moment to strike.

This sudden silence, though, after so many weeks of frenzy, is indeed eerie. Nina and Sergei remain at Gagra, and sometimes I wonder if I will ever see them again. I try to keep my spirits up by having Rafik supply me with a regular store of girls—but they are the usual coarse, overeager whores from the Ministry. Really, there is no delicacy left!

At the estate I keep the boys on constant alert: even their spare moments are filled with pistol practice. (I myself have become proficient enough to hit a target in the head with a Tula .32 from fifty meters—even with my shaky hands!) I also have a new collection of long-playing records of Dinu Lipati's Chopin preludes, which help pass the long evenings.

The possibility of escape to the West still has its attractions: it would certainly be interesting to see how those smug bourgeois Americans would react to the appearance of the dreaded architect of Communist Terror himself! And, of course, even these random jottings would no doubt secure me a pretty fortune—and who can deny that a little nest egg of dollars is not something to cherish in one's old age? Better, at least, than ending one's days in a hut at Vorkuta!

Still, there would be dangers—and I am not thinking so much of a repetition of the Trotsky affair, but rather of the Nazi Hess. For who is to assure me that these softheaded bourgeois leaders will not take into their heads to treat me as a monster criminal? For while the Boss is still regarded by many Westerners as a heroic partner in the Great Patriotic War against fascism, I am a mere policeman with blood on his hands. I can just see those so-called Social Democrats climbing onto their moral pulpits to deliver a pious homily on the Rights of Man—remembering that I am the murderer of their late beloved Jan Masaryk, not to mention the Katyn affair. Nor would it be any good trying to shift the blame onto the Boss's shoulders—Nuremberg has taught us all that lesson! In any case, I can just hear the Old Man using all his velvet-voiced cunning to wheedle them over, offering to exchange me in return for some crafty new diplomatic ploy—perhaps a phony offer to intercede in the Korean problem? He would have them eating candy out of his hand, while they would take me and squeeze me for what information I have, then toss me away like a sucked orange.

Still, it is a happy pastime, just imagining what I could give those Westerners to think about!

But no. I have decided. Only one solution remains. The Boss is an old fruit who has grown overripe and turned bitter at the top of the tree. The time has come to shake him off.

There were three men in the parked car. The driver was a youth in a windbreaker sitting beside an older man with a flattened nose, who had a canvas carryall in his lap. They were both wearing leather gloves. The man in the back seat wore a dark suit and was smoking a cigarette through an ivory holder.

The car was an old Buick with stolen New York State license plates. Under the dashboard was a short-wave radio which was tuned to the wavelength of the local police patrol car.

It was a dark night, and blobs of summer rain were beginning to fall. The patrol car reported its position on East Forty-second Street, driving west. The man in the back seat consulted a gold watch and said, "Time to go. You have forty minutes." He spoke with a slight Middle European accent.

The other two got out and began walking up the pavement, past rows of darkened brownstone houses. They counted the numbers, then stopped. The youth in the windbreaker ran up the steps to a door with a brass panel on which was engraved Burn, Hirsch, Inc. The door was of dark polished wood with a triple security lock. Behind him the older man stood watching the street.

From inside his windbreaker the youth took a folded plastic bag containing what looked like a row of surgical instruments; he selected a short steel pin with two inverted hooks and inserted it into the first lock. Forty seconds later the door opened. No alarm went off. The youth entered the house, followed by the older man, who closed the door soundlessly behind him.

They both carried pencil flashlights. The older man led the way to the stairs. There was no elevator. On the first floor they stopped at a door marked EDITORIAL OFFICES. It was unlocked. Inside was a large room lined with desks, covered typewriters, In and Out trays heaped with papers, and a filing cabinet. The older man jabbed his thumb at the ceiling, and the youth returned to the stairs.

The older man went over to the filing cabinet. It was unlocked. He pulled out the drawer marked "B" and began riffling through a stack of documents, letters, press clippings, a few photographs of authors; but the only thing he removed was a cablegram that read: "ADVISE REBERIA THREE HUNDRED THOUSAND DOLLARS PAID GREGORY VOLKSKANTONALE BANK ZURICH DETTWEILER." It was dated eleven days ago. He took out a notebook and in a laborious hand copied the words down, then put the cablegram back and closed the file.

At that moment the young man appeared from upstairs. "Nothing in the desks. Just a safe—looks about a hundred years old. You should be able to crack it with a penknife."

The older man followed him upstairs to the third floor, where there was an open door marked S. MISKIN, EDITOR IN CHIEF. PRIVATE. Beyond lay a white-haired carpet, black leather chairs, curtains the color of a blood orange, an abstract nude, paneled refrigerator and drink cabinet, dictating machine, three telephones, a twenty-four-inch color television set and a miniature jacaranda tree. Behind the tree was the safe, which looked like

218

a Victorian trunk, with a brass handle and a dial with Roman numerals.

The older man opened his canvas carryall and took out a stethoscope, placed it against the door of the safe, and began gently turning the dial. The minutes passed. Headlights from passing cars swung across the ceiling; somewhere a police siren howled and died into a distant street.

The older man paused to look at his watch. "Fucking cast iron," he muttered. "They sure knew how to make 'em in those days! I may have to use the torch," he added, "but it'll take a good twenty minutes."

"Shall I go down and warn him?" said the young man.

"I'll give it one more try," said the other. "I got three of the combinations already. And he said not to make it look like a break-in."

Three minutes later there was a click, the brass handle pulled down and the iron door swung open. Inside were three shelves. On the first lay a heap of sealed documents; on the second, several stacks of dollar bills, still wrapped in their bank seals. Two of the piles were hundreds, the rest twenties and tens. The man left them untouched and turned to the top shelf. Here were a number of books bound in plain gray paper, and five carbon typescripts with blue plastic covers on which was printed the word BERIA, and underneath, in neat red ballpoint, *Not to be removed from office.* He took the top copy, closed the safe door, and said, "Right, let's go!"

Two minutes later they were back in the Buick. The older man handed the typescript and the copy of the telegram to the man in the back seat, who slipped both into a thick envelope marked *Herr Dietrich Rosch. Air Freight Express. Pan-Am— Copenhagen.* "Kennedy Airport," he said, "and make it fast— we do not have much time."

They reached the airport in thirty-five minutes. At the Pan-Am building the man in the back seat got out and hurried through the automatic doors, while the Buick headed back toward Manhattan.

He walked over to the air-freight counter, filled out a duplicate form, paid out thirty-five dollars, and handed the package to the girl behind the desk. Outside he hailed a taxi, giving an address on Long Island.

Pan-Am Flight 427 took off fifty minutes later. At 10 A.M. local time it landed at Kastrup Airport, Copenhagen, where a blond man with a Swiss passport which identified him as Herr Rosch collected the package and took it across to the Aeroflot counter. He spoke a few words to the man behind the desk, who opened the gate and showed him into the back office.

Two hours later the package left on Aeroflot's Flight 099 to Moscow. It arrived three hours and fifty minutes later, and was collected directly off the Ilyushin by two men who drove up to the plane in a ZIS sedan. In less than half an hour the package lay on a desk in the building in Dzerzhinsky Square with the inscription over the entrance KOMITET GOSUDARSTVENNOI BEZOPASNOSTI.

This course of events had been set in motion less than thirty-six hours earlier, when the editor in chief of Burn, Hirsch, Mr. Sy Miskin, had called a press conference in New York's Plaza Hotel. It had been attended by about a dozen journalists, most of whom were from the international news agencies, together with the literary editors of the more serious magazines.

The conference had been in progress for less than five minutes when it became clear that what Sy Miskin was breaking to them held the promise of a world political sensation. "But definitely not for the squeamish," Miskin had said, with his head wagging to one side, while the newsmen scribbled furiously in their notebooks.

He had gone on to explain that the original typescript had been written in the Georgian dialect Mingrelian, and that Burn, Hirsch had hired, under the greatest secrecy, three of the country's leading linguists to translate the work into English. The Mingrelian original had already been submitted to forensic experts, who had been able to confirm that both the paper and the make of typewriter were of Soviet origin, and between twenty and thirty years old. So far no evidence had been produced to prove that the typescript was not authentic.

Miskin's speech was followed by a barrage of questions, mostly centered around the identity of the man who had brought the typescript out of Russia.

"We have a signed affidavit," said Miskin, "at present lodged in a New York bank, from an East European citizen describing in detail how the work was smuggled from the Soviet Union into a certain satellite state, from which it was then brought by a second party to the West."

"How much is Burn, Hirsch paying for the book?" someone asked.

Miskin hesitated. Charles Whitmore had been reluctant to disclose any details about the option or the full price until the work was published.

"It is in excess of one million dollars," Miskin said at last, "which entitles us to world exclusive rights."

There were several more questions as to whether the State Department had been consulted on the possible political repercussions—to which Miskin declined to comment—and what opinions, if any, the Sovietologists had given on the book. To this Miskin replied that Professor Otto Krull, of the Harvard Center for International Affairs, had been unable to find any positive reason to doubt the authenticity of the work.

On this point he thanked the newsmen and declared the conference closed.

AP and UPI flashed the first bulletin on the wires at just after 8:45 P.M. Eastern time. Ten minutes later a copy was on the desk of a junior official at the State Department, and another with the Central Intelligence Agency at Langley, Virginia.

Tass monitored the report—which it pirated off the wires without paying for the service—at 4 A.M. Moscow time. The bureau immediately called the American desk of the Foreign Ministry, where the night duty officer decided that the news merited a call on the secret line to the home of the Deputy Foreign Minister. After some deliberation the Minister rang the Foreign Minister, Andrei Gromyko.

Gromyko's response was prompt. A top-level conference would be held at the ministry at 7 A.M. at which Yuri Andropov would preside in his capacity as Chairman of the Committee for State Security. At this conference a single decision was reached: an official of the Soviet Embassy in Washington would fly direct to New York and contact a man called Rittinger, a naturalized Lithuanian who ran a small photographic agency and did occasional errands for the embassy, dealing mostly in low-grade classified information. He was not thought to be under suspicion from the U.S. authorities, and also had contacts with the New York underworld. Rittinger would arrange, for a payment of three thousand dollars, to hire a pair of burglars to do a second-story job on the offices of Burn, Hirsch, and procure a copy of the English translation.

As soon as the typescript reached KGB headquarters, a team of English-language experts were engaged on a twenty-four-hour rota in compiling a detailed synopsis of the work (there was no time to render it into a complete Russian translation), with orders that it be ready on Chairman Andropov's desk by noon next day.

Meanwhile, the State Department had requested that copies of the book be delivered to it at once, with the undertaking that the work would be treated as a classified document. Miskin telephoned this request to Whitmore, who had already anticipated it and gave his assent.

At the same time Miskin was seriously disturbed by the discovery of the missing carbon copy of the translation. He discreetly questioned all the staff who had access to his office, but without result. He had the whole building searched, then checked with the typing firm that had made copies of the typescript, but still without success. There was no sign of a break-in, and Miskin did not report the incident to the police, or to Whitmore, since he was aware that the copies should have been deposited at once in the bank, along with the Mingrelian original.

That same day, the English typescript was delivered to the printers, on the understanding that the work be undertaken only by the most reliable men, and that the proof copies be delivered within ten days. Miskin also had to fend off a number of demands from Professor Krull's academic rivals that they too be allowed to study the work and give their own opinions as to its authenticity.

By evening Miskin had swallowed three tranquilizers and four double martinis, before disconnecting his private phone and falling into an exhausted sleep, praying that the next few weeks would not turn up some drastic revelation to destroy the greatest project of his career.

Alexander Dimitrov, known to his friends and colleagues as Sasha, was deputy feature editor of a Moscow magazine with the largest circulation in the world—some thirty million readers, mostly among the youth from all over the Soviet Union.

On the afternoon following the high-level conference at KGB headquarters, he left his offices and entered his chauffeur-driven Mercedes 280, put his feet up on the front seat, and lit a Romeo y Julieta from a pigskin case.

The driver had the engine running; he glared at Sasha in the mirror and started the car with an angry jolt. Sasha was nearly twenty minutes late for his appointment at Dzerzhinsky Square, but he was not worried. He gave the impression of being worried by very little. His position in the Soviet hierarchy was both unique and paradoxical. Besides his job with the magazine, he was an official adviser to the Ministry of Culture and an unofficial adviser to the KGB. During the "Thaw" after 1956 he had gained the reputation of being one of the brightest young "liberal" stars in the early Khrushchev days, when he had been responsible for many controversial Western books and films appearing in Russia. He had also traveled widely in the West; spoke fluent French, German, Italian, and English with a transatlantic accent; and was on close terms with the leading intelligentsia in these countries. He also had a detailed knowledge not only of the Western cultural scene, but also of the workings and psychology of the various Western mass media. It was on account of this that the Committee for State Security had called on him in this threatening crisis over the alleged Beria papers.

Sasha was a tall, dashing man in his early forties, though he looked younger: very dark-skinned for a Russian, with sloping eyebrows, black and glossy like horsehair. In Paris he had been described as *"le type cowboy"*—an image which he enjoyed cultivating. Today he was wearing a dust-colored jacket over a floral shirt unbuttoned at the throat, with his tie pulled loose; he also needed a shave.

There was a heat wave in Moscow, and the driver had closed all the windows and turned on the car's air conditioning. It was a five-minute drive to the KGB headquarters, and after a moment Sasha picked up a battery-operated electric shaver off the shelf under the back window and began rubbing it across his dark jaw.

He knew that his association with the Committee was constantly precarious. Many senior officials and *apparatchiki* despised and distrusted him; but the more astute Party leaders realized his worth. Apart from his specialized knowledge and experience, Sasha was the joker in the pack. Important Western visitors, depressed by the gloom and rigidity of the regime, were delighted and reassured by him; he confirmed their happiest illusions about the Russians: he drank and womanized and made irreverent jokes at the expense of the regime. But above all he was a loyal Party member. The numbing bureaucracy of the system, the police interference, censorship, the suppression of the arts, were all things he considered transitory. Sasha Dimitrov was an ambitious romantic; he was also a shameless *bon viveur,* living on an extravagant salary in a four-room apartment overlooking the River Moskva and a dacha on the Black Sea. His masters had judged him accurately: there was little danger of his defecting; he had too much to lose.

The Mercedes drew up outside the six-story building in Dzerzhinsky Square. Sasha showed his pass at the door, straightened his tie, still without fastening his top button, and rode up in the elevator to the fourth floor.

MALLORY'S REPORT

Five days after Miskin's news conference, Tatana and I had lunch with Frank Smollett in the Wig and Pen Club at the top of Fleet Street.

We had flown in from Paris the day before and were staying at a hotel in South Kensington, where we'd registered as Mr. and Mrs. Forster. Boris, who had remained in Paris for what he called *"un séjour gastronomique,"* had meanwhile transferred from his numbered Swiss account in the name of J. Gregory enough money into my London bank to clear my ancient overdraft and leave me with a few hundred pounds in hand. (I was trusting him to settle our finances more equitably when the full payment was made on publication day.)

Two days before, I had telephoned Frank Smollett from Paris and told him I had someone important I would like him to meet, but emphasized that it would be a delicate meeting and begged him to remain moderately sober.

Tatana played her part impeccably. She was dressed in demure black and wore no makeup, her manner remote and nervous. In the bar she asked for a sherry, while Smollett ordered himself a large whisky. "With water?" asked the barman. "Water? I wouldn't drink water!" Smollett cried. "Fish fuck in it." The barman had evidently heard the joke before and did not even smile; but for a moment I thought Tatana's façade was going to crack into laughter. She managed to restrain herself, and even appear mildly shocked, while I diffidently introduced her to Smollett as a friend I had met at a reunion dinner at King's, leading into her background gradually, casually, careful not to give Smollett the least hint that he was being set up for a story. I was merely doing an old colleague a favor, as I'd promised him in Budapest.

Tatana spoke very little and left her meal almost untouched. She answered Smollett's questions obliquely, often in monosyllables, until I began to fear that Smollett might even lose interest. I had finished my steak-and-kidney pie, and Smollett was through the best part of a bottle of burgundy, when I said, "Frank, it's about these Beria papers the Americans say they've got hold of."

"Oh, yes?"

"Tatana knew Beria. At least, she had one encounter with him. A most unpleasant one." I turned to her, and she dropped her eyes.

"Please! It was awful. Horrible."

For a moment none of us spoke. "Would you rather not talk about it?" I said at last, putting my hand on her arm.

She took a sip of wine and said, "I suppose if it's very important . . ." She gave Smollett a quick, almost beseeching look. "You tell him, Tom. I can't bear to think about it—even after all this time."

I took a deep breath and nodded. "I'll tell you, Frank, because I think it's honestly in the interests of history. But on one condition. I don't want Tatana harried by your people. She's going abroad tomorrow and this will be the only chance you have to talk to her." Then I told him the whole story: how she

227

had been a pupil at the Bolshoi Junior Ballet School in 1952 when she'd been twelve years old: how Beria's car had drawn up at some Moscow traffic lights and his aide-de-camp had got out and asked her to come that evening to the house in Malaya Nikitskaya . . . Here Smollett took out his notebook and asked me how to spell the name. At the same time Tatana excused herself and retired to the ladies'.

I continued with a brutal account of her subsequent rape, and how the next day her father had been summoned to the Lubyanka and had disappeared. When I was through, Smollett gave a chortle. "Christ, you should be back in journalism! But how do we prove all this is true?"

"You don't think it's the kind of story a girl like that would make up, do you?"

Smollett's pink eyes squinted at me across the table. "What's she getting out of it, old boy? Or you, for that matter?"

I paused. There was no harm done in his thinking we had come to him out of mercenary motives. "That's up to you and your editor," I said at last. "I'm not so worried, but she's pretty broke, poor girl. A few hundred quid would help her a lot."

Smollett frowned into his glass. "I'll have to talk to my editor first. And he'll probably want to see her, too. It's not so much the question of money—it's proving the damned thing. And as you say, this could turn out to be a very big story."

"Well, let's look at it from another angle," I said. "According to this American publisher, these diaries of Beria are full of his sexual escapades. And it's a generally known fact that he was keen on very young girls. It's quite possible that he describes this story himself."

Smollett gave me a leery grin. "You wouldn't by any chance have read these diaries, would you? I mean, you weren't in Budapest just for Flanagan's piss-up. And would I be far wrong if I were to guess that you met up with that Hungarian poet in order to collect these diaries and bring them out?"

I stared him in the eye. "No comment, Frank."

He chuckled. "If you *were* the courier you must have made a mint!"

"When these diaries appear there's going to be one hell of a stink. And the people involved are going to have to be bloody careful."

At that moment Tatana returned. Whether she had applied a little makeup or not I couldn't tell, but she looked paler than when she'd left us. She sat down without a word.

Smollett looked at her and said, "Tatana, would you mind very much coming back this afternoon and meeting my editor? He's a very understanding fellow. It's just that a story like this—" he waved his hand vaguely—"it's too big for me to decide on myself. Especially if you're going abroad tomorrow."

There followed several minutes of ritual argument, while I ordered her a large brandy, after which she began to relent, and finally agreed to accompany Smollett to his office. I settled the bill and saw them both into a taxi; but just before it drove away I said to Smollett, "If you drop her or me in the shit, Frank, I'll bust you to the Inland Revenue."

He laughed. "With over a million dollars in the kitty, old boy, you can change your name, get a new passport, new nationality —even get yourself fixed up with a bit of plastic surgery!"

"So long," I said, "and I'll be reading your column very carefully in the next few weeks." I smiled briefly at Tatana and watched the taxi drive away past the Law Courts.

Smollett's editor was a quiet, even diffident man, she told me later that evening. He had been very sympathetic, very reasonable, and, despite his controlled manner, obviously excited. She eventually allowed herself to be persuaded to have a photograph taken; and it was finally decided to postpone publication of her story until the Beria book was published—which, according to the editor's latest information from New York, was scheduled for a couple of weeks' time. He had drawn up a contract with her, under which she undertook to discuss her experiences with absolutely no one; then had written her out a check for five hundred pounds.

That evening she was in high spirits and stood me dinner at Wilton's. Next morning we flew back to Paris.

PART
SIX

It's a double pleasure to trick the trickster.
                    —La Fontaine

Paper Six

Moscow, February 1953
Last night received a summons to Kuntsevo for Saturday night.
The Boss gave no reason, though he appears at last to be giving
one of his dinners again. As a farewell, perhaps? But for him or
for us? For Georgi M. tells me that he is sick, in body as well
as mind.

I thought of refusing, but this would only postpone matters.
The only precaution I am taking is to bring along Nadoraya and
two carloads of the boys.

Meanwhile, I have made my plan—confiding it only to Rafik,
who will, of course, take the secret to his grave. The Boss, I told
him, has arrested the one man in Russia who can save his life:
Vinogradov.[1] On the other hand, everyone knows how we Georgians can defy Nature and live to be over a hundred! And
although the Boss's health may be in decline, there is no absolute
guarantee that this is the end. I therefore came to the conclusion
that our best hope lay now with Lukomsky.[2] As a member of the

---

[1] Professor V. N. Vinogradov, a leading Soviet heart specialist.

[2] Professor P. E. Lukomsky, another leading Soviet cardiologist, who escaped
the Doctors' Plot and is known to have attended Stalin in his last hours. Believed to be still alive.

233

Soviet Academy of Medical Science he has so far escaped the Plot —but his arrest can only be a matter of time.

We therefore agreed that the boys should pick him up in the morning in one of the unofficial cars and bring him straight to me —not to my office or Malaya Nikitskaya, but to Rafik's place on the Arbat.

He arrived pale and shaking. He is an old man, obviously not in the peak of condition himself. I offered him a glass of the finest French cognac, and this steadied his nerves enough for me to be able to talk to him man to man. I began by giving him a brief account of what I had heard of the Boss's present state of health. (I am no medical expert and was careful to add nothing that might prejudice his final diagnosis.)

"He is seriously ill," I told him. "However, he may live for a few more weeks—perhaps months. And in that time you know well what can happen!" I could tell by Lukomsky's face that he did not need reminding. Then I said straight out, "Now, look, Comrade Professor! For you the choice is a simple one. Either you cooperate with me or you wait till the Boss has you picked up with the others and beaten to a powder. So which is it to be? You are an expert on heart diseases. And you know the Boss's drinking habits. It should not be difficult for you to arrange for that old heart of his to stop beating."

He sat with his empty glass in both hands, and his face was streaming with sweat, although it was a cold day and the heating in the apartment was not excessive. I then spent some time trying to put him at ease. I pointed out that I could be a useful friend in these troubled times—that I had at my personal command more than one million troops, which made me indisputedly the second most powerful man in the Soviet Union. This seemed to calm him slightly, though he was obviously still in a state of shock and ter- ror. Nor was I entirely at ease myself, for there was always the chance that this old doctor might try to curry favor with the Boss and his cronies by going straight to them and reporting our meet- ing. So I was careful to point out to him that I still commanded the ear of the Boss, and that one word from me would be enough to ensure a bullet in the Professor's neck.

He began to bluster that he was under constant surveillance, etc., but I assured him that Rafik would deal with that problem. At three o'clock that afternoon he returned to Rafik's apartment and handed me four blue capsules. He said they were a new American drug, originally developed as a pain-killer for cancer; the normal dose was one every four hours, but administered in one dose they would induce a coma whose first symptoms were deep sleep, and later stentorious breathing, such as after a heavy night's drinking. They were quite tasteless, and effective within a couple of hours; but he warned me that with a strong constitution the coma could last sometimes for a few days, unless the dose was repeated.

I gave the old Professor another cognac, and made it clear that if his knowledge was in any way defective, he would wish he had never passed his medical exams. He left in a sober mood.

Moscow, March 1953

At five yesterday afternoon[3] Poskrebyshev phoned and spoke to Rafik, telling him that we were all to meet the Boss in the Kremlin cinema at 8 P.M.

When I arrived I found all the familiar faces: Georgi M., Khrushchev, Mikoyan—even the wretched Molotov and that coxcomb Voroshilov. In fact, it was quite like old times. The Boss seemed in better health than I had expected, though he looked gray and wizened, and moved slowly, with his withered arm stiff at his side. I was also struck, for perhaps the first time, by how small he was.

But he greeted us all with an almost exaggerated *bonhomie;* and when it came to my turn he punched me playfully in the ribs and cried, "So, my good Prosecutor, you have not been idle during this

[3] Saturday, February 28, 1953—the last known social appearance of Stalin before he fell ill.

235

new Witches' Sabbath! I see your men have occupied the Kremlin?" There was the usual glint in his eyes, as I replied, "I was acting in the interests of special vigilance and security, Master."

He turned away and cracked a few jokes with the others, even teasing Molotov on how pale he looked. "You should take some fresh air, Scriabin![4] Get away from that desk of yours and do some honest work!"

I could see it was not going to be an easy evening.

The film we watched was a prewar French one about gangsters, but I paid little attention to it. Afterward we all rode out in convoy to Kuntsevo. The Boss made no comment about Nadoraya and his two cars full of my Georgians. When we got to the dacha I observed that he began drinking more than was usual for him. He also seemed in surprisingly good spirits, and continued joking with us—which included forcing Molotov to swallow half a bottle of French burgundy before he would allow him to sit down at the table.

The hours seemed to pass slowly. And I noticed that the Old Man's color grew worse; his eyes had a dull glazed look and his speech had begun to lose its customary fire. It was not until past 3 A.M. that I got my chance, when he retired with several others to the toilet, leaving his wineglass almost full. I broke open Lukomsky's capsules, as he had instructed—all four of them—and found they dissolved easily.

I had a bad moment when he came back and took the wrong glass, which I pointed out with a laugh was Voroshilov's and might easily be poisoned. He took this in good heart, although the Marshal turned the color of toilet paper.

The party broke up about an hour later, with the Boss saying he was tired. I must say I have never been more pleased to see Nadoraya and his boys waiting in the cars outside!

[4] Scriabin was Molotov's family name, of noble origin, before he took the pseudonym "Hammer Man." Stalin's form of address was clearly derogatory.

Moscow, March 1953

Georgi M. was the first to raise the alarm. It was after midnight on Sunday. Apparently, they had let him sleep through the day—as was routine after one of his late-night sessions—but Khrustalyov[5] had raised the alarm when there was still no movement by midnight. He had been found asleep on the floor of his study. They had let him sleep on, having put him on the sofa which he used as a bed, but had later become anxious, and Georgi M. had called Khrushchev.

At this time I still had heard nothing. Then in the afternoon Georgi called to say that the Boss was definitely very ill and that Lukomsky had been summoned. (I had already insisted that L. was the only remaining doctor at large who was up to dealing with the Boss's complaints.)

When I got to the dacha he was still in a coma. The Professor was there, looking the perfect part in his black suit, with a black bag. The others had also already arrived—including his daughter, who seemed very composed, with a certain poetic sadness about her, although she had less reason to love and respect her father than most of us.

At 7 A.M. Lukomsky told us there was little point in our staying. Just before I left, I had the chance of a word with him, and he told me that the coma might last two or three days—to which I replied that if he changed his mind and decided to be indiscreet, my word would always be accepted before his. I could see he took my meaning to heart.

Two nights later the Boss's condition deteriorated rapidly. We were all called to the Kremlin inner study, where Poskrebyshev told us that he believed the Old Man was dying. (It was the only

5 Chief of Stalin's personal bodyguard.

237

time I have ever noticed the least trace of sentiment in the man, except when he broke down over the business with his wife.) I must say I too experienced a curious sensation at the news; it was almost like hearing of the approaching death of a stern and dreaded father—an emotion which would no doubt be shared by most of the common people.

Next day he regained consciousness, and for a bad moment I thought that either Lukomsky had failed me or the Old Man's Georgian constitution had proved too strong even for the Americans' new drug.

He was still lying on the sofa in the little downstairs room he used as a study. Several times he half opened his eyes and tried to speak, but the words were unintelligible, and his breathing was tight and shallow like an asthmatic's. He also looked very small and shrunken, his pocked skin like a slice of stale bread; and gazing down at him, so stricken and helpless, it was hard to believe that this was the man who had ruled the Soviet Union with an iron fist for thirty-one years—who had made Roosevelt jump through hoops, and had even outwitted the crafty Churchill.

We took turns watching over him, while a nurse fed him tea, which he could hardly swallow. Svetlana was also there, holding his hand when he was not in a coma. Sometime in the afternoon Lukomsky, pale and perspiring, and looking close to death himself, declared there was little more he could do. Poskrebyshev, who had never left the room, now called in a quack to apply leeches to the back of his neck—insisting that it was a time-honored ritual among the Russian peasants, which would assure them everything had been done to save the Boss's life.

At the same time, his son Vasily appeared, reeling drunk, shouting and moaning and playing a besotted Hamlet, until we had him thrown out. He then began abusing the servants in the kitchens, until Nadoraya's men drove him home. Some people have no respect!

There were other doctors and nurses there now, and the Boss was fortunately in a coma again when the leeches were applied; I

238

had to leave the room and get myself a drink. The end could not be long now.

It came at 9:30 P.M., when he began to make a horrible croaking noise. His face went mauve, almost black, and saliva drooled from his mouth. It went on for twenty minutes, as though he were being strangled.

At 9:50 he was pronounced dead. Poskrebyshev had already alerted Radio Moscow with the final bulletin that we had prepared earlier in the day; and also instructed the radio station to stand by with Tchaikovsky's Sixth. The others, including the doctors and nurses, were gathered around the sofa, many of them in tears. I saw no point in waiting, and drove back to the city.

I called Rafik at once and told him to prepare the Special Purpose Forces and a unit of riot-control troops, together with tanks and flamethrowers—both in case of panic and against the possibility of one of the others trying to pull a fast one.

Radio Moscow, on our instructions, did not announce the news till 8 A.M. Almost immediately large crowds began gathering in the Arbat and along the river, converging on Red Square. Khrushchev had taken charge of the funeral arrangements, and Lukomsky—I was relieved to hear—was to carry out the autopsy. At 4 P.M. he announced that the Boss had died of a hemorrhage to the center and left of the brain. The body was then taken to the Kremlin mortuary to be embalmed.

By evening the streets and squares were filled with crowds, most of them weeping hysterically. By 9 P.M. I observed that the situation was getting out of control. I called Rafik and had him block off all the side streets leading to Red Square. Unfortunately, this led to panic, as some of the crowds were being forced forward, while the rest could not get out, and many casualties have been reported.[6]

[6] According to eyewitness accounts, including those of the poet Yevgeny Yevtushenko, more than 500 people in Moscow were crushed to death by Beria's riot trucks, and many thousands injured, as the grief-stricken crowds tried to storm the Hall of Columns where Stalin's body was lying in state.

All the while the Kremlin bell has been tolling, the radio playing *La Pathétique* and Chopin's *Funeral March*. Today the body lies in the Hall of Columns, where it will remain for three days. In the city order has finally been restored.

So sets the "Shining Sun of Humanity."

Sasha Dimitrov arrived in London one week after *The Beria Papers* had appeared in the American bookstores. The latest edition of *Time* proclaimed it top of the best-seller list, while the magazine also queried whether Brezhnev, Kosygin, Marshal Grechko *et al.* could survive the allegations; *The New York Times*, in a strong editorial, asserted that, genuine or not, *The Beria Papers* were a dangerous precedent in smear campaigns against world leaders. The Soviet press remained ominously mute. The Royal Institute of International Affairs in London had given its opinion that the book was not genuine, as it had done in the case of the Khrushchev memoirs; and a handful of left-wing M.P.s had introduced a motion in the House of Commons asking if the Attorney-General could not issue an injunction to prevent the book from appearing in Britain, where bidding for the rights was hectic. Outside the Communist bloc, only Finland—notoriously sensitive about upsetting her powerful neighbor—had banned the book. Burn, Hirsch had sold out its edition of 100,000 and was reprinting 250,000; an unsuccessful homemade bomb had been tossed through the

241

ground-floor windows of its offices on East Forty-fourth Street, and the U.S. paperback rights had been sold for two million dollars. Charles E. Whitmore had even consented to give a small party in the book's honor, calling the work "an important but lurid contribution to modern history."

Before leaving Moscow, Sasha Dimitrov had received a copy of the American edition, for which he had had to sign four receipts, as well as a written undertaking that he would communicate it to no one and would hand it back on his return. He had read it on the plane from Moscow to London, and had been morbidly amused. It was a good hoax. He did not believe that a man as calculating as Beria would ever have committed such dangerous words to paper; policemen took minutes, they recorded names and dates and meetings, they did not indulge in lewd, self-incriminating confessions. Besides, they were too busy. Still, there was that tiny doubt at the back of Sasha's mind, which made him all the more anxious to track down the authors and call them to account.

His visit to Britain had been arranged without trouble under the auspices of the Arts Council. Officially he was there to facilitate an exchange between a leading London drama company and the Mayakovsky Theater. He was booked into the Strand Palace Hotel and paid only a fleeting visit to his embassy, where he contacted the committee's chief agent in Britain who gave him a list of possible contacts. At the top of this, as Sasha had anticipated, was Mrs. T. Bernstein, nee Shumara.

Sasha was aware that the latter was a Georgian name. On the other hand, there were many Russians with names of Georgian origin who did not speak a word of the language. At the same time, the possibility that this Mrs. Bernstein had described a true incident had to be considered seriously. The files showed that her father had disappeared in the early fifties, although the details were not recorded, since most of the dossiers kept during the Beria period had been either destroyed or "mislaid."

Sasha's first visit was to Cambridge, where he posed, as he

242

frequently did in Britain, as an American graduate student. At King's College he learned from the head porter that he had understood Miss Shumara was going to stay there for the long vacation, but that she had left suddenly over two months ago without even giving a forwarding address, and the college hadn't heard from her since, except for the interview in last Sunday's newspaper.

Sasha then interviewed her tutor, a former White Russian who lived out at Huntingdon. He was a garrulous, foolish old man who thought highly of Miss Shumara—so intelligent and beautiful, with the manners of a true aristocrat and the melancholic gaiety of a gypsy! No, she had not told him where she was going, but he thought she had probably gone abroad to escape further publicity over the terrible incident in her childhood. He feared that she had been forced to sell the story to the newspaper for money—she was very poor, and had to make do on a small grant from the college. "Poor child! To have to be exposed to such infamy—and after all these years!"

"You wouldn't happen to know, sir," Sasha asked casually as he was about to take his leave, "if she speaks Georgian?"

"Certainly," replied the old man. "She *is* Georgian. And her Russian is excellent, too."

Later that day Sasha made inquiries about her friends in the university, but by the little he learned she seemed to have led a solitary life, and the few people she did know were away for the summer vacation.

Sasha's next appointment, back in London, was with Frank Smollett—and here he struck it lucky. He introduced himself as an American writer who was working on a book about the British press. He had read and admired Smollett's column, and wanted to pick his brains about the workings of Fleet Street. Next day he invited Smollett to lunch at the Connaught.

His embassy contact had already informed him of Smollett's weakness for alcohol, and Sasha prepared to take advantage of it. He began by suggesting that they have a Bikini Special—

243

named after the Bomb, not the bathing costume. He instructed the waiter on its ingredients: a large bourbon, benedictine, a dash of green chartreuse and a twist of lemon. After three of these they went in to lunch: roast beef and a bottle of Mouton Rothschild '61. It was Monday, a day of rest on a Sunday paper; and by the end of the meal, which was washed down by a couple of large brandies each, Smollett suggested an afternoon drinking club in Soho where there was an excellent Negro pianist.

Toward five o'clock, and the end of a second bottle of Krug, Smollett had become wild-eyed and drooping, until Sasha decided it was the moment to strike. Casually he mentioned the Shumara–Beria story, and Smollett responded with a hoarse cackle:

"Lovely girl! Fucked at the age of twelve. Just fancy. You like that kind o' thing? Y'know, Lolita stuff?"

Sasha strung him along for a few minutes, discussing the virtues of very young girls, then asked Smollett how he had come by the story.

"S'pose to be hush-hush, old boy—promised the bloke not to tell, and the girl's sworn to secrecy. Disappeared—dunno where."

Sasha was careful not to press the point. He poured Smollett the last of the bottle, and after he had drunk it Smollett said, "Tell you the truth, the whole business was bloody weird. You read about that shindig in Budapest last month—the Flanagan birthday party—and how a couple of blokes were thrown out?" Sasha had not heard the story. Smollett went on: "I was there. Not at the party. But had this friend, author bloke, used to be a journalist—turned up at the hotel and got an invitation. He went with some Hungarian—old ex-Communist who writes poetry. They got into some kind of fight with Flanagan—this Mallory bloke had been in the revolution as a student and got all steamed up and lost his temper."

"Mallory?" said Sasha gently.

244

"Yeah. Tom Mallory. Writes novels. Don't know whether you've ever heard of him. Shall we have another bottle of bubbly?"

"If you like. Let me pay, though."

"Piss off. Only members are 'lowed to pay."

"That'll be ten quid, Frank," said the barman, a chunky young man with carefully waved hair.

"Put it down on the slate, Tony. And give us 'nuther bottle."

"How did this man Mallory fit in with the girl?" said Sasha as Tony popped the cork and filled their glasses.

"Rang me up and introduced me to her. Out o' the blue. And you know what my editor paid her. Five hundred bloody quid! And without anything to go on 'cept her word. Mind you, Mallory's straight. Come to think of it, I shouldn't be telling you all this. Off the record, understand? But I'd say the girl's story was probably true. No reason to make a thing up like that—and anyway, it's in the book. Y'read it?"

"Not yet, I'm afraid," Sasha lied.

"Bloody hot stuff. Wouldn't wonder if it brought down half the bloody Kremlin!"

"This guy Mallory lives in London, does he?" said Sasha.

"No. Got a job in Germany—some radio station, working for the Americans. Munich, I think. Then he got the push, or his contract finished—anyway, he's gone back abroad again." Smollett suddenly fixed Sasha with an angry squint. "What d'yer want to know for, anyway? You got some special angle on this? CIA, perhaps?" He turned to the barman. "Hey, Tony, I think p'raps we got a member of the CIA here! Is that against the club rules?"

"Not so long as you pay your bills, Frank. You got sixty-eight pounds on the slate now."

"Ah, fuck off," Smollett said cheerfully. He turned back to Sasha. "You really a writer?"

"Well, I write books," Sasha smiled.

"Oh, yes. Don't s'pose I read any. Don't get much time to

read these days. You gonna write a book about this Beria business? Book about the book? Bloody good story, I reckon. You're not drinking," Smollett added accusingly.

"I'm fine," said Sasha, picking up his full glass and pretending to sip it.

"Tell you what I think," said Smollett, "if you promise you're not the fucking CIA."

Sasha laughed. "Do I really look that bad?"

"You look too bloody sober. Now, swear on the Krug! Say 'I swear . . .'" They went through a ponderous ritual in which the barman was made to act as witness.

"Well, I'll tell you what I think," Smollett continued at last. "Can't do much harm now the story's broken. I think Mallory was in Budapest to contact this Hungarian and collect the Beria book. I dunno how he got onto the girl—'cept he said he met her at Cambridge. Bit of a coincidence, if my hunch is right. But that's my opinion—for free!"

"Do you know who this Hungarian was?"

"Oldish fellow. Looked like a death's head. Had some crazy name, but Mallory said it wasn't his real one. All very hush-hush, old boy."

Sasha nodded and did not pursue the matter. Instead he tried asking Smollett more about Mallory, but Smollett's reply, when it was coherent, might have fitted most Englishmen in their mid-thirties. The barman was making another halfhearted attempt to get him to settle his account, but the man was now irretrievably drunk. He stumbled into the hall to telephone a girl; and Sasha slipped into the toilet, where he began to scribble down the information he had just learned, under the notes he had taken after his trip to Cambridge—*Shumara, Tatana (Bernstein). Israeli passport. Georgian origin. Left Cambridge six weeks before B. announcement. Interview ten days before publication. Alleged poor but has money to travel.*

To this he now added: *Mallory, Tom. Novelist, youngish. Recently worked U.S. radio station. W. Germany. Munich? Intro-*

246

duced Shumara to Smollett. Was in Budapest for film star Flan-
agan party. (Check date.) Accompanied by elderly Hungarian
ex-Party poet from whom M. alleged collected B. MSS.

When he got back to the club room he found Smollett lolling against the bar.

"If I was you, sir, I'd take him home," said the barman.

Sasha smiled and heaved Smollett up under the arms and carried him like a child down the narrow staircase into the street. He was worried at first about what he was going to do with him, when suddenly, with the reflex of the experienced alcoholic, Smollett became both articulate and mobile.

"Got to get home, old boy. Got to make some calls."

At that moment Sasha saw an empty cab. Smollett crawled into it and was just able to give an address, then slumped back as the driver pulled out into the traffic along Shaftesbury Avenue.

Sasha Dimitrov wondered how much of their conversation Smollett would remember in the morning.

The first thing that Sasha did next day was to go to the National Book League, where he found the name of Thomas Mallory's publishers. Then he went to a phone box, following one of the Committee's basic rules for agents in the West: all local calls must be made from public phones, and all foreign calls put through the Soviet Embassy; for even a cultural envoy like Sasha Dimitrov could not be certain that his line from the Strand Palace Hotel was not tapped.

A girl secretary at the publishers' told him that Mr. Mallory was abroad and that they had heard nothing from him for several months; the last address they had had was Apartment C, 25 Elisabethstrasse, Munich, but she understood that he had now left there. She suggested that Sasha call his agent, and gave him the number.

247

Another girl answered the second call. Sasha told her he was anxious to contact Mallory about a business deal; he gave his name as Bob Manning, a scout for one of the big American movie companies. The girl told him to hold on. A couple of minutes later a man's voice came on the line: "Can I help you, Mr. Manning? My name's Hennison."

Sasha said he was in London for a short stopover and had an important message for Mr. Mallory, and could he know where to contact him?

The voice sounded doubtful. "Mr. Mallory's abroad at the moment."

"Where?"

Hennison hesitated. "He phoned me last week to say he doesn't want to be disturbed—he's working. But I can take any message for him."

"I gotta talk to him myself," Sasha said.

"I'm sorry, Mr. Manning, but, as I told you, my client left his instructions. You know how neurotic these authors get when they're working?" There was humor in the voice, but Sasha was not rising to it.

"How the hell am I expected to do business with him, then?"

"You can do business with me—that's what I'm here for," said the agent smoothly.

Sasha blustered: he was assigned to ask Mallory to do a treatment of his last book, and in order to arrange this he must talk to him personally. No, he could not meet the agent; he was only in London for twenty-four hours before flying back to L.A. All he wanted was to call Mallory, put the proposition and get yes or no. "There's three thousand bucks for him," he said finally, "in advance. And another three thousand when the treatment's finished."

"I can call him myself," said the agent, "and ring you back."

"Listen, Mr.—" The pips sounded, and Sasha put in another coin. "Mr. Hennison, I can't talk business with your client through a third party—that's not the way I operate. If your

248

client insists on playing hide-and-seek, then someone else gets the job."

There followed a silence. When Hennison's voice came back, it was quietly resigned. "All right, Mr. Manning. He's at a little place in France. Telephone, Verdun-sur-le-Doubs twelve. Department of Saône-et-Loire." He spelled both names, which Sasha scribbled down.

"Thank you, Mr. Hennison. You'll be hearing from me." Sasha hung up and now called International Inquiries, and asked for the number and subscriber's name of Apartment C, 25 Elisabethstrasse, Munich. A voice with polite Asiatic precision said that it was a number without a subscriber's name. Sasha then rang Verdun-sur-le-Doubs 12 and was told it was the Hôtellerie Bourguignonne.

He took a taxi to the grim Soviet Embassy mansion in Kensington Palace Gardens. Here a room had been put at his disposal, from which he called the Committee headquarters in Moscow and instructed them to contact their agent in Munich —a man called Eckhardt, who was in the export-import business. Eckhardt would call a number which belonged to a Chinese restaurant off Queensway. This, unknown to the proprietors, was one of half a dozen drop numbers used by Soviet intelligence in the London area.

Eckhardt was a competent agent who had worked for the KGB for ten years and earned good money; but he was known to have no political loyalties, and recently, during a severe appraisal of the Committee's Western free-lance employees, there had been suspicions that he might not be devoting his entire energies for the benefit of Moscow. At least one report had hinted—though without any proof—that he had been selling material to the Gehlen organization, the West German intelligence agency. Since then Eckhardt had been entrusted only with small local assignments, while all important work was handled by the Bonn and West Berlin bureaus.

Eckhardt arranged to call the drop number that afternoon.

Meanwhile, Sasha invented an excuse to postpone his negotiations with the Arts Council and booked himself first-class on the noon flight next day to Paris. He also passed on what information he had so far gathered to his contact at the embassy, who switched on a tape recorder as soon as Sasha began to speak and listened without interrupting.

Sasha was in the middle of his Chinese lunch when Eckhardt's call came through, at just after three. Sasha instructed him to find out the name of the occupant of Apartment C, 25 Elisabethstrasse, and everything else that could be discovered about the man, such as nationality, profession, how long he had lived there, and any guests or subtenants he might have had over the past year. He also told Eckhardt to check with the two anti-Soviet propaganda stations in Munich, Radio Free Europe and Radio Liberty, and learn what he could about an Englishman called Thomas Mallory—what work he had done for RFE and for how long—and to make discreet inquiries at the Radio Liberty archive library as to whether this Mallory had had access to any of their files, and if possible find out which period these had covered.

Eckhardt agreed to call back next day at ten, to another drop number, this time at a coffee bar in Earl's Court Road.

When Sasha returned to the embassy, his contact informed him that a Thomas Mallory had recently been involved in a much publicized incident in Budapest, and went on to corroborate Smollett's account of the film star's birthday party there —though so far Hungarian intelligence had been unable to positively identify Mallory's Hungarian companion at the party. (The newspaper photographs had been too blurred, and the hotel authorities were unable to help.)

This last detail worried Sasha. So far the scent was a faint one, but the fact that Mallory wrote fiction and had been employed by a leading anti-Communist organization was encouraging. The question now was whether his presence in Budapest had been coincidental or whether his contact with this Hungarian had ulterior motives. The latter suggested the unpleasant possibility that the original manuscript could indeed have come from a source within the Communist sphere. In which case this man Mallory would have been merely a courier and of little importance. It was not a possibility that would be welcome with the Central Committee.

At exactly ten next morning Sasha was called to the phone in the Earl's Court coffee bar. Eckhardt sounded enthusiastic. Number 25 Elisabethstrasse was owned by RFE for its employees, and Apartment C was leased to a Russian defector called Boris Drobnov who had worked for RFE for two years. Eckhardt had learned that the Russian had left nearly five months ago, subletting the apartment without permission. He had also, over the previous six months, had a guest staying with him, an Englishman also working for the radio. Asked if this Englishman was called Mallory, the *Hausmeister* found the name familiar but could not be certain.

Eckhardt had then encountered a problem. He had called the personnel department of Radio Free Europe to check on Drobnov and Mallory, but as soon as he mentioned the names an American voice had asked him who he was. Eckhardt had begun to explain that he was a business associate of Herr Drobnov when the American had asked him to hold on. Several minutes later the American had told him that if he would drop in any time before 5:30, they'd be glad to give him all the information he wanted. But something about the man's voice had warned Eckhardt. He had no wish to identify himself in person and risk busting his whole cover, so he had had no further communication with RFE. Sasha told him that he had behaved correctly.

Eckhardt then reported how he had next called the archive library of Radio Liberty and had been informed by the duty officer, an innocent-sounding young American, that Drobnov had spent a number of evenings between March 26 and April 14 doing research in the library covering the period 1945 to

251

1953. The American had added that this was the second such inquiry he'd had in the last few days. Had this Russian guy done something wrong? he asked. Eckhardt had assured him that it was a routine inquiry and had hung up.

Sasha thanked him and promised a bonus for the information, which he emphasized was classified top-secret. It all added up to far more than anything Sasha had hoped for at this stage—although it also told him that other people had been following a similar trail, and Sasha did not have to think far to guess who these people were. He decided the sooner he got down to Verdun-sur-le-Doubs the better.

When the waitress came he ordered a coffee. He would save his appetite for the caviar and pâté de foie gras on the first-class flight to Paris.

Two days before Sasha Dimitrov arrived in London, Max Frome was in Munich. A top operative from the Central Intelligence Agency, he was a sour, white-faced man with shrewd careful eyes. His first call had been to the director of RFE, another American called Don Morgan. The appointment was arranged at an hour's notice.

"Boris Drobnov," Morgan repeated. "Yes, he's your most likely candidate. Defected in '61 and spent some years in the States. His father had been a top scientist in Uncle Joe's time, so Drobnov had a lot of difficulty getting security clearance. Personally, I thought he was okay, but that wasn't everyone's opinion. A lot of people here were glad to see the back of him."

"When did he leave?"

"About five months ago. Because of his security trouble I had only been able to take him on as a junior researcher. I tried to get him a job with Radio Liberty, but it was hopeless. You have no idea how touchy these emigrés can be. Anyone who's had direct association with the regime is more or less taboo. It was a pity, because Drobnov was a bright boy and a good worker —even if he did upset a lot of people. Absolutely no tact."

Frome listened patiently, his face blank. "I checked this morning," he said at last, "with the Radio Liberty archives and it appears he spent a lot of time there—at about the period he gave his notice in—going through official records on the Soviet regime between the end of the war and '53. Which, as you well know, is the period covered by the book."

"It's a very serious allegation," the director said.

"It's a very serious business," Frome replied. "The State Department wants us to get to the bottom of it—and the sooner the better."

Morgan said, "Unless the publishers decide to bring an action for fraud—which they're hardly likely to do if the book makes money—I don't see what any of you can do."

"My job at this stage is simply to establish that it *is* fraud," Frome said, "and, if so, find the people responsible. What then happens depends on the State Department. Now. What about Drobnov's political views? Fanatically anti-Communist?"

Morgan shrugged. "No more than most of the people here, I guess. He was under a ten-year sentence *in absentia* for defecting—whatever that's worth."

"Does he speak Georgian?"

"Not that he ever let on."

"And he wasn't a member of any secret underground group?"

"I'm fairly certain not. We keep a careful check on that kind of thing." Morgan gave an official smile. "We aim at being an impartial organization, Mr. Frome. Crude propaganda is something we try to avoid."

"I've checked with the NTS and the Ukrainian Socialist Party," said Frome, "and they vigorously deny any knowledge of the book. Although a lot of them seem to accept it as authentic."

Morgan sighed. "That's the trouble. Personally, I've been having one helluva headache trying to decide how we should treat it here. Of course, we've had to mention it in our newscasts—but so far we've kept off any direct comment."

"That's your problem," said Frome. "Ours is more difficult. What sort of passport does Drobnov hold, by the way?"

"German *Fremdenpass*. Although he's been in the West more than ten years, he absolutely refuses to renounce his Russian citizenship. Case of Slav sentimentality, I guess."

Frome looked satisfied. "Too bad for him! It means he has to get a visa for every country he visits. Have you got a photograph of him?"

"We have one in our files."

"I'd like a couple of copies. What does he look like, by the way?"

"Very heavily built, about five feet nine—large, rather fat features, getting a little thin on top."

Frome nodded. "That pretty well ties in with the description we got from the New York publishers of the contact man who made the original deal with them." He stood up. "Well, that about takes care of it for the moment, Mr. Morgan. If you could just let me have those copies of his photograph."

"I'll have it photostated for you right away." Don Morgan smiled pleasantly as he opened the door.

Max Frome kept one of the photograph copies, a good full-face likeness blown up to eight by twelve inches and mailed the other express to Langley, Virginia. Then he returned to his room in Munich's Eden Hotel, where he made calls to the Company's resident agents in London, Paris, Geneva, Rome, Vienna, Stockholm and Madrid, instructing them to check with the immigration authorities as to whether Boris Drobnov, a Russian traveling on a *Fremdenpass*, had been issued a visa at any time during the last five months.

All the replies were in by 6 P.M. Five were positive: Drobnov had been granted visas for Italy five months ago, Britain and France six weeks ago, and Austria and Switzerland in the past month. Frome now instructed the agents to check with these countries' various police bureaus which dealt with the registration cards of all foreign visitors—with the exception of Britain, which did not employ this system. Since it was the height of the holiday season, it was a process that could involve several million card indices, and, despite the latest computers, it would take up many hours of arduous police work. Frome decided that a little well-placed pressure from the Langley headquarters might help speed the process, and made the necessary request—though he still did not expect a full list of addresses much within twenty-four hours.

In the meantime, he made further inquiries about Drobnov among his former colleagues at RFE. Most of them confirmed Morgan's assessment of his character and reputation; but, more important, Frome learned of Drobnov's close association with an Englishman, Thomas Mallory, who had left RFE at the same time as Drobnov and was furthermore a novelist.

Frome now called the Company's five agents once again and instructed them to press the respective police departments to check whether a Thomas Mallory had cards filed for the same hotels as Drobnov. It was at this point that the agent in Vienna connected this same Mallory with the celebrated fracas at the Flanagan party in Budapest a few weeks earlier.

The pieces were now beginning to fall into place. Frome was by nature a cautious man; his trade had taught him to distrust all speculation in favor of facts; but until he had the answers to the police files, he would have to be satisfied with a highly plausible explanation of how Burn, Hirsch had been deceived in what might turn out to be one of the great cons of the century.

Drobnov and Mallory had written the book, using their respective talents in Sovietology and creative literature, had somehow acquired paper and a Georgian typewriter of the right age and origin, and had had the work translated into Mingrelian. Mallory had then somehow contacted the Hungarian who had signed the confidential affidavit that was now in the vaults of a New York bank. Frome had to concede that the whole scheme possessed a certain admirable simplicity, and was only thankful that he was not the one who would have to decide what action should now be taken against the culprits.

By next evening he had not only received confirmation of his previous theories, but had also been supplied with the one missing piece to the puzzle—the identity of the translator.

Drobnov and Mallory had left Munich together for Italy on April 20, staying overnight in hotels off the Autostrada del Sole; then there had been a period of three months for which the Polizia Turistica had no record of them, before they had returned north again, after which Drobnov had paid a brief visit to Britain. He and Mallory had then traveled to France, staying in a hotel in the Somme *département,* in the company of a naturalized Israeli citizen, a Mme. Tatana Bernstein, née Shumara, born 1939 in Zugdidi, Georgia. The same woman who had given the sensational interview on the Beria rape to a London Sunday newspaper.

The police files further confirmed that a Herr Drobnov and a Frau Bernstein had stayed at Sacher's in Vienna at the time that Mallory had visited Budapest; after which the Bernstein woman had disappeared for a few days—no doubt to give her newspaper interview in London—and then the three of them had returned to France. The Bureau pour la Documentation des Étrangers had meanwhile reported that six days ago the three of them had checked into the Hôtellerie Bourguignonne, in Verdun-sur-le-Doubs, Saône-et-Loire. These were the last *fiches* in the bureau's files.

It was all very clever, thought Frome. Damned clever. Just a pity for them they were amateurs.

The evidence was still basically circumstantial, but it was now too strong to be held in much doubt. That night Frome filed a top-priority coded report to Langley, requesting orders.

These he received direct from his chief. He was to proceed immediately to France and keep the three under close surveillance until further instructed.

The next morning he took the train to Lyons, where he hired a Renault R-16—a common enough model, with a top speed of around ninety or a hundred miles an hour—and by midafternoon drove into the sleepy little town of Verdun-sur-le-Doubs.

MALLORY'S REPORT

It was an L-shaped town, shuttered and pigeon-gray, on a bend in the River Doubs. There was a narrow humpbacked bridge and a triangular *place* with a café where workers used to stop in every morning to swallow their *marcs* before setting off for the vineyards, and old men sat all afternoon playing dominoes.

The Hôtellerie Bourguignonne had a glass-fronted porch leading to the restaurant, large windows with wine-red curtains, and big brass bedsteads and spacious stone-tiled bathrooms. Boris had chosen it for strategic as well as sentimental reasons: it had one star in the *Michelin* and was only two hours' drive from Geneva, on a secondary "yellow" road leading to the Swiss frontier; it also lay in the heart of the Côte d'Or—what Boris called "the world's wine heaven"—where the surrounding country rolled away in miles of neat terraced vineyards, the hills dominated by gray-stone châteaus.

We had been there almost a week now. Boris had gone to Zurich to finalize arrangements for transferring money abroad, and we were to join him next day in order to open separate numbered accounts in our own names: $300,000 for Tatana, and half the balance—$1,350,000—for myself.

There seemed to be few regular guests in the hotel, though

the restaurant was usually full, mostly with French tourists who stopped off the *autoroute* on their way south. The regulars were three stout Frenchmen in dark suits, whom I put down as wine merchants, and who ate copious meals in almost complete silence. There was also a pale, glum-looking man who'd arrived the evening before and sat alone in the corner drinking Vichy water; and at the next table from ours a little man with a huge wife who talked continuously at him in a very loud voice.

The day before we were due to join Boris in Zurich, Tatana and I planned an excursion. The *patron,* who had taken a liking to us, prepared a hamper of pâté, cold *poulet de Bresse,* strawberries, and a vintage Meursault wrapped in a polythene bag full of crushed ice. The day broke clear and calm, with the promise of becoming very hot. We were alone at breakfast, except for the pale man, who was sipping coffee in his corner. When we went out to the car, he was taking photographs of the bridge. A couple of workmen came out of the café opposite, but otherwise the town seemed deserted.

We decided to avoid the *autoroute* and take the yellow road to Beaune, then across to Pouilly. Tatana began to talk happily about settling in France—buying an abandoned château, doing it up and filling it with her friends for weeks on end, throwing huge parties that would become famous throughout Europe. During the past week her attitude toward us both had changed, subtly, almost imperceptibly, but the change was there, and it was in my favor. She still treated Boris with extravagant affection, laughing and hugging him and whispering soft words to him in Russian, but I soon deduced that she was no longer sleeping with him. We still had separate rooms, and the only times we had made love had been once in the afternoon following a heavy lunch, and again after a long walk through the vineyards, when we'd disappeared up to her room for the *cinq-à-sept.* Her physical energy had remained unabated, but if anything her manner had become even more distant and enigmatic.

We stopped in Beaune, at a café in the old cobblestone square where we had coffee, and she joked about how funny it would be if Boris simply disappeared with the whole three million and we never saw him again. Around noon we found a track that led down to a river. There was not a dwelling in sight, and Tatana stripped naked and bathed in the slow-moving water. I followed her. Afterward we laid out the lunch on the long grass. Once we heard a car passing on the road leading to the track; but otherwise it was quiet except for the humming and ticking of insects. Tatana persuaded me to have some Meursault, which we drank out of paper mugs, and we began talking about Cambridge; I told her about our old provost, a tiny man with long white hair who had been one of the greatest classical scholars of his day and was a devoted gambler: how every vacation found him at Deauville or on the Riviera, and how one year he'd been invited to lecture at the University of Houston, Texas, where he'd spent whole nights in the bars— still dressed in his black gown and dinner jacket—playing poker, and on the way home had dallied in Las Vegas, where he was rumored to have lost a small fortune.

She laughed and sipped her wine, lying on her back with her hips and breasts a pale olive against the rest of her body, which was a deep brown that matched her eyes. "Make love to me," she said.

We moved with the air heavy with the scent of thyme and honeysuckle; and when we broke apart, she lay with her eyes closed, smiling at the sky. We finished the wine and strawberries, and fell asleep. I was woken by her hand caressing me gently, artfully, as she leaned over me, kissing the lobe of my ear. "Let's do it the French way this time," she murmured.

In the same moment I heard another car approaching above, then stop. "There's somebody up there," I said.

She giggled. "So much the better. We'll show them the French aren't the only people who know how to make love."

I curled round with my head between her thighs, and the

taste of the Meursault mixed with the salty juices of her body, which quivered into a perfectly synchronized climax. "We're getting very good at it," she said, when it was over. "I've never known it as good with anyone before." Later we swam, then lay side by side until the sun began to lose its heat. I had not heard the car drive away, but there was no sign of another human being anywhere on the sloping green hills. We packed up the picnic and returned to the Citroën. About a quarter of a mile away, as we rejoined the road, we passed a car parked under some trees. It was empty.

I had promised to telephone Boris at his Zurich hotel at six, so we took the *autoroute* back, collecting the punched card at the toll gate outside Pouilly, and headed south again toward Beaune. After about twelve miles we reached a petrol station. The Citroën tank was still showing half full, but I pulled in and asked for five gallons of *super*, told the attendant to check the oil and water; then put a franc piece into the automatic machine and got two plastic cups of black coffee.

Five minutes later we were on the road again. I was now sure we were being followed. It was the same car we'd passed near the track down to the river—a big Renault with Lyons number plates. I'd seen it reach the toll gate a few hundred yards behind us, and it had pulled into the petrol station a couple of minutes after we did. The driver had been too far away for me to see him clearly, except that he was wearing a straw sun hat and dark glasses.

I didn't say anything to Tatana for the moment, while I concentrated on a plan of action. The Citroën's top speed was at most ninety miles an hour. I doubted whether I could hope to outpace the Renault, and the next big town was Chalon, where I thought of trying to lose him by backtracking through side streets; but I didn't know the town, and he probably did. Then I considered simply stopping by the roadside and waiting to see what happened: the driver would hardly try anything reckless on a crowded *autoroute*.

261

Then the idea came to me. Between the two carriageways was a flat sandy verge with a partially completed crash barrier of corrugated steel. But I noticed that at intervals there were gaps, to allow diversions for road works. I told Tatana to fasten her seat belt. We were doing more than eighty in the fast lane, and I could just glimpse the Renault keeping well up, about a quarter of a mile behind. Ahead I saw another short gap in the crash barrier, about three hundred yards away and closing rapidly. I checked in the mirror, pulled into the center lane and told Tatana to sit well back and hold on. Then I slammed my foot flat on the brake, wobbling the wheel to correct a possible skid, slipped down into second gear and felt the whole car rear up on its hydraulic suspension like a bucking horse. The engine howled as I swung the wheel hard over to the left. There was a shriek of rubber, the end of the steel barrier came swerving dangerously close, the car bounced onto the verge, then down again onto the oncoming carriageway.

I stamped on the accelerator and passed the Renault flashing by a few seconds later. The driver was braking hard, but not hard enough. I wondered if he'd risk making another U turn at the next gap: but then there was the problem of the toll card. I'd already decided to say that mine had blown out of the window. They would make me pay the full rate from Lyons; but two cars arriving at the same gate, one after the other, and both without cards, would be inviting too much suspicion. I guessed that whoever had been following us had reasoned likewise, for there was no further sign of the Renault. But I was taking no chances, and decided to turn off again at the Pouilly exit. I found my hands were sweating on the wheel. It was only then that I began to explain to Tatana what had happened.

"It could have been a coincidence," she said doubtfully.

"I'm not going to risk a coincidence for three million dollars," I said.

"Who could it have been?"

"Probably someone from the hotel." I had thought immediately of the pale man taking photographs that morning on the bridge; and I remembered those press photographers who use cameras with a right-angled lens so they can take pictures while pointing in a different direction.

"It could be someone working for the Russians, the Americans, even the Swiss," I went on. "But whoever it is, we're going to have to get out of here fast. And warn Boris. He's got that damned stateless passport, which means they can check on everywhere he goes, through his visas."

"I hope to God it is only the Swiss," she said.

I nodded. "They're very efficient—and if Boris has opened those accounts for us, it's just possible they're running a quick check on us." But it was not just her I was trying to reassure, but myself too.

"As long as it isn't the Russians," she murmured; she sat very stiffly in her seat, staring straight ahead.

When we reached the Pouilly exit I explained how I'd lost the toll card, and the man at the gate wrote out a long receipt, charged me twenty-two francs and, with an appreciative glance at Tatana, let us go.

While this had been going on, I'd been studying the map, and decided that the safest as well as quickest way back would be on the *autoroute* south again. I was reckoning that the Renault would be well ahead of us by now—probably making it back to the hotel, if my hunch was right.

We crossed the flyover to the opposite carriageway, and had passed through the toll gate when Tatana said, "If it is the Russians, we are in real danger."

I smiled grimly to myself: her words were an exact repetition of my impotent arguments with Boris back at Frabecchi. Finally I said, "Boris is in more danger than we. He's still a Soviet citizen, remember."

"So am I," she replied. "Once a Soviet citizen, always a Soviet citizen. That's how they reason."

"It's more likely to be the Americans," I told her. "The publishers may have got suspicious and asked the CIA to investigate."

"But how can they have got onto us so quickly?"

I didn't answer at once. I had been wondering the same thing myself. I thought of Smollett and Laszlo Laszlo—they were probably the two weakest links so far. Then there was Boris himself, and his Georgian friends in Paris. Was it possible that one of them had shot his mouth off? Or that Boris could have left some fatally incriminating piece of evidence back at the flat in Munich?

"There may be some quite simple explanation," I said lamely. "The main thing is, we've got the money. If necessary we can be on a plane tomorrow and halfway across the world by next day."

Tatana made no comment, and for the rest of the journey we rode in silence. The first thing I noticed when we reached the hotel was that the Renault was nowhere to be seen. I turned the Citroën round and parked it a couple of hundred yards up from the hotel, facing in the direction of the Swiss frontier. It was a quarter to six. The hotel was quiet, the bar and restaurant empty. We went up to my room—it was the first time, I realized, that Tatana had been inside it—and placed a call to the Hotel Schweizerhof, Zurich.

I was put through almost at once, and a moment later Boris' voice came bellowing down the line: "It is all in the bag, *mon cher*! You cannot imagine how simple—a child could have done it! All you have to do is show them your passport and give them a specimen of your signature."

I told him that was just fine. "Now listen to me carefully, Boris'—and I described to him what had happened that afternoon.

"You are sure?"

"Ninety-nine percent. We're under surveillance and we're going to have to get out tonight. The same goes for you . . . Don't interrupt! Check out right now and tell them you're go-

264

ing to Paris. Give them the forwarding address of the American Express. Then get a taxi and wait till you're in a busy street. It's rush hour now, so it shouldn't be too difficult. Wait till you see a free taxi coming the opposite way, then pay yours off and get into the other one. It's an old trick, but it's still the best there is. Then find a small hotel and ring me back with the address. We're going to leave here in the early hours of the morning, so expect us around six."

"I think you are being melodramatic, *mon cher.*"

"I hope so. I hope to hell so!" I hung up, then went down and found the *patron.* "Something's cropped up," I said. "We have to leave tonight for Paris. If anyone tries to contact us, tell them they can reach us through the American Express there. By the way," I added, lowering my voice, "can you tell me who the man is who arrived the night before last? The very pale one who eats by himself at the corner table?"

"Ah, that is the American. A Monsieur Frome. He is not a friend of yours?"

"Not exactly. Why?"

"He was asking about you too—the first evening he came."

"What did you tell him?"

The Frenchman frowned. "I told him your names. He was very persistent, you see." Then his face cleared and he gave me a sly wink. "I thought he might be interested in Madame, perhaps?"

I forced a smile and said, "I'd like you to do me a small favor. I don't want this American to know we're leaving—not until to-morrow, at any rate. You're quite right," I added, "there are complications with Madame. We'd like to leave at about two in the morning, so he doesn't hear us. Can we have a key to get out?"

"Trust me—I will arrange it!" He smiled, enjoying the con-spiracy. "You can put the key through the letterbox. You will be returning?" he added, as he began making out our bill.

"I hope so," I lied. "We'll telephone you first."

Boris called back less than an hour later. "I'm in the Hotel Bahnhof—really shabby! But I have booked two rooms for you." He added quickly, "And I played your taxi trick beautifully! In fact, I played it twice—a really good game."

I told him again that we'd see him at around six in the morning, then went down with Tatana to dinner. In the restaurant there was no sign of the American, Frome. Tatana was very quiet; I ordered her champagne, and she drank the whole bottle, but hardly touched her food. My own anxieties must have been infectious, for even the champagne seemed to do little to cheer her.

We were having coffee when Frome came in. He walked straight across to his table without giving us a glance. But I noticed that his face was faintly pink, with a white ridge on his nose where he'd been wearing dark glasses. Mr. Frome had spent the day in the sun. I also noticed that he ordered very little and seemed in a hurry to finish.

I left Tatana at the table and collected the key to the outside door from the *patronne*, then went upstairs to pack, putting my luggage next to the things Boris had left behind. Tatana came up a few minutes later and I joined her in her room. We were both exhausted by the sun and lay together on her bed and dozed. But I kept coming wide awake at the slightest noise from outside; and finally, around midnight, I crept out, locking the door behind me, and went downstairs. The hotel was as quiet as an empty church. Outside there was a half moon; the café across the way had closed and the town was silent. There were four cars in front of the hotel, all with French number plates, but still no sign of the Renault, either in the square or in the street by the river. I checked the Citroën in case someone had thought of immobilizing it by letting down the tires or disconnecting the distributor head; but all was in order, and the engine fired first time. As I returned to the room Tatana stirred in her sleep, but did not wake.

266

I waited till 1:45 before disturbing her. She had a headache from the sun and the champagne, and insisted on a cold shower before we left. It took us a couple of slow, stealthy journeys to get all the luggage out to the car. The only sound was the shriek of two cats who flitted across the street and vanished up an alley.

It was a few minutes past two when we finally started. No light came from the hotel, or from another car. The Citroën headlamps threw a long beam down the country road, which stretched straight and empty between the dark expanses of vineyards. I drove flat out until we joined the winding road that climbs into the Juras, the natural mountain barrier between France and Switzerland.

Tatana had let her seat right back and lay curled up asleep again. In the next half hour the only vehicle we passed was a trailer truck, snorting and hissing round the steep hairpin bends. Ten minutes later we came to the frontier. I didn't bother to wake Tatana, but took her passport from her handbag and showed it with mine to the two drowsy officials, who just nodded and waved me on.

We now began the sharp winding descent through the pine forests toward Lac Leman, the road bordered by red-and-white poles to mark the edges during the winter snows. We passed only one car—a small family Peugeot with a couple inside— whose lights were soon lost behind us. I'd been checking in the mirror every few minutes, and was now sure there was no one following.

After ten arm-twisting miles the road flattened out to join the lakeside *autoroute* from Geneva; and twenty minutes later we were in the outskirts of Lausanne. I made a slight detour to the railway station, where there were lights in the entrance hall. I woke Tatana; we went into the all-night *brasserie* and drank two black coffees each, and she had a cognac.

"Everything's all right," I said. "We've lost him. With any

luck, the old *patron* will tell him we've gone to Paris, and he'll spend the next few days sitting in the American Express waiting for us to turn up."

She did not look entirely reassured. "If they're already onto us, there are other ways of tracking us down—registering in hotels, for instance. We'd be better off going back to Frabecchi."

"We have to get the money side fixed up first." I tried to sound casual. "We'll think of something, love. We're going to have a full council of war with Boris the moment we arrive."

She finished her cognac in silence, bought another packet of Corporals, and I got an early edition of *Le Journal de Genève*; but there was no mention of *The Beria Papers*, let alone of an Englishman, a Russian and an Israeli wanted for fraud.

Five minutes later we were heading north to Bern. The traffic was mostly all-night trucks; but I had now ceased to worry about the odd pair of headlamps coming up behind us. Of course, Frome—if it *was* Frome—would have the number of the Citroën, but unless he was using the Swiss police to help him out, I didn't see how he could keep a close watch for us, even assuming that he had found out that we'd left. But at the same time I decided that the sooner I got rid of the old car the better.

It was 4:30 when we reached Bern, and another hour and a half to Zurich. The sky was growing pale over the gray apartment blocks and behind the steeples along the river. A few early-morning workers were beginning to appear in the streets, and the first trams were humming down the Hauptstrasse. I found the station, and the Hotel Bahnhof opposite. An old man was sweeping out the lobby, but the desk was empty. I rang a hand bell, and after a moment the old man came limping over. I told him we had rooms reserved by a Herr Drobnov, but did not give our own names. He bent down under the desk and brought out two registration cards. "*Bitte*," he said; then, without asking to see our passports, limped back with his broom and continued his sweeping.

I realized our luck and filled in my name as David Markham, company director, and Tatana's as Mrs. Elizabeth Markham, housewife. I cursed Boris for having reserved separate rooms, but decided that if there were any queries, I'd simply say we were expecting a friend. There was a guest list under the desk, and I found B. Drobnov in Zimmer 277—only wishing that Boris had been able to play the same trick with his registration.

After a lot of knocking he finally opened the door to us; he'd evidently been asleep, fully dressed in his electric-blue suit, cream silk shirt and alligator shoes. "Ah, comrades!" He closed the door and lumbered over to a side table where there was a half-empty bottle of Schnapps. "I have nothing for you, *mon cher*," he called to me. "You will have to drink water. They don't serve any coffee till seven." He poured two glasses, handed one to Tatana, and threw back his own in one gulp. "So," he said, turning to me, "you think we have problems?"

"Very serious ones. I don't know how the hell they twigged, but they have."

"Who is they?"

"An American called Frome."

Boris began pacing the room, while I dropped into an armchair and Tatana stretched out on the bed. "An American?" he said at last. "You have proof of it?"

"That's what his passport said."

"Passports can be forged or bought or stolen. They prove nothing." He stood in the middle of the floor with his hands clasped on top of his head. "But you think we are in danger staying here?"

"For the moment, yes. Certainly in hotels, where we can be checked. But what I want to know is how they got onto us. Could one of your Georgian friends—the old man who gave you the typewriter—have said something?"

Boris gave a yelp of rage. "You don't know him—you have not even met him—or you would not even suggest such slanderous things! These Georgians, they are as firm as rock!" And he

269

rolled his eyes at Tatana, who shrugged. "They do not talk idly to strangers!" he roared.

"All right," I said quietly, "it's just that someone must have talked. Unless you left a piece of evidence in your flat?"

"I threw out everything we did not need. And I did the same thing after we left Frabecchi—burned everything. I am not a fool! Anyway, what about you? That spectacle you made of yourself in Budapest, huh? You don't think they got a few ideas from that?"

"That was just show biz. There was nothing there to connect me with Beria." But I knew that I'd overplayed my hand in Budapest. "Then there's always RFE," I added. "As I told you before, that's one of the first places they're likely to check."

"RFE has a staff of one thousand," said Boris. "You think they have put spies to follow every one of them?"

"They followed us," I said, but I could see I wasn't going to get anywhere with Boris. He did not even seem to accept that we were in any real danger.

"Look," I said at last, "we've got the money. We sort out the bank accounts today, and tomorrow we move. We go somewhere far away. Somewhere we won't have any trouble getting money transferred, and, above all, somewhere the KGB and the CIA—if it *is* the CIA—are going to find damned near impossible to penetrate."

Boris gave a hoarse cackle. "And where the hell would that be? The moon?"

I looked at Tatana. "There are more than a hundred member states of the United Nations. Let's say about ninety that aren't in the Communist sphere of influence." I got up and fetched some hotel writing paper off the desk. "Let's start at the beginning," I said, "with A."

"Albania," said Boris, and they both laughed. I looked at my watch. We had just three hours to think of some safe corner of the world before the banks opened.

270

Max Frome knew he had behaved like a fool. Worse, like a damned amateur. I'm getting too old for this kind of field work, he thought bitterly. Chasing people around in cars was strictly for the James Bond school. Frome had done it only because he thought the pair were checking out that morning. The Russian had already gone, then he had seen the other two carrying the wrapped parcel into the car, and he thought he had missed them loading the rest of their luggage. Instead, they'd gone for a picnic and a good screw in the grass.

Frome should have kept tabs on them through the *patron*; the trouble was, the old guy and his wife had seemed on very good terms with their two clients, and Frome hadn't wanted to arouse their suspicions by making too many inquiries and have them alert his quarry. Still, the incident on the *autoroute* had been disastrous. There could have been no mistake about that—they had seen him, and beaten him at his own game. If only the place they had chosen for their dalliance hadn't been so damned remote. It was there they must have first spotted the car. Later the same afternoon he had gone to the Avis people in Chalon

271

and exchanged the Renault for a Simca—not that it was going to make a damned bit of difference now. And then, to cap it all, he'd been too sleepy after his day in the sun to stay up and keep a proper watch on the hotel. And now the birds had flown.

Frome had been completely frank in his report to the Company; no good playing this sort of game after you've been rumbled. Not only would it jeopardize the whole operation, but there was always the chance that the opposition might turn nasty. And Frome was looking forward to a good pension with which to spend the autumn of his life in the Bahamas doing some deep-sea fishing.

He had checked out of the Hôtellerie Bourguignonne that morning and driven to Lyons, where he filed his cable to Langley from the central post office. Ninety minutes later he received the reply:

DEEPLY AGGRIEVED YOUR MISFORTUNE STOP TAKE NECESSARY LEAVE STOP SUGGEST HOTEL MEIERHOF ZURICH WHERE WANGER MACLEAN WILL BE MOST HELPFUL STOP ALSO ADVISE FRIENDS HAVE CONTACTED VOLKS-KANTONALE BANK ZURICH STOP THOMAS.

"Friends" meant the opposition, and "Thomas" was his boss.

Frome called the station to ask about trains for Zurich and was told there was one leaving in just under an hour. He turned in the Simca at the Avis office and took a taxi to the station, where he had a couple of beers, fretting away the twenty-odd minutes until the train arrived. The Company, of course, had done the only thing possible: it had pulled him off the job and given it to Wanger and Maclean, whom Frome was now instructed to brief at the Meierhof Hotel. Ted Wanger was an American employed as a senior sales representative for the Nestlé factory in Vevey; and Maclean was the Company's chief man in Geneva, who ran a small, respectable finance company. Frome had never met either of them.

At 11:40 the train for Zurich pulled in and he boarded an

empty first-class compartment. As the neat suburbs slid past, he wondered how the opposition had managed to get onto the Volkskantonale Bank. That must have been a bad blow for the Company—though nothing like the blow it was going to be for Drobnov, Mallory and Mrs. Bernstein. The trail seemed to be hot once again—at both ends now.

Frome settled back and hoped there was a decent restaurant car on the train. He had found it difficult to appreciate his meals at the Hôtellerie Bourguignonne.

🖋

Sasha Dimitrov drove his hired Mercedes sports 280-SL into Verdun-sur-le-Doubs at 4:30 that afternoon, having covered the two hundred miles from Orly in just over two hours. But he was still forty-one hours too late.

At the desk he was told that the Englishman and the Israeli girl had left for Paris two nights ago, giving as their forwarding address the American Express. The Russian, Drobnov, had disappeared earlier, apparently leaving the Englishman to pay his bill.

Sasha's first reaction was to wonder why they should have bothered to give an address at all. It was probably a blind. Unless they were expecting some important mail, of course. He drank a Pernod at the bar and placed two calls, to the Committee's bureaus in Paris and Geneva. When they came through he was careful to speak English, since the phone was behind the bar: French could have been too easily overheard and Russian would have attracted too much attention. Sasha had put away his Soviet diplomatic passport and was now posing as an American expatriate, resident in Liechtenstein.

His Paris call came through at once, and he gave his instructions for the American Express to be watched, especially the *poste restante*; and to his surprise was told that the French Bureau had already received photographs of the three suspects.

His call to Geneva took longer: it was rerouted from the central Swiss Bureau, which took calls twenty-four hours a day, and a few minutes later was put through to an unlisted number. The voice that now came on identified itself as being that of a Monsieur Rolland; it was clear and abrupt, speaking faultless English, with a slight Swiss-German accent. "Where are you?" When Sasha told him, the man said simply, "Leave at once and meet me at Apartment Three, Forty-six Rue des Granges." Before Sasha could say anything more, the line went dead.

There were already some good smells coming from the kitchen, but he contented himself with a sandwich and a large coffee before setting off again on the drive to Geneva. It was not until nearly eight o'clock that he entered the Rue des Granges —that sanctum of the *grande bourgeoisie genevoise* whose bronze-grilled, lace-curtained fortresses conceal the banking secrets of billions of dollars in every currency, often from furtive sources.

Monsieur Yves Rolland occupied a duplex on the top two floors of one of the few houses in the street to have been converted into apartments. Sasha edged his Mercedes into a space in the row of American cars outside, and pressed the top bell in the panel beside the door. A Swiss-German voice rasped out of the intercom, and Sasha identified himself by his new American name. The door clicked open.

The apartment was starkly sumptuous, like a showroom for expensive Scandinavian furniture. Its owner was an old man with gray hair combed carefully across his scalp; his eyes were the color of dirty ice, his lips bloodless and immobile. He was not a man who smiled often, even to be polite.

"You have lost the suspects in France," he said in Russian, closing the door and slipping the double catch. "Moscow is not pleased."

Sasha shrugged and sank into a yellow foam-rubber chair shaped like a huge egg. "I'd like a drink," he said.

Rolland poured a small measure of German vodka. Sasha

tasted it without pleasure; it was coarse and unchilled. "What did Moscow expect me to do?" he said. "Hire a private jet from London to Beaune?"

"Do not be facetious, please." Rolland's Russian had the precise, elegant accent of Leningrad; there was no trace now of Swiss-German. "Moscow expects positive results," he went on, settling himself into another leather-covered egg. "Your inquiries in London and Munich have been useful, but they have not been conclusive. The suspects are still at large." He handed Sasha three photographs: the first looked like a studio portrait, of a young man with a brooding expression; the second, of a dark, full-faced girl; the third, a blurred image of a man with untidy hair and heavy features.

"Thomas Mallory, Miss Tatana Shumara—as she then was— and Boris Drobnov," said Rolland. "The last two are from our own identity files. They are not very recent, particularly the one of Drobnov, but they are adequate. The one of the Englishman was taken from the jacket of his last novel." He paused to light a thin black cheroot. "Something you did not think of getting yourself, Dimitrov."

Sasha suddenly felt tired and depressed. He was not up to this kind of game: he was too excitable, too restless; he lacked the essential patience and perseverance of a good agent—the attention to every fact, every detail, until the final deduction was reached without imagination, with no inspiration or flights of fancy, just the well-oiled machinery of a clinical mind.

Yves Rolland had just such a mind. He was also a highly important man in the Committee—head of the Swiss Bureau, which controlled the central Soviet network of espionage and counterespionage in Western Europe, and who was known to the Swiss authorities as a successful dealer in paintings and antiques. The fact that Sasha had been summoned face to face with him could only mean that a decision had been reached and action was about to be taken.

"While you have been running around in England and

France," the old man continued, "we have been making investigations in the People's Republic of Hungary. We consider it unlikely that the presence in Budapest last month of both the Englishman, Mallory, and your alcoholic journalist from London was coincidence." He tapped a finger of ash from his cheroot into a green onyx bowl. "The journalist reported to you that Mallory had been in contact with a certain Hungarian. Our agents in Budapest have been making inquiries and have had this Hungarian detained for questioning. A troublesome fellow who has spent two terms in prison, the second time for his part in the counterrevolution. Last autumn he managed, through contacts in the Army, to get a visa to the Soviet Union, where he visited a certain highly undesirable individual." He added the name of a well-known dissident writer whom Sasha had read in *samidzat*.

"We do not think," Rolland went on, "that this Hungarian was able to remove any illegal material during this visit, but his character and background make it possible that he agreed to draw up the document which the American publishers claim to have in their possession."

"What does he say to this?" Sasha asked.

Rolland dropped the stub of his cheroot into the onyx bowl and sat back, his fingertips steepled together, and stared at the ceiling.

"He denies everything, of course. He also claims to have powerful military friends in Moscow, which may be true. Unfortunately we have been unable to carry out the investigations ourselves, except in the presence of the Hungarian authorities."

"What about the staff in the hotel where the film star's party was held?"

"They are unable to help. They know the man well—it is a big tourist hotel, just the kind of cosmopolitan place he likes to frequent. But they cannot identify him on the night in question, or in the presence of the Englishman, Mallory. Hungary is a very loosely-governed country," Rolland added, with a little

276

sigh. "It is their bourgeois imperial heritage, which calls for a firmer hand than we are giving them at present. However, that is another matter. As far as our problem is concerned things will be easier when we have got Drobnov." He stood up and went over to a white pine desk, unlocked it and took out an envelope.

"Dimitrov, this is your chance. The Committee is entrusting you with a most delicate duty. If you succeed you will be well rewarded. If you fail—" He gave a shrug. "You will not fail."

Sasha stared at the envelope in his hands. Across the front was written in red: *For the eyes of Alexander Dimitrov only.* He broke it open and drew out a single typed sheet of thin pink paper. It bore no signature.

Rolland settled back in his chair and watched him read it. Sasha tried to keep all expression out of his face; he read it twice, refolded it and said, "Just Drobnov? What about the other two?"

"The other two do not concern you. They were followed yesterday morning from the Volkskantonale Bank in Zurich to the airport here, from which they left last night, having bought single first-class tickets to Nairobi on a flight to Johannesburg, stopping at Cairo. They are now the responsibility of our African Bureau."

"And Drobnov?"

"Drobnov is still with us. He is staying at the Bahnhof Hotel in Zurich, where I have posted three men. Drobnov has applied for a South African visa, which we can assume—with his *Fremdenpass*—will take a few days. Enough to give you an opportunity, Dimitrov, to carry out your instructions." Rolland looked at his watch. "I would like to offer you coffee, but I think it best you leave now for Zurich. You are booked into the Marienbad Hotel, which is close to the Bahnhof." He stood up again and opened the door. As Sasha came level with him Rolland said, "You have forgotten something."

Sasha looked around, then groped quickly in his pocket for

his orders. Rolland brought out a gold lighter and lit the pink paper, letting the ashes drift onto the pale wooden floor. He nodded as Sasha went out. They did not shake hands.

※

"We've had a piece of luck," said Ted Wanger, putting down the telephone. "Or perhaps luck's not quite the word? That was a pal of mine with the old Gehlen organization. One of the KGB errand boys working out of Munich has peddled them a piece of info my friend thought might interest us. The opposition is onto Drobnov and Mallory—and they appear to have moved in at fairly high level. Even sent a special man from Moscow."

"Goddam." Max Frome sat chewing a cold turkey sandwich. "That's all we need—a face-off with the Russkies! Just Drobnov and Mallory? Not the girl?"

"The tip-off didn't mention any girl. The agent was simply asked to check on Drobnov's address and background in Munich. Came up with his roommate, Mallory—that they'd both worked for RFE and that Drobnov had spent a lot of time at the Radio Liberty archives checking on the Beria period. The guy put two and two together and contacted the Germans—he peddles 'em stuff every now and then which they find useful enough not to pick him up. Sort of *quid pro quo.*"

Frome scowled at his plate. "So what's the catch, Ted? Don't tell me your Gehlen friend gave you this out of love?"

Ted Wanger grinned. He was a big, blond, all-American boy aged about forty. "This double-dealer tried to hustle the Germans into giving him fifty thousand D-marks for the info, but they beat him down to half, and they'd be quite happy to split it half again with us."

"Cheap at the price," said Frome. "Just for the pleasure of knowing we've got the opposition working alongside us on the same scenario—and probably right here in Geneva at this moment."

278

The telephone was ringing again. Wanger answered it, nodded several times, made a quick note on a pad beside him, said, "Good man!" and hung up.

"We're back in business," he said. "Mallory and the girl just checked into the airport here and are booked on Swissair's Flight 287 to Nairobi—leaving in one hour, fifty minutes."

"And Drobnov?"

"Still holed up in the Bahnhof Hotel, Zurich. Kershaw and Tipping are staking it out. His South African visa application ties in with this latest development—though Nairobi's probably just a blind stop-over. At least, I hope so. South Africa's a lot easier than some of those black African states."

Frome nodded. "The security boys out there are pretty good. And they'll make it damned tricky for the opposition."

Twenty minutes later Wanger was in a taxi speeding toward Cointrin Airport. As a top man at Nestlé he was virtually his own boss, and his colleagues were now used to his taking off on foreign trips at sometimes only a few hours' notice.

Ted Wanger made no conscious effort to remain inconspicuous when he reached the airport. He arrived with a pair of pigskin cases and a matching overnight bag, and collected his first-class return ticket to Johannesburg from the Swissair counter. He had changed into an oyster-white suit crisscrossed with elaborate camera equipment, the kind carried by rich tourists, and when he had passed through Customs and Immigration, and the routine check for hidden weapons, he went straight to the duty-free shop in the departure lounge, where he bought four bottles of the most expensive whisky and six hundred of his favorite king-size cigarettes. Ted Wanger looked exactly what he was: a highly paid American executive on a business-with-pleasure trip to South Africa.

He recognized Mallory and Tatana Shumara as soon as he entered the lounge: not only had Frome described them in detail, but there were also the photostated photographs of them both which had been circulated to all Company desks—Mallory's obtained from his English publishers, the girl's from the London Sunday newspaper—as well as the more recent photos taken by Frome outside the hotel in Verdun, thus confirming that the two sets of suspects were indeed the same.

They were sitting at the far end of the lounge, studying each new passenger with the scrutiny of two judges at a beauty contest. Wanger strode over to the bar, which was close to them, and ordered a Bloody Mary in loud cheery English, then sat down a few tables away from them and read the *Daily American*.

Ten minutes later he saw Skip Maclean. He too, far from appearing inconspicuous, seemed dressed for effect: a long-limbed man in a suede jacket over khaki shirt and tie, with snake boots and bush hat. Wanger decided he could have been anything from an aging playboy to a white African mercenary, but was surely too good to be a conventional secret agent.

The Boeing 707 was less than half full; it was winter in southern Africa, and most of the passengers were obviously businessmen. Ted Wanger had been allocated a window seat across the aisle just behind Mallory and Miss Shumara. In the tourist compartment Skip Maclean sat alone near the back of the plane and began to read a paperback of *The Godfather* in French. The stewardess' voice welcomed them aboard in three languages. The flying time to Cairo would be two hours, fifteen minutes.

MALLORY'S REPORT

Cairo International was black and airless, with a parched oven-heat that smelled of dust, urine and diesel oil. The plane was stopping for forty minutes, and we were ordered out. A group of Arabs sidled aboard with brooms and cleaning rags. There were soldiers on the runway and around the ill-lit airport buildings; they carried Chinese AK-47 machine pistols, made under license in Czechoslovakia, and watched us with indifference. In the transit lounge, Levantines in baggy trousers tried to wheedle us into buying plastic models of the Sphinx and facsimiles of Nasser and Tutankhamen.

A young barman served us thimbles of black coffee, giving us a look of hatred as he handed me the Egyptian change for a ten-dollar bill. Tatana and I were each carrying about one hundred dollars in cash, five thousand dollars in travelers' checks, and credit cards for one of the biggest international banks in southern Africa.

I had given up trying to guess which of the passengers might be a secret agent, even a hired killer. Most of them appeared to be prosperous single men, any one of whom, for all I knew, could have been on the payroll of the CIA or the KGB.

When we reboarded there were three new faces in the first-class compartment—two smart young Africans and a small waxen-faced man with bulging eyes who looked like some nocturnal animal. The lights were dimmed and we slept for the next four hours, humming through the purple darkness high above the desert, tracing the course of the Nile south over the mountains and plateaus of Ethiopia, then across the wastes of scrub and savanna that cover the great Rift Valley from the Sudan to the Congo.

At 5 A.M. we landed at Nairobi. It was hot and damp under a dawn sky mottled with clumps of dirty soapsuds. The Kenyan officials looked neat and officious in their Sam Brownes and peaked caps, while sleepy-eyed Africans moved about the arrivals hall with mops and pails. I changed some money, and a grizzled African with scars on his cheeks like grooves of polished steel shined my shoes for a shilling in the lavatory, and another, younger African, with white mess jacket and bare feet, brushed down my collar.

The loudspeakers were now calling, "Flight SR-287 to Johannesburg." This was to be the first real test. If any of those anonymous men from the plane was following us, now was when he would have to make himself known. For Tatana and I stayed in the airport after the flight was called; we had a breakfast of fried bacon and eggs, washed down by Kenyan coffee, and heard the scream of Flight SR-287 taking off.

The arrivals hall was now crowded, but I recognized only two passengers off the plane from Cairo: a little pop-eyed creature and a tall man in a broad hat who'd boarded at Geneva and was straight out of Central Casting for one of Hemingway's African stories.

We finished breakfast and went over to the BOAC counter, where I bought two single first-class tickets to Johannesburg on the flight leaving at 7:30. When it was called I noticed the

Hemingway character striding across the tarmac to the tourist-class door. I looked out for the man with the thyroid eyes, but he seemed to have disappeared.

We landed at Jan Smuts Airport, Johannesburg, at noon. A dapper little man with gray beard came aboard, asked politely for our vaccination certificates, and handed each of us a customs declaration in which we had to tick off whether we were carrying "firearms, dangerous drugs, livestock, books, magazines and literature . . ." Inside the terminal, huge pink men in white shorts and khaki knee socks examined passports and luggage with stolid efficiency. I saw the Hemingway man being greeted outside the barrier by an attractive middle-aged woman who kissed him discreetly while an African carried his bags out to an American car. I watched them drive away, but could think of no satisfactory explanation as to why he should change planes on a through-flight and add two and a half hours to his journey. There might, of course, be some quite innocent explanation: that he'd had to meet someone in Nairobi, send an urgent message, that his wife was expecting the BOAC flight and he'd caught the Swissair one by mistake—although why should he prefer waiting in Nairobi rather than Johannesburg?

I felt uneasy, but decided not to share my suspicions with Tatana until I was more certain. Instead I took her across to the Air Madagascar desk—known locally as "Mad-Air"—which ran a thrice-weekly flight to Tananarive, the capital of Madagascar. We were in luck, as there was a plane leaving that afternoon.

We were welcomed aboard the Mad-Air Caravelle by two blond South African hostesses and a young steward who looked like the captain of a school cricket team. Most of the passengers were sleek silent Indians in immaculate business suits, and women in graceful saris. At Durban the plane almost emptied. A few middle-aged Frenchmen came aboard, and a fat African in a white suit with gold rings on both hands. There was also a change of cabin staff: two gorgeous African hostesses with scarlet lips and hair piled up under silk bandanas, and a black steward who brought the fat African a bottle of champagne the moment we left the ground.

Two hours later we landed at Itavo Airport, Tananarive. The fat African was the first to leave, bowed off the plane and shown through the smiling Customs and Immigration without producing a scrap of paper. For the rest of us it was an unwelcoming place. A pale Malagasy with Polynesian eyes and a button missing from his uniform stamped our transit visas upside down in our passports.

Before leaving, we bought single tickets to the island of Réunion, on the morning flight from Paris; then we took a ramshackle taxi into Tananarive. Swamp and scrawny jungle were broken up by corrugated-iron huts, small brick houses, gray villas, and finally the railway station, a late-baroque edifice with fan windows surrounded by cherubs and half-naked marble maidens.

The taxi dropped us at a hotel opposite. It was hot and dark, with wooden floors and high stone rooms where fans swung from the ceiling with a clanking swish like breaking surf. Our window looked onto the square in front of the station, and I watched for several moments to see whether any other cars drew up. There had been several on the road from the airport, but none of them now appeared; and from the silence of the hotel, interrupted by the groans of ancient plumbing, we might have been the only people staying.

The long hours of flying had left me agreeably, erotically exhausted. I closed the shutters, locked the door, and in the half-dark pushed Tatana back across the bed, tearing her dress open like an envelope. She gave a little cry of protest as I ripped off her pants and bared her breasts, which I crushed with my hands, pressing her down into the bed, her fingernails stabbing into my back, her muscles contracting round me and squeezing me dry in less than a minute. I collapsed across her, feeling her heavy breathing and the steady draft of the fan lapping against our bodies.

284

It was early evening when we awoke. Downstairs, I checked if there had been any inquiries for us, but the African boy smiled and apologized: there had been no calls. Later we walked up the main boulevard, which was as wide as the Champs Elysées and bordered by yellow arcades full of cafés and glass-fronted restaurants. At the top a steep honeycomb of tiny streets climbed round a terracing of formal gardens with a statue of Voltaire, and ended at the gloomy walls of the former royal palace, built by Queen Ranavalona I, who is reputed to have eaten on average one man a week throughout her forty-six-year reign, and which is now the presidential residence.

We were now limp and sweating, and went into an air-conditioned restaurant where we ate rough pâté and *biftek avec pommes frites*. No one followed us; we saw no one familiar or suspicious; and the local French-language newspaper, *Le Journal malagache,* contained no mention of *The Beria Papers*.

The Air France Boeing began its descent to Réunion at 10:15 next morning. Through the window all I could see was a wall of dark-green mountain ribbed with lava flows, disappearing into cloud that covered the island like a layer of damp cotton wool.

The decision that had eventually brought us this far had been reached after long, bitter and often frivolous wrangling during those early hours up in Boris' hotel room in Zurich. The first, most obvious suggestion had been somewhere in Central or South America; but I'd pointed out that with the exception of Chile, which was nominally a Marxist state, Latin America was thoroughly infiltrated if not controlled by the CIA.

We had next considered the neutral countries and respectable tax havens, including Switzerland itself, until Boris convinced me that more political murders have been committed there by the Soviet secret police than in any other country outside the Communist bloc. I then suggested Sweden, which Boris vetoed on account of the drinking laws. Malta attracted none of us; and the Bahamas were too close to the States for comfort. The Arab countries were out of the question because of Tatana's Israeli passport; India and Ceylon were too friendly with the Russians; and the Far East was, again, riddled with the CIA.

Finally we were left with Africa. Or rather, white Africa. Tatana was in favor of it because she wanted to see the wildlife. But as for South Africa, I suspected that the U.S. government, despite all its pious protestations against apartheid, secretly treated the white republic with the respect due to one of the cornerstones of the Western economy, and that, again, the ubiquitous CIA would have plenty of influence when it came to extraditing undesirable foreigners.

Rhodesia was more promising. I remembered the recent case of an English businessman who had been given a twenty-year suspended sentence and had been deported for working for the CIA; and the Rhodesian security service would certainly be a fair match for the KGB. On the other hand, I had awful images of cocktail parties with men in crested blazers discussing cricket and rugby while the women chattered about their morning's bridge game. In Darkest Surrey, I thought, with food no different from an English boardinghouse—which was enough again to secure Boris' veto on Rhodesia.

Then I had my inspiration. I'd been thinking about Madagascar, which was obscure and wild enough, but with a legacy of French civilization, when my mind had moved farther east across the Indian Ocean, to the little island of Réunion—still technically part of French territory, but a part where Frenchmen who are not welcome back in Metropolitan France can settle in relative peace, untroubled by the overzealous attentions of the Palais de Justice. Several leading OAS gunmen from Algeria were said to have taken refuge there, as well as a number of former guards from Devil's Island who live in terror—so I had once been told—that some ex-inmate will one day land to wreak a long-awaited revenge.

286

For our purposes the island offered several important advantages. The French secret service, SDECE, was notoriously uncooperative with other foreign agencies, unless it was to its direct advantage—and particularly so with the Americans, since the recent drug scandal in which the French service was alleged to have run a vast heroin smuggling operation into the States. At the same time, SDECE could no doubt hold its own against the KGB. The island was also sufficiently remote—I suspected that most people outside France had never even heard of it—as well as comfortably civilized: French cooking, which pleased Boris, and a French monetary system. It also lay within a few hours of South Africa and Rhodesia, as well as on a direct air link to Paris.

So it was that finally we decided on Réunion.

The day after Mallory and Tatana had left, Boris Drobnov decided to treat himself to a gastronomic adventure—no doubt his last for a long time, although he did not know at this stage just how long.

There was only one place that complied with his exacting tastes: the Pyramide in Vienne, just south of Lyons. Three stars in the *Michelin*, and what Boris claimed was the best food in the world. That morning he had been allowed to collect his passport from the South African consulate, where he had been told they were still awaiting his visa confirmation from Pretoria, but would telephone the hotel the moment it arrived. Boris' French and Swiss visas entitled him to multiple visits within three months. He had reserved a table the night before, and now took the morning train to Lyons, and a taxi down to Vienne.

The restaurant lies in a cul-de-sac off the Rhone, with the words Chez Point Traiteur in discreet gold lettering on a black plaque above the door. Boris passed under them with the humble excitement of a pianist about to give his first recital. He

288

had already rehearsed his meal, which he knew by heart and spelled out to the waiter in his high-pitched, execrable French: a half bottle of 1943 Taittinger, followed by a Château Grillet '55; *truite farcie au porto, volaille de Bresse en vessie,* strawberries with kirsch, all rounded off with a selection of cakes. He ate slowly, luxuriously, savoring every mouthful. Toward the end of the meal he got into conversation with an American two tables away, who was also eating alone. Boris, feeling sated and mellow, invited him for a cognac. The man's name was Gavin Caskey; he was a writer who had just finished a novel and was celebrating. "I don't usually eat in this kind of style," he said, laughing, "but this is a special occasion!"—and Boris grandiosely made the order doubles. But he was careful not to let on too much about himself, and encouraged the American to do most of the talking, which Caskey earnestly did, beginning to tell him about his novel—a kind of autobiographical stream of consciousness from his early childhood in Brooklyn, through school and university, ending in free-verse invective set in Vietnam. Boris listened contentedly and at ease, interrupting with an occasional burp.

The restaurant has a tradition that in order to facilitate its clients' digestions, guests are supplied on request with a chaise longue in the formal garden and a free liqueur of their own choosing. It was past four in the afternoon when Boris and Caskey, on the American's suggestion, availed themselves of this extra luxury. They lay in the shade of the trees, balloon glasses of *fine champagne* in their hands, as Caskey's voice droned on about self-expressive violence, and Boris began to doze off. Caskey waited until he was fully asleep, then got up and waved through the railings. A stocky man came through the gate into the garden. Boris was lying without his jacket in a short-sleeved shirt. The man took from his pocket a hyperdermic needle and dexterously jabbed it into Boris' forearm.

He woke with the sudden muscular pain; opened his eyes wide at the sight of the stranger and was about to cry out, when a euphoric dizziness swept over him; the glass dropped from his fingers onto the grass; and within three seconds he was unconscious again.

Caskey settled both their bills, explaining that his friend had drunk a little too much; and together he and the stocky man carried Boris out to a car parked in the cul-de-sac facing the river.

Twenty minutes later they were at the little airport outside Lyons. The officials here were familiar with the stocky man, whom they knew as an Austrian doctor and owner of the Piper Cherokee which had flown in from Vienna only two hours earlier. He had already explained that he had come to collect a friend who had suffered a heart attack. He was going to fly him straight to Geneva, where the man had his own cardiologist.

They now waived the usual formalities, and the one CRS man there helped carry aboard Boris, whose breathing was heavy and whose color bad. The slender twin-prop plane taxied up to the end of the runway, turned and revved its engines with a sudden roar that coincided with the shriek of tires outside the small terminal building, as two men leaped from a big American car and ran inside, waving wallets with cards in little plastic windows at the bewildered officials. The CRS man came back and the two newcomers began speaking at him in rapid French, pointing out to the runway, where the Piper's engines had steadied themselves and the plane began moving forward. A moment later it rose in a steep turn and headed east into the clear evening sky.

🖋

Boris opened his eyes and felt a throbbing through his whole body. He was strapped into a seat beside a small window through which came the glare of snow-capped mountains. The American writer called Caskey was sitting next to him, in the narrow vibrating hull of an eight-seater aircraft; and in front

290

was the square fuzzed back of a man with his head encaged in earphones.

Boris blinked and tried to focus. There were deep shadows on the snow outside, drifting by very fast, and from their direction he knew that the sun was behind them and that they were flying due east.

He looked at his watch and began to sweat. It was almost 7 P.M. How long had they been flying? One hour? Two hours? He tried to remember the last moments—trees, late-afternoon sun. His mouth tasted of bile, his stomach felt swollen and cramped. Due east from France. Switzerland—then Austria. If it was Austria, he didn't have much time left.

They were flying low, dangerously low, which could only mean they were avoiding radar. Ahead, in front of the man with earphones, was a plastic bowl of deep blue. The mountains were beginning to break up. His whole body felt cold. He struggled against the seat belt, and Caskey said, "Relax and you will not be hurt."

It took him a moment to realize that the man had spoken in Russian. Boris reacted in panic, swinging his arm back and aiming the wedge of his hand at the man's carotid artery; instead, he struck bone, while his left hand struggled to free himself of the seat belt. But something was wrong: it had a special catch and would not come undone. Caskey hit him twice. Boris' head bounced back against the seat and he could feel blood and snot down his chin.

"I want to go to the toilet," he muttered, this time in Russian, too, and the man answered, "You stay where you are."

"I'll shit in your plane," said Boris; then shouted in Russian at the pilot, "I'll shit all over the seats of your beautiful plane!" But the man didn't seem to hear.

The Russian who had called himself Gavin Caskey now went forward and spoke to the pilot, who removed his earphones for a moment, glanced back at Boris, nodded, and reached down beside his seat, handing the Russian a snub-nosed automatic.

291

"If you don't behave," Caskey said, turning back toward Boris, "I'll shoot you—in your kneecaps so you don't walk again."

"You're a bastard."

"I know. I'm also an amateur—like you, Drobnov. So let's try to treat each other with respect." He sounded for a moment genuinely aggrieved, although the wide menacing barrel of the gun still pointed steadily at Boris' left knee. "You really want to use the toilet?" he added.

Boris gulped and nodded. He felt sick now and he no longer had to pretend that his bowels were loose. Caskey leaned down, keeping his distance and hardly moving the little gun, and with his free hand did something to Boris' belt buckle, snapping it open; then stood back while Boris clambered to his feet.

"And keep the door ajar!" the Russian called; but just then the floor tilted and Boris fell forward, grabbing the edge of one of the rear seats. The pitch of the engines had changed, and his heavy weight swung sideways, pressing against the thin wall of the fuselage.

At the same moment he heard the pilot shout back, "Four minutes to go and we're across!"

The floor sloped still further and Boris vomited. His whole nervous system had revolted against that single, massive terror which had lurked like a persistent nightmare at the back of his mind for the past eleven years: his return to the hands of the Communists. And now it had happened—or was about to happen in four minutes.

He was dully aware that his bowels had emptied themselves. He felt drained and ill: he wanted to faint, die—even risk a bullet in the kneecap. Anything better than this. The Russian with the gun hadn't moved. Boris turned and found he was leaning against the outside door. There were words in French: *Gardez la Poignée Toujours à DROITE. Pour Ouvrir Tournez à GAUCHE.* Only part of his mind registered the words; but it was that part which was now in control. Very deliberately he seized the handle and with all his remaining strength jerked it over to the left.

292

A second later the concave shield swung outward under his weight, and with a roar of air his body disappeared into the icy slipstream.

Ψ

They found what was left of him on a hillside just north of Gattendorf, two and a half miles from the Austro–Hungarian border. He was still carrying his *Fremdenpass*, and had on him 280 new francs in French money and nearly five thousand Swiss francs.

Subsequent police inquiries could discover no next of kin.

293

MALLORY'S REPORT

Gillot Airport outside St.-Denis, the capital of Réunion, was very modern, very French: the CRS men, in their dark-blue uniforms and smart white sashes, were black-skinned Creoles; and the one who stamped our passports spoke accentless French. A pretty French redhead changed two hundred dollars for me into Communauté Française Africaine francs; and another girl at the Bureau de Tourisme—a blonde this time, and even more pretty—hired us a Simca convertible and gave us a sheaf of brochures and a map of the island. This showed it to be the shape of an egg, with a narrow coastline. The interior, even from the colored contours, appeared strange and menacing: behind the rim of volcanic mountains that rose from the coast lay three dark shaded circles. These, the girl explained, were vast prehistoric craters, each called a *cirque*, the highest of which reached to almost ten thousand feet. Inside these craters, little towns and villages clung to the lava walls, and some of them were great beauty spots—the most famous, she told us, being Cilaos, which stood at more than 6,500 feet and from where you could see, on a clear day, the whole island.

294

She went on to show us, in the lower right-hand corner of the map, a yellow space with what looked like a red eye in the center. This was the island's active volcano, surrounded by a lava desert. "It is a fabulous spectacle," she said, giving us a dazzling smile.

I wanted to ask her about the ex-guards from Devil's Island, but I saw Tatana beginning to scowl with impatience; so instead I inquired about hotels. The girl recommended the Bougainville in the center of town, then led the way out to the car. On the way I stopped to buy a first edition of *Le Figaro*, fresh off the Paris plane, as well as the latest *Time*, in which I saw that *The Beria Papers* again headed the best-seller list.

The Simca was outside with the roof already down. The girl checked the odometer, wished us a happy *séjour*, and gave us another brilliant smile, which I returned. Tatana just nodded and climbed in.

"You were flirting with that girl," she said, as I turned out of the airport gates.

I grinned, trying to conceal my satisfaction: the thought of Tatana being jealous, particularly on such feeble evidence, would have seemed impossible a month ago. "She was flirting with me," I said teasingly. "I thought I was being very restrained."

"You let her go on telling us about the island. She's not a guide."

"It was very interesting being told about the island—especially if we're going to be here for some time."

"We have plenty of time to find out about it for ourselves," she said stiffly; then picked up the newspaper and began ostentatiously reading it, despite the wind from the open roof.

We were driving down the wide coast road with the ocean on one side and rows of sugarcane on the other; clusters of villas behind well-tended gardens; glimpses of a shantytown—mud, naked children, tattered Communist posters; Creole police directing the traffic with white batons; more Creoles drinking apéritifs under bright café awnings; the town center neat and white, with palm trees along the ocean front and fountains playing in the squares. Except for the black beaches and black faces, it reminded me of one of the less spoiled towns on the Riviera.

I was about to stop and ask where the Place Bougainville was when Tatana let out a shrill cry in Russian, then moaned, "Oh my God! *My God.*" She sat forward, gripping the copy of *Le Figaro* so hard that she almost ripped it apart. I pulled up sharply and had to prize the paper from her clenched fingers, while she began to sob hysterically.

I saw it at once, in the Stop Press:

Man Falls from Plane.
Body of man found last night near Gattendorf, southeast of Vienna on Austro–Hungarian border. Believed to have fallen from private plane. Identified as Boris Drobnov, Russian emigré, Munich. Police anxious to interview Dr. Felix Radin, Austria, owner of Piper Cherokee which took off from Lyons airport 16.20 hrs. yesterday.

I read it twice, then had to put my head between my knees to keep down the nausea. Tatana was still weeping and moaning, her hands over her face, the tears streaming between her fingers and down her arms. For the moment I was too stunned to speak. All I could do was think, somehow they'd got him, and he'd killed himself rather than be taken back alive. He *must* have killed himself. There were other, tidier ways of doing away with someone than tossing him out of a private plane without even removing his identification papers. Poor Boris. Poor bloody Boris! And I remembered miserably how I'd tried to warn him—reason with him, plead with him, even threaten him—and all I'd got was a crack on the head with a jugful of wild daisies. I thought of Boris' huge body lying broken somewhere near the mine fields and tank traps of the Iron Curtain.

Tatana was still crying, as I started the car again and drove slowly round the town center, taking several wrong turnings before I found the hotel. I stopped at a café next door and bought her a large brandy.

"He couldn't have felt anything," I said, holding her hand. "He'd have been unconscious before he hit the ground."

"The bastards," she muttered, "the dirty, evil, fucking *bastards*." And she swallowed the brandy in a gulp.

The clouds had crept down from the mountains and now covered the sun; but it was still very hot, and little bubbles of sweat stood out on my face and arms. I left some money on the table and took her into the hotel. Here there was no chance of avoiding registering. A businesslike Frenchwoman at the desk demanded our passports and told us she would fill in our *fiches* herself. Then she summoned a French porter who took us up to a double room, clean and functional, with the dry chill of air conditioning.

I took a shower, while Tatana flopped down on the bed, still weeping intermittently. "I can't believe it," she kept saying. "Boris—dead—it can't be true! He seemed so—so *indestructible*."

But I believed it only too well; and now that I was over the shock and able to think about it more rationally, I began to consider the implications that his death held for us. Moscow's intentions seemed obvious enough: to capture one of us and take us to Russia, where we would be made to reveal the source of the book. Boris' danger was therefore now our danger.

Then an even uglier thought occurred to me. They had carried out the kidnapping in France, if the report of the plane taking off from Lyons was correct. Réunion was also France—and, by jet, only eight hours away. I wondered if Rhodesia wouldn't have been a better choice after all.

While Tatana still lay distraught on the bed, I picked up the copy of *Time* and found a lead story entitled "Beria Inc." The magazine traced the main strands of the conspiracy, but came to no positive conclusion as to whether the book was genuine or not; then concluded that if it was a hoax, the forgers were likely to be the Number One target of the Soviet security service. The edition had gone to press at least two days before Boris' death.

We had little appetite for lunch; and afterward drove south along the coast road, beside the emptiness of the ocean, which heaved like the skin of a huge reptile. Eventually we found a bamboo beach bar that opened onto a strip of black sand. The sun was obscured behind a glaring haze. We bathed in the tepid water, then took refuge under the roof next to a revolving fan, where Tatana asked for brandy; I ordered a *citron pressé*.

There were only two other people in the bar—a couple of dark-skinned youths with long hair and bikinis the size of handkerchiefs who stood snapping their fingers to a jukebox. They both stared deliberately at Tatana while the Frenchman poured her a glass of three-star Hine and stared even harder when she told him to leave the bottle.

"Maybe we should go back to Jo'burg, then up to Salisbury?" I said at last.

She looked at me with swollen eyes. "What good will that do? If they want to get us, they'll get us wherever we go. We're Number One on their list, you can be sure." She had not read the *Time* story, but was reflecting it with dreadful accuracy, her voice spelling defiance rather than fear.

"They'd have a lot of difficulty in Rhodesia," I persisted, "and with all that money we might even do a deal with the authorities—get special police protection."

"Yes, like Trotsky." She closed her eyes and smiled. "He not only had the Mexican police guarding him, he also had his own private guards. But they still got him."

"They got him through a trick. Trotsky was careless," I said. "Besides, the Russians are probably out to kidnap us, not kill us. And with proper police protection they couldn't hope to do it short of bribing a whole platoon of Rhodesian police—and I don't somehow see even the KGB doing that."

She stared into her brandy. "If you're so sure of these wonderful Rhodesians—well, go there. Go and live in a little fortress where pigheaded policemen watch you twenty-four hours a day. I'd rather go to prison." And I realized, as I had so many times with Boris, that it was useless to argue. I was up against that immutable streak of Russian obstinacy which even the threat of death did nothing to demolish.

Just then one of the long-haired youths came over and asked her to dance. She gave him a casual glance and shook her head without replying. He glared at her, then shrugged contemptuously and strolled back to join his companion at the jukebox. A few minutes later they left, still in their bikinis, and through the bamboo screen I saw them drive noisily away in an open two-seater.

Tatana had finished a third of the bottle of Hine, and was still sober, when it began to rain—thick vertical spears of water that bounced off the lava beach in clouds of steam. I ran out and put up the hood of the Simca, though the seats were already drenched; and on the drive back, the mountains were blotted out and the road was like a swirling canal. At the hotel I asked if there'd been any inquiries for us, but the woman shook her head. Upstairs Tatana refused to let me kiss her, because of the taste of brandy in her mouth, and insisted that I make love to her on her belly, which I did to the rhythm of the rain and the sucking drone of the air conditioner. Later she fell into a heavy sleep; and I lay beside her and wondered again whether it wouldn't be better to take the next plane to Johannesburg and go straight to the British Embassy and make a clean breast of everything: arrange for a press conference, give them the whole story right up to Boris' death, then offer to pay Burn, Hirsch the balance on what they'd reckon to lose—since the paperback, magazine, and foreign rights would presumably be made void the moment the truth was out. Then perhaps we could do a further deal, as Clifford Irving had done, and get a contract to write the book-about-the-book—the whole background story of the hoax, right up to its last, terrible climax. But first I needed someone to talk to. Not Tatana. Someone uninvolved, who could sympathize and give advice, and perhaps even offer a safe way out.

After dinner we went to a cinema and saw an old Jean Gabin film which broke down three times. The audience were mostly Creoles who chattered and shuffled and cracked nuts in the dark, howling and hooting each time the lights came on.

We were in bed by eleven; but for a long time I was kept awake by the murmur of a radio from some open window outside.

I wondered what sort of funeral they would give Boris.

We slept late, and I was woken by the phone purring by the bed. It was the woman at the desk. *"M'sieur Mallry? Il y a deux messieurs qui vous demandent en bas."*

I felt as though the air conditioner had been turned on full, and shivered under the sheet; then I got up, careful not to wake Tatana, who was still in a deep sleep; pulled on my clothes and went along to the lift.

I saw them the moment I stepped into the reception hall. They were sitting across from the desk, drinking coffee at a low table. One was a large blond man whom I thought I recognized from the transit lounge at Cairo International. The other was the now familiar Hemingway figure. He stood up slowly and said, half extending his hand, "Mr. Mallory? My name's Maclean. Skip Maclean. This is Ted Wanger." He pulled up a chair as he spoke, and I sat down and called to the woman at the desk for a third *café filtre*.

"We might as well put our cards on the table, Mr. Mallory. You're blown—wide open."

I looked at him and said nothing. I felt neither surprise nor

300

dismay; though I remember thinking that nearly seven hundred dollars for the single fare to Réunion seemed rather a lot when we could just as well have had this conversation in a hotel in Geneva.

"We're not here to accuse you or criticize you," Maclean continued. "In fact, if anything, we're here to try and help you." He reached under his chair and handed me a copy of yesterday's Paris *Herald Tribune.* The story was in headlines on the front page:

Mystery Plane Death of Russian Emigré
Believed Connected with 'Beria Papers'

There followed a dramatic account of how Boris had been carried unconscious on board the Piper at Lyons Airport by two men—the alleged Dr. Radin and an unidentified American—and how the plane had been subsequently picked up by Austrian radar south of Vienna, close to the Hungarian and Czechoslovak borders, where it had disappeared in the direction of Sopron in Hungary.

There was also a lot of detailed information about Boris' background which suggested more than even the keenest newshound could have dug up in so short a time—the story was under an agency byline—and I detected the helping hand of the CIA. There was no mention of myself by name, although it was stated that Drobnov was believed to have had at least one accomplice; and the story ended with a recap of the London newspaper interview with Tatana. Sy Miskin had also been contacted, but had refused to comment, and was reported in another story, datelined New York, to have been given special police protection, along with several other executives of Burn, Hirsch.

I handed the paper back. "Next deal," I said, and the man called Wanger smiled.

"All right, deal it is, Mr. Mallory. But it'll have to be our game."

I spread my hands and shrugged, as the woman put down my filter coffee.

"We'd better be frank with you right away," Maclean said. "We work for the U.S. federal government."

"I'd never have guessed," I murmured.

Maclean smiled and continued, in his gentle voice. "You've seen what happened to your friend Drobnov. They were taking him back to make him spill the dirt. Now that they've lost him, they'll concentrate on you. And we happen to know, from a pretty reliable source, Mr. Mallory, that they were after you and Drobnov together. We're not so sure about the girl, but if they've followed the same leads as we have, they shouldn't be far behind you both."

I still said nothing.

"I have to hand it to you, though," Maclean added, tilting his lean weathered face and giving a small chuckle, "your trick of flying here via Jo'burg and Tana nearly had us foxed. We still don't know how the opposition is making out, but in South Africa the Russkies are pretty thin on the ground. They'll take a little time to catch up—but catch up they will. And when they do, you're going to need friends."

"You mean I should treat the CIA as friends?" I asked, blowing steam off my coffee.

They both sat watching me patiently. "Look at it this way," said Maclean. "You and the girl are on your own. In fact, at this moment you're perhaps the two loneliest creatures in the Southern Hemisphere."

"We're not here to hunt you down and persecute you," said Wanger. "The legal side doesn't interest us. You may not be able to visit the States for a few years—but even that we might be able to fix if you play ball."

Maclean took over again. "The deal is this, Mallory. You give us a complete account of how you forged *The Beria Papers*. Every detail right from the beginning—your trip to Budapest, the affidavit from the Hungarian, the girl's confession to the

London paper. Everything. And you make a public statement repeating this account to the press. In return we guarantee, first your immediate safety, as well as immunity from any subsequent prosecution, and secondly, we get the State Department to try and reach an agreement with Moscow to call off their dogs. Remember, once you've confessed, the Russians aren't going to want to pursue this damned thing any more than we are. All everybody wants is for the story to lie down and get forgotten!"

As I listened I felt like a patient who's just been told by a doctor that he is not after all suffering from an incurable disease. Of course, Maclean and Wanger could be lying or bluffing; but somehow I trusted them—perhaps just because I longed to trust someone, anyone, and Maclean and his blond partner looked tough and straight and reliable, and I fancied them as a better bet than hanging around with Tatana, alone and friendless on this volcanic outpost.

"To tell you the truth," I said finally, "I've been thinking of doing the same thing myself. Fly to Jo'burg and give myself up."

"Keep out of Jo'burg," said Wanger. "Just stay right here. Jo'burg's where the KGB's trail got to—though it seems to have stopped there for the moment—and we've told the South African boys to pick up anyone who tries making inquiries there about passenger lists on Air Madagascar to Tananarive in the last few days."

"But check out of this hotel," said Maclean. "It's a little too central, too obvious. Go up somewhere quiet inland. There's a place called Cilaos, near the volcano. Nice hotel—swimming pool, ideal holiday resort. You may have to spend a few weeks lying low while we iron things out."

"Will you be staying?"

"One or the other of us will," said Wanger. "You won't be on your own, believe me."

"Just one condition," I said. "If I write up this story for you,

303

I want to keep the copyright. That is, I want to try and sell it."

Maclean's voice hardened. "You don't think you've sold enough already?"

"Look," I said, "I'll make a deal myself—to repay Burn, Hirsch, if they guarantee me a decent advance on the real story. Is that something else you can help me fix?"

Maclean began to smile. "I'm not a literary agent, Mallory. And I wouldn't lay odds that the boys at Burn, Hirsch have too much love left for you! But I will say this. If you and the girl pay your shares of the money back, it's going to make things a lot easier all around—for you and for us." He nodded solemnly, then added, "By the way, you'd be better off with new passports—at least till the worst of the heat's off." He handed me a couple of brand-new British passports. "Use these from now on. With any luck, they'll throw the scent completely."

Mine had me down as Richard Grenville Forsythe, sales representative, born Bromley, Kent, 1935. My photograph had been taken from the dust jacket of my last book; and the passport even contained entry and exit stamps from Cointrin Airport, Geneva, as well as one from the Sûreté here at Gillot Airport. And Tatana was entered as Mrs. Laura Forsythe, nee Maltini, housewife, born Milan, 1940. Hers contained the same entry and exit stamps, and both passports had been validated by the Foreign Office for ten years from a date six and a half weeks ago. We had even been provided with the necessary vaccination certificates for cholera and smallpox, issued by the Swiss Ministry of Health in Geneva. The only items lacking were our signatures.

I nearly asked them how they'd managed to do it at such short notice—it couldn't have been more than twenty-four hours —but decided the question would be naïve, as well as slightly impertinent. These were real professionals; what was more, they were offering me—if they were on the level—the sort of deal I'd been secretly praying for ever since reading of Boris' death.

As we all got up to leave, Maclean gave me a card. On it was printed *Michel Drouet-Lemont. Cie. Navigation France-Afrique, S.A.* There followed two addresses and telephone numbers, in St.-Denis and St.-Paul. "He's your contact man," he said, "in case anything goes wrong and you want to call one of us."

Neither of them smiled. "We trust you," Maclean emphasized, "because we're not playing you for a sucker, Mallory. If you want to go on living, at least in freedom, you got to trust *us*. You try and make a break for it—even using those new passports—and just see how far you get."

"You'd hand me over to the Russians?"

"We wouldn't need to," he said. "We'd just let the Russians find you. It would take time, but they'd do it. We're the last people to underestimate the opposition."

I had a sudden, nasty suspicion that this might be the most convenient solution for them: issue us both fresh identities, then tip off the KGB and let them get on with the rough stuff, leaving the CIA's hands clean. But, as Maclean said, I had to trust them, or risk finishing up like Boris.

"Well, good luck," said Ted Wanger.

"And don't worry," Maclean added. "Just take it easy and sit tight. Remember, Hotel Bellevue, Cilaos."

This time we all shook hands.

As soon as they had gone, I went up and woke Tatana. When I told her about my two visitors she was furious.

"You should have called me at once!" she cried. "After all, I'm in this as much as you!"

I tried to calm her, but she was never at her easiest just after waking, and I decided to break Maclean's conditions to her in gentle stages. If I judged her even half accurately, she was not going to give up those $300,000 without a fight. I gave her her new passport, told her to sign it "Laura Forsythe," and not to forget who she was now—namely, my wife—and assured her that the visit downstairs had been a thoroughly friendly one.

She went into the bathroom, grumbling through the door about having to leave for Cilaos so soon; but I shouted at her that the weather tended to break in the afternoon. We left the hotel half an hour later. The sky was still clear, the sun reflected off the ocean with diamond brilliance, filling the streets with an aching glare. I just caught the shops before they closed, and bought two reams of typing paper, explaining to Tatana that while we were cooped up here I was going to start work on a new book.

"Haven't you made enough money to retire?" she asked.

"Money must never be allowed to stifle creative activity," I said pompously; but I could sense that greedy streak in her character which had made her so amenable to our scheme from the beginning, but which I feared again would provoke problems; and so I decided to postpone all explanations of the deal, at least until we had reached Cilaos.

However, now that I had time to think more clearly, certain aspects of that deal, and of the conversation leading up to it, began to worry me. For instance, the preparation of the passports showed a contingency planning that must have originated before the news of Boris' death—for I doubted that even the CIA could arrange such things in a few hours. But then, if the planning had been that detailed, why had Maclean said it might take a few weeks to get things ironed out? With whom? The CIA chiefs? The State Department? The British Attorney-General? Or Moscow? And why insist that I stay in Réunion? They had already admitted that the KGB's trail had reached Johannesburg, and even if it had stopped there, they would catch up in time—as Maclean had been careful to point out. So why the hell keep us hanging around just waiting for them? Surely, if the CIA had been able to arrange false passports for us both, they could arrange for us to be accommodated in one of their private hideouts, instead of stranding us at the top of a dead volcano, with only the name of an unknown French shipping agent to contact in case of trouble?

I considered all this as I drove south again along the coast road, and cursed myself for not having been more alert at the time; for I'd been so numbed by the appearance of the two men, and so relieved by their skilled, solicitous manner, that I'd been lulled into accepting everything they said. But now I began to wonder. I wondered, too, about taking that next plane to South Africa and giving myself up. Two things deterred me: the airport was in the opposite direction, and the planes to Johannesburg left only in the morning. There was, of course, the night flight to Paris, leaving at 10 P.M.—which would give me enough time to change my mind after I got to Cilaos.

The truth was, I preferred to trust Maclean and Wanger. At least, trust them more than risk running out on them, even with those false passports. "Just see how far you get," Maclean had said, I decided to obey him.

At the tiny town of St.-Louis I turned left into the mountains.

For the first part of the drive, through the pass, the road was fairly good: narrow and steeply cambered against the rains, but reasonably straight, between green cliffs that rose more than a thousand feet on either side, with dense fauna growing almost horizontally out of the rock and spouting many waterfalls—spews of white that turned to spray long before they hit the ground.

We came to a last bend and everything changed. We were now in the great Cirque de Cilaos, the largest and highest of the three extinct craters. The road had narrowed to what seemed scarcely twice the width of the car, and had been carved out of the lava face in a twisting spiral that climbed up the inside of the crater like the rifling of a gun barrel. The floor of the crater was in deep shadow, and the top, some ten thousand feet above, was hidden by dark swirling cloud. Somewhere

307

up there was the famed beauty spot of Cilaos.

I checked the fuel gauge, which registered three-quarters full, and just hoped the brakes were in good order, for I was rarely able to get out of second gear. Although the road was climbing, it would suddenly, with no warning, dip into a sharp corner with the edge protected only by white-painted stones.

Once the slope was so severe that even with my foot flat on the brake I couldn't make the turn in time and only managed to pull up a few inches from the edge. Then, either through panic or because I was still unused to the gears, I couldn't get into reverse. Each time I eased off the hand brake and tried to engage the clutch, I could feel the car slip forward another few inches nearer the drop, which was now many hundred feet deep. I ordered Tatana out; then, somehow keeping my eyes away from the chasm, I took a deep breath, tensed my muscles, and began a slow, careful, routine hill start. When I'd done it, and had the little Simca facing back up the road, my shirt was stuck to my back and I could feel the sweat itching down the calves of my legs; and I cursed not only Messrs. Maclean and Wanger, but even the luscious blonde at the airport. In fact, I'd have gone back to St.-Denis then and there, except that I could see absolutely no room in which to turn round.

Nor was the geography of the road the only hazard. For although it was a weekday, and the weather was fast closing in, the road was by no means empty. Looking up at the weaving dotted line of white marker stones above, I could see the insect shapes of cars crawling in both directions. Usually I could judge their distance well enough in advance to be able to draw in to the side and wait until they'd passed; but I had to keep my hand almost permanently on the horn, ready to slam on the brakes and pull over against the lava wall at any moment—especially as twice a couple of sports cars came shrieking round a bend, bearing down at me almost in the middle of the road. I began to think that the route to Cilaos constituted some perverted national sport in Réunion.

308

After two painful hours of this we had covered less than twenty-five miles, but were now close to the ceiling of cloud. The rock face was beginning to change. Instead of black lava, the walls were broken up into columns of bald rock like shanks of bone, between clefts of spongy, leprous moss. Once, when I stalled again on a bend, I was aware of the silence. It was a deathly hush, made even greater by the tiny grating echo of a car changing gear somewhere far below.

Ten minutes later the cloud closed round us in a white fog that shut out even the bends ahead. Occasionally there would be a glow of sun and we could glimpse the rim of the crater, still far above, rising like a row of black fangs.

We reached Cilaos without warning. The cloud cleared long enough for us to see a huddle of small white houses piled up the side of the rock like sugar cubes. In the center of the town were a couple of modern concrete buildings—one a school, the other a small supermarket, which was also a bank. The hotel lay on a ridge just above the town, a long two-story building lined with shuttered balconies. We drove up past a sloping lawn the color of green baize, with clumps of brilliantly colored flowers, some of them shaped like half-open mouths, others covered in sharp evil-looking spines, or sprouting leaves that drooped like fleshy green tongues and gave off a rich overripe smell.

The lobby of the hotel was large and bleak, with glass murals painted in a pseudo-primitive style. There was a bar at the end where a fat, sulky-looking girl was reading *Elle*. The reception desk was empty. I handed her our new passports. She told us we were the only guests, and I asked her, half jokingly, if many people got killed on the road up here. She shrugged. "Two or three a month, maybe. Usually at weekends. Young people, they come up for the dancing and drink too much, then—*boom!* —over the edge."

She took down a key and slouched ahead of us, up some concrete stairs and into a big white room equipped with both air conditioner and central heating. She pulled up the shutters, and through the drifting mists I saw an oval swimming pool with a deserted bamboo bar and a few forlorn chairs and tables.

I put my typewriter and reams of fresh paper on the table by the balcony window. Tatana asked the girl to send up a bottle of brandy.

Half an hour later I had finished putting Maclean's basic proposal to her, and to my amazement she accepted it almost without argument. The only detail I did not mention was the little matter of her paying back the $300,000. That was something, I decided, that could wait till the more important problems were settled.

᙭

We have now been at the Bellevue Hotel, Cilaos, for seventeen days. The weather is usually clear between sunrise and noon, with an alpine brilliance that is wonderfully invigorating. At such times, as the girl at the airport told us, we can see the whole island—a vast sweep of emerald and black-edged mountains rolling layer upon layer down toward the dim gray-green line of the ocean.

The hotel remains almost empty, except for occasional guests who stop overnight, mostly middle-aged couples on holiday from Metropolitan France; and on Saturday nights they hold a dance downstairs when for a few hours the hotel comes alive with long-haired youths and girls and thundering pop music that echoes across the mountains. Otherwise the place is morbidly quiet.

Tatana spends all day reading, lying by the pool in the morning and on her bed in the afternoon. I have taken to rising with the sun and working sometimes ten hours a day, reporting the whole course of our enterprise from that first evening when we'd begun cleaning out Boris' flat, until now.

Skip Maclean paid us one unexpected visit, with our contact of the France-Afrique Navigation Company. They were both

310

friendly and businesslike. Maclean was also keen to know how my work was progressing. I told him that it contained much that would not interest an intelligence agency; but he promised me that by the time it had been evaluated and digested by a computer, only the barest facts would remain. As far as the original was concerned, providing I changed nothing and retracted nothing, I would be free to dispose of it as I pleased.

I then tackled him about why things were taking such a long time. He replied airily that matters of diplomacy always took time. Particularly with the Russians. The State Department, he assured us, were making important overtures, through the usual cautious and elaborate channels, to convince Moscow that the Beria scandal would soon be cleared up to everyone's satisfaction; and he promised us that positive results were expected within the next couple of weeks. As for us having to stay holed up in Réunion, he thought it was still the best place. The KGB's trail had been killed off in Jo'burg, where a couple of their agents had been picked up at Jan Smuts Airport; they had confessed that they were from the KGB's African Bureau, based in Conakry, Guinea, and had been sent to track down myself and Tatana, but were still awaiting final instructions from Moscow. BOSS, the South African Bureau of State Security, had kept the trail hot by making the two agents send normal coded messages back to Conakry, and they had finally received orders pulling them off the chase. Either Moscow had been tipped off or they had given up. I wasn't entirely satisfied with either explanation, nor do I think was Maclean; but he had his instructions, too, and although he continued to be friendly, he was also firm: Tatana and I were to stay at the Hotel Bellevue in Cilaos. Two weeks was not a lifetime, he reminded us cheerfully; and if there was anything we wanted, we could always ring Monsieur Drouet-Lemont.

But two weeks still seems a long time. Not so much for me, as I am working; but for Tatana the days pass heavily, and I have noticed her becoming restless and morose. We arrived

311

here with about a dozen books between us, and these she had read and reread, besides a stock of Simenon paperbacks from the little supermarket. Often, while I've been working in the morning by the pool, she's come down and swum, then prowled round the edge like a prisoner in an exercise yard. She has also been drinking a lot—mostly brandy, but with no evident ill effects—and chain-smokes all day.

Afternoons and evenings are particularly difficult, when the clouds close in, and from noon onward it is like dusk outside, with the skies weeping a thin miserable rain that fills the hotel with a smell of damp concrete and rotting vegetation. We make love regularly, but even this has begun to assume the regularity of a forced ritual.

Then yesterday we broke the monotony by making a trip to the volcano. This was against Maclean's instructions, which are not to leave Cilaos until he tells us to; but I didn't see how one small sightseeing trip could put us in any danger. The night before, I had got the girl at the bar to prepare us a packed lunch, and we set off before sunrise, because the weather on the volcano begins to close in by midmorning.

Fortunately we did not have to negotiate the Cirque again, as the road led farther inland, south from the crater through a landscape of lunar rocks and sulphuric sands washed by the rains into a dull yellow pancake. The road became little more than a track and bore many tire marks, although at this hour we saw no other vehicle. It ended at a low rusted fence with a sign in red, above a black skull-and-crossbones: *DANGER! FALAISE ABRUPTE.*

I stopped the car a few yards away and got out. As soon as I reached the fence I stepped back. Beyond was a precipice, perhaps a thousand feet deep, perhaps more, and below and beyond stretched a wasteland like a wrinkled black skin covered in scars and pustules. The clouds lay below us, and there was no sign of the ocean.

I approached the fence once more, this time with Tatana,

and together we gazed. It was almost possible to believe that the world was flat and that we were standing on the edge.

In the middle of this desert rose a rust-red cone, its rim smoking gently like the bowl of a well-worn pipe. At the same time I noticed the smell—a sour dead smell in the clear mountain air, a smell of sulphur and cold ash and rotting matter, although we had not passed a single sprig of vegetation in the last five miles.

Tatana took my arm. "Tom, let's get away from here."

We got into the car. Clouds were already blowing up from the mountains behind as we started back. It looked as though our packed lunch would not be needed.

We'd been going about three miles, and the first mists were sweeping round us, when we turned a sharp bend beneath an overhanging excrescence of lava, and a Land Rover came swinging round in the opposite direction, swerved and just missed us. I hadn't had time to see the driver's face, and a moment later it was lost in the mist.

A few hundred yards farther on we passed a signpost which I'd missed on the way out, directing us off the track: *À la Cratère Colombier—100 Mts.* I slowed down. "It's only a little more than a hundred yards," I said. "It seems a pity to come all this way and not even see a crater."

Tatana did not sound enthusiastic; but I was still feeling shaken by the near-miss with the Land Rover and needed some air. I pulled up, and we got out and followed a well-trodden path up to an extinct cone about twenty feet high, its sides covered in small boulders which we had to clamber up on our hands and knees. At the top was a hole about six feet wide. Its sides were sheer and black.

"It must be a basalt crater," I said, "one of the hardest minerals there is. This is what the volcanologists call a 'chimney'—the vent at the bottom of the crater floor out of which the molten lava and gases are forced up through the crust of the earth. Long after the lava's crumbled away, the basalt stays intact. Careful!" I shouted, as Tatana leaned over the edge and

313

peered in. "God knows how deep it is. It may go down for several miles."

"Into the center of the earth," she murmured; she had picked up a loose boulder and flung it in. Through the silence came a dreadful thumping that grew rapidly fainter, then died out altogether. At that moment I heard the engine. It must have been approaching for some time, but we'd been too absorbed to notice it. I turned and saw the Land Rover that had missed us a few minutes earlier. It had stopped at the end of the path. At first nothing happened.

Tatana had begun to scramble down the side of the cone. "Come on, it's just another tourist," she called.

I began to follow her, when the door of the Land Rover opened and a man in a fawn coat got out. I was halfway toward him when I recognized our French contact, Michel Drouet-Lemont.

He gave us a faint smile and held up his hand. "I'm sorry— I thought it was you. I was driving rather fast, I'm afraid!" He stepped forward, still holding up his hand. "They told me at the hotel that you were here—but then I saw that you had not gone down to the volcano. I have to fly to Mauritius this afternoon," he added, "and I wanted to see you before I left."

"Why? What's happened?" I said.

He smiled again. "It is good news, I think. Monsieur Maclean desires you in St.-Denis tomorrow at noon—packed and ready to leave."

"Did he say for where?"

"That he will inform you himself—in the bar of the Bougainville, at noon tomorrow," he repeated.

"And you came all this way to tell me? Couldn't Monsieur Maclean have telephoned or come himself?" I asked suspiciously.

The Frenchman gave a little shrug. "Monsieur Maclean is not in Réunion today. And he prefers that you should receive your instructions personally." He started to turn back to the

314

Land Rover, then added, "But I advise you to wait until tomorrow morning before driving down. Do not attempt it today—there is going to be bad weather in the Cirque. And you know what the road is like!" He climbed in and drove off.

We followed a moment later; but Monsieur Drouet-Lemont had already disappeared into the cloud.

🦋

I am writing this in our shuttered room, with the rain splashing on the balcony outside; and although it's only four in the afternoon the lights are on. Tatana is on the bed reading; our luggage is packed, except for our toilet things; the bill has been paid, and we're ready to leave at dawn.

So this seems to be the end of the story—except for what Skip Maclean has managed to arrange with the powers-that-be back in Europe and the States. As for Tatana's share of the money, we still haven't discussed it; but when I think of what happened to Boris, even $300,000 doesn't seem worth it. In fact, if I'd had any idea how it was going to turn out, I'd never have done it.

315

EPILOGUE

But that was not quite the end of the story.

At 10:20 next morning the driver of a Renault station wagon drove up to St.-Denis police headquarters and reported a serious accident in the Cirque de Cilaos, halfway down from the town. A car had gone over the edge and lay smashed in a gulley several hundred yards below the road.

When the police arrived on the scene an hour later they had to use ropes and tackle to reach the wreck. On a ledge about fifty yards down they found a man lying unconscious. Four gendarmes, using an improvised sling, managed to bring him back up to the road, where the ambulance had arrived with a doctor. The man's condition was grave: the doctor diagnosed severe concussion and internal bleeding; one leg was shattered and his rib cage crushed.

Another team of gendarmes had now reached the car. It was a white convertible Simca that now looked more like a piece of crumpled tissue paper. Several yards from the wreck lay the broken body of a girl. She was obviously dead; indeed, one of the gendarmes later remarked to a colleague that it wasn't even possible to tell if she'd been pretty or not.

On the doctor's insistence the ambulance returned to St.-Denis without waiting for the girl's body to be brought up; and with its headlights on full-beam and the siren's panting scream echoing around the walls of the crater, it covered the thirty-three miles to the hospital in just under an hour. The victim was still alive when they rushed him through emergency and into the operating theater, where two surgeons were already waiting.

The police, meanwhile, were trying to determine the cause of the crash. There had apparently been no other vehicle involved, and no witnesses. The weather had been clear, and the accident had occurred on one of the relatively less dangerous stretches of the road—a shallow bend where the white-painted stones at the edge had been scattered by the impact. The sergeant in charge was surprised that a car of that size could do such damage, even driven flat out; but the state of the wreck ruled out any chance of detecting a mechanical failure. There were a pair of recent tire marks close by, but these were too broad for the Simca; nor did it seem likely at that hour for the driver to have been drunk—although blood tests would be carried out in due course on both the man and the dead girl.

The police were also confronted with another problem. Each of the victims had been found to be carrying two passports—altogether three British and one Israeli. The inspector of police immediately called M. Brian Armitage, the honorary British consul on Réunion.

Armitage was an elderly widower who worked for a fruit-packing firm in St.-Denis and represented the interests not only of the British but also of several other nationalities—including the Israelis, although such a duty had never before come his way. He was at his apartment, about to take his siesta, when the call came through. The inspector summoned him with some urgency to the hospital.

318

Here Armitage found several doctors and nurses crowded around a bed in the emergency ward. The patient, he was told, appeared to be an Englishman named either Forsythe or Mallory. In either case, the inspector remarked ruefully, the mystery was likely to continue, since the doctors doubted that he would last the hour. He was now in a coma, although he had recently recovered enough to mutter a few words which the others had not been able to understand.

While a nurse adjusted the saline drip-feed and blood-transfusion equipment, the inspector took Armitage aside and began to explain about the dead girl and the two sets of passports. "According to one, she is his wife, Madame Forsythe—of Italian origin, it would appear. But her second passport puts her down as an Israeli, Madame Bernstein."

Armitage was aware that the problem of identification was that of the police, while he would be left with the irksome business of arranging the funerals. And in a climate like that of Réunion, this had to be done with promptitude. Armitage's main worry, as he saw it, was going to be to decide what kind of religious service he should arrange for someone who had been either a Catholic or a Jew.

At that moment one of the doctors beckoned him. The patient was beginning to mumble again—the same words as before. Armitage leaned over him, putting his ear close to the man's parched lips. At first he could not make out any words at all; then the man made a desperate effort to raise his head, and Armitage heard just two words, repeated once, before he sank back on the pillow. A moment later the chief surgeon pronounced him dead.

Armitage explained to the inspector that it had been nothing of importance—merely a formality concerning the funeral arrangements for the girl. The patient's last words had been to demand that she be interred, not cremated. Armitage had heard the words quite distinctly. The man had said, "Bury her! Bury her!"